FROM PRAIRIE TO PLANES

FROM PRAIRIE
TO PLANES

How Dallas and Fort Worth Overcame
Politics and Personalities to Build one of
the World's Biggest and Busiest Airports

Darwin Payne and Kathy Fitzpatrick

DALLAS/FORT WORTH INTERNATIONAL AIRPORT
25TH ANNIVERSARY

Three Forks Press
Dallas

THREE FORKS PRESS
P.O. BOX 823461
DALLAS, TEXAS 75382

ISBN: 1-893451-00-3

PRINTED IN THE UNITED STATES OF AMERICA

FIRST PRINTING

Table of Contents

Acknowledgements

Anyone writing the history of an institution as large as DFW International Airport owes an immense debt of gratitude to a large number of individuals without whom it simply would not have been possible. We would like to emphasize that while this work was commissioned by DFW Airport, we were left free to shape the story as we saw fit and as the record—insofar as we could discern it—indicated. This required, we know, much forbearance on the part of DFW officials who supported us in all our needs for gathering information but who very carefully refrained from comments about how the work should be written.

The one official at DFW with whom we regularly dealt and whose idea it was to commemorate the airport's twenty-fifth anniversary with a history was Joe M. Dealey Jr., director of public affairs. As keen as was his interest in the subject, Mr. Dealey stepped aside to give us free range for writing the book. He became a good friend.

We're also grateful to all other employees in the Public Affairs Department, and especially Clarees Vesey and Angel Biasatti.

A great deal of our research was done in the Records Management office, which we found to be a most congenial and friendly setting during our searches through the records and documents which they store. Thanks to Gary Wittmann, Jo Bartoszek, Joyce Cheser, and Sarah Reiling.

A number of individuals graciously consented to personal interviews, and all of them were helpful and pleasant experiences. We are especially saddened that Bayard Friedman, who was unusually candid and helpful, died shortly before this book was published. Uniformly cordial and helpful as well were Vernell Sturns, J. Lee Johnson III, Len Limmer, and Jeffrey P. Fegan. Marshall L. Lynam gave us documents that aided in our understanding of the Wright Amendment.

Libraries we used included our own at Southern Methodist University, the aviation collection at the University of Texas at Dallas, the Dallas Public Library's Texas/Dallas History and Archives Division, the Fort Worth Public Library, and the University of Texas at Arlington.

DARWIN PAYNE and KATHY FITZPATRICK
October 30, 1998

FROM PRAIRIE TO PLANES

ONE

DFW International Airport

✈

"He who transports, sustains."
Leonardo da Vinci

As the twenty-first century draws near, it might seem unlikely to most people that the world's second busiest airport—apparently on a certain track to become the busiest—is found deep in the heart of Texas. Most likely, one might think, such an airport would serve a glamorous international destination—New York, London, Paris, Tokyo, or Los Angeles. It may seem even stranger that this busy airport, Dallas/Fort Worth International, was constructed after years of often bitter feuding between the two cities who own it and gave it their names. And, moreover, it might seem odd that the two cities that built this airport—enormously successful and profitable—did so only after the federal government issued an ultimatum that forced them to do it.

When it opened in early 1974 DFW encompassed 17,638 acres, about twenty-seven square miles. (It is now bigger, having added 341 acres.) It was the world's biggest airport, larger even than Manhattan Island in New York City. The acreage at DFW could contain New York's JFK, Chicago's O'Hare, and Los Angeles International airports with room to spare.

More than 2,300 flights are recorded every day at DFW. Transportation forecasts project that early in the twenty-first century it will surpass Chicago's O'Hare and Atlanta-Hartsfield both in number of flights and passengers served. By 2015 it is expected to accommodate the astonishing figure of one hundred million passengers a year.

Such figures correctly suggest that the airport's success has been a tremendous boon for the North Texas economy. In the year 1997 alone it generated more than $10.8 billion, a figure so large it is difficult to comprehend. In simpler terms, this amounts to $1 million every hour—24 hours a day, 365 days a year.

These distinctions might have surprised those who planned and built Dallas/Fort Worth International Airport. Even though they were visionaries with determination to build a great airport, how could they have anticipated such incredible growth when they came together in 1964 and began planning their mid-cities airport? Perhaps, even without fully anticipating their creation's ultimate success, they were mindful of what Leonardo da Vinci said: "Que transit sustinet," or, "He who transports, sustains."

DALLAS AND FORT WORTH are only thirty-five miles apart. Their airport, located almost precisely mid-way between their downtown centers, became in the last three decades of the twentieth century a unifying force after long decades when all efforts to cooperate had failed. Until their eventual airport partnership they had a long history of rivalry—sometimes friendly, but insofar as aviation was concerned, always serious and often bitter.

The seriousness of it became apparent again in the 1990s when a difficult and emotional issue that had a familiar ring to it once more erupted—what limitations should be placed on commercial passenger flights out of Love Field, a facility owned solely by Dallas and not shared with Fort Worth? This was an issue which for a long time had seemed to be resolved. Despite its potential for volatility and a return to the courts, the resumption of additional and longer flights out of Love Field did not appear to seriously jeopardize the underlying reservoir of goodwill between the two cities that had developed during a successful partnership of twenty-five years.

The two cities remain dissimilar in many ways. Dallas—"Big D"— emphasizes an image of sophistication and urbanity. Fort Worth describes and promotes itself as "where the West begins." In recent years, though, Dallas has shown evidence of trying to recapture some of its pioneer past, and Fort Worth has surged forward in the arts.

Even during the earlier years of their rivalry both cities shared a common bond—they were bursting with ambition. From their days as tiny frontier settlements in the mid-nineteenth century until deep into the middle of the twentieth century, both desperately sought to escape the handicaps of their locations far from the nation's major population centers. Older cities along the East Coast—Boston, New York, Philadelphia, Baltimore—were blessed with navigable ports and a direct route via the sea to Europe. Remote, too, was North Texas from the railroad center of Chicago and the automobile industry of Detroit, both favored by their locations on the Great Lakes. Also, Dallas and Fort Worth were far away from the West Coast, where port cities such as San Francisco, Los Angeles, San Diego, and Seattle looked directly across the Pacific to the Orient. Nor did Dallas and Fort Worth enjoy the advantages of St. Louis at the juncture of the Missouri and Mississippi or of New Orleans at the point where the mighty Mississippi drains into the Gulf of Mexico. Geography denied Dallas and Fort Worth the advantages that were so critical to the growth of these cities.

The best chance for Dallas and Fort Worth to compete economically with these geographically favored cities arose a couple of decades after the dawn of the twentieth century. It came via Wilbur and Orville Wright and the development of heavier-than-air flying machines. The rapid maturation of the aviation industry offered as early as the mid-1920s the direct transportation links the two cities so long had desired. No longer would deep-water ocean ports or navigable rivers or railroad connections be the essential keys to a city's potential. Open spaces were available to all. The possibility of outlets to the rest of the nation and the world became clear. They would be through invisible avenues where no well-trod pathways were visible— through the ocean of the air. Dallas' and Fort Worth's location in the heart of the nation suddenly emerged as a major blessing.

Nowadays, ninety-five percent of the nation's population lives within four hours flight time of DFW. The major cities of Mexico and Canada are also no more than four hours away. European cities require only an overnight flight. The Orient is reachable before the sun sets.

THE AIRPORT'S builders had rare foresight as they planned in the 1960s. They acquired far more property than most people thought necessary. DFW was twenty times the size of the principal airport it replaced, Dallas' Love Field.

In purely commercial terms, the more than $10 billion a year DFW was bringing into the area's economy in the late 1990s was estimated to support more than 200,000 jobs. The airport clearly is the principal economic engine for Dallas, Fort Worth, and North Texas. Its creation became not just the icing on the cake for an area economy that already was booming; it became the main ingredient. DFW opened a new dimension for regional growth. Its presence, added to the other attributes of North Central Texas, prompted the relocation to the area or the expansion of hundreds of corporations, including such Fortune 500 giants as Exxon Corporation, J.C. Penney Company, Inc., and AMR, parent corporation for American Airlines.

Through its marketing efforts the airport even spawned a new word that became standard for describing the Dallas, Fort Worth, and Mid-Cities area. In that word, the "Metroplex," all of the communities, not just Dallas and Fort Worth, became part of a single unity.

DFW is the only airport in the world with three control towers. It is the only airport in the world with seven operational runways capable of landing four aircraft at the same time. Nearly 900,000 landings and takeoffs were taking place at DFW in the late 1990s. More than half of all domestic air passengers in the state of Texas were enplaning at DFW; nearly two-thirds of all the air cargo in Texas is handled at DFW.

Long runways were recognized as vital when the airport was built. They will be even more vital in the future as bigger and bigger airplanes are built. A new runway in 1996 increased landing capacity significantly. An eighth runway is planned to be constructed after the year 2000, and three runways will be given 2,000-foot extensions. DFW will be one of the very few airports in the world capable of handling the new giant aircraft to be built by Boeing and Airbus and scheduled to be available in the year 2003. Dubbed the New Large Aircraft (NLA), it will be as long as a football field and almost that wide between its wingtips.

DFW property reaches primarily into four separate mid-city municipalities—the towns of Coppell, Euless, Grapevine, and Irving. It straddles the border of two counties, Dallas and Tarrant. To the south it incorporates the old Amon Carter Field, later Greater Southwest. An airport whose property lies in so many separate municipal jurisdictions has the potential for encountering unusually complex zoning problems, but a special state law gave DFW the right to control its own development without being bound by separate municipal zoning ordinances.

TO THE CASUAL eye, DFW appears to be far less busy than it actually is, and this is not just because of its generous boundaries. Its architects deliberately chose decentralization as the guiding concept. Instead of a single huge and dominating terminal packed with huge crowds of passengers, four half-loop terminals are spread apart on both sides of the parkway that serves as a north-south spine down the middle of the airport. The advantages are several. Basically, dispersal brings easier accessibility for people, especially for those arriving or departing by automobile. It also permits easier access for airplanes at the terminal gates.

Linking the terminals together is an automated transportation system called AIRTRANS, which has sixty-six separate cars operating on thirteen miles of guideway and making stops at various points alongside all of the terminals. The cars have no drivers—they stop and go automatically. They make a full loop of the airport terminals, traveling in one direction only. An entirely new "people-mover" is planned for the future at a projected cost of $650 million. It will be the largest single construction project ever undertaken at DFW.

DFW'S board of directors and staff emphasize that their airport is a work-in-progress, a facility destined never to be completed. The new "people mover," runway and runway extensions, and new terminals are part of the Airport Development Plan completed in late 1997. The plan projects to the needs of the year 2015. It has anticipated costs of some $3 billion, more than four times the $700 million it cost to build the original airport.

DFW is the home base and primary hub for one of the world's leading carriers, American Airlines, which has a pervasive presence and strong historical ties to Fort Worth and Dallas. Some 70 percent of all passengers at DFW traveled on an American Airlines flight in the late 1990s. The volume of traffic American generates at DFW is astonishing. In a 39-minute period in late 1997 (8:19 a.m. to 8:58 a.m.) the airline had forty-four flights arriving, better than one flight per minute. This dominance by a single airline is not so unusual. Delta sells 80 percent of the airline seats at Atlanta-Hartsfield; Continental has an 80 percent share at Houston International; and United has 71 percent of the business at Denver International. DFW also serves as a strong secondary hub for another of the world's elite airlines, Delta.

In all, some twenty different carriers were serving the airport and offering flights to nearly 200 destinations, including about forty international destinations in the last years of the twentieth century. There were non-stop flights to Tokyo, Osaka, Honolulu, London, Frankfurt, Paris, Lima, Santiago, and other parts of the world. More than thirty non-stop flights a day were offered to eleven Mexican destinations. For travel within the United States, a passenger had a choice of more than fifty daily flights to Houston, nearly forty to New York City, about thirty-five to Atlanta, some thirty to Chicago, and more than two dozen to Los Angeles.

Passengers seem to get most of the attention, but air cargo is a vital part of the airport's operations. The volume handled grew from 660,000 tons of cargo in 1992 to 894,000 tons of cargo in 1997, a jump of more than 35 percent. International cargo is a big part of this, constituting 48,000 tons of the 1997 total and growing rapidly.

The needs of the 60 million passengers or so who pass through DFW annually—about 160,000 a day—are met by some 45,000 airline and support employees. Everything that sustains the basics of life, especially modern life, is present. At the core are the personnel, equipment, and facilities directly required for providing air transportation. But DFW also has police officers, fire fighters, paramedics, a post office with its own zip code, a jail, chapels, barber shops, salons, shoeshine stands, internet cyberbooths, more than a hundred restaurants, a golf shop, clothing shops, newsstands, a high-rise hotel with 1,400 rooms, a country club, two golf courses, tennis and health club facilities, an internal transit system, parking for some 35,000 vehicles, a public works department, currency exchange outlets, an independent weekly newspaper, and much more, including a Texas winery.

Big airports, truly, are like big cities. Their enormous sizes, the complexity of their operations, their value to the communities in which they exist, their vital roles in American life, and their important links to the outside world are essential elements in the history of the twentieth century. The manner in which airports are conceived, built and operated over a span of years is often complex. As the following pages will show, the roots of DFW International Airport go back to the earliest days of aviation in the separate cities of Dallas and Fort Worth.

TWO

Dallas and Fort Worth Encounter the Wonders of Aviation

✈

The French pilot looked warily at the tree limbs whipping about in the brisk breeze, eyed the awaiting crowd in the grandstand, and declared, "I'm going to fly."
Roland Garros in Fort Worth

Much of the nation seemed obsessed with the possibility of escaping the bonds of gravity and soaring into the air in a flying machine as the twentieth century first began unfolding. Whether or not it could be done was a popular topic of debate. *Floating* above the ground in a substantial basket tethered to a huge balloon was possible and had been done—everybody knew that. In fact, Texas' first recorded balloon ascent had been made in Dallas on April 16, 1861, when a "Professor Wallace" went aloft to the delight of spectators. But propelling a heavier-than-air machine into the sky and staying up there was a different matter. To many learned people the notion seemed ludicrous. A famous mathematician, Simon Newcomb, had "proved" conclusively in 1901 through detailed calculations published in the nation's most popular magazine, *McClure's*, that flying was impossible. Even if man did fly, Professor Newcomb pointed out, since the speed alone would sustain him, how would he ever stop?

Others, though, most notably the esteemed secretary of the Smithsonian Institution, Samuel P. Langley, were utterly convinced that flying not only was possible, but that technology had advanced to the point where "power flying," as opposed to "gliding" (which had its own advocates as the key to sustained flight), could be achieved at any time. Langley and others were working toward that very goal. In 1903 Professor Langley and his helper, Charles M. Manly, aided by a $50,000 grant from the U.S. government, believed that they had created a flying machine—they called it an Aerodrome—that would lift off the earth and take to the skies. Nation-wide publicity preceded and accompanied their first effort on October 7, 1903, but the attempt was a dismal failure. Similar interest—much of it now especially mocking in tone—accompanied their second effort on December 8, 1903. This attempt also failed miserably. The ridicule directed toward Langley and his absurd notion that he could fly was shattering. When this distinguished gentleman died six years later it was said that he had never recovered from the humiliation.

How ironic that only nine days after Langley's very public failure, two unknown bicycle-makers from Dayton, Ohio, Orville and Wilbur Wright, made four distinct flights in their home-made machine over the sand dunes at Kitty Hawk, North Carolina. No one was there to see them; nor, given Langley's recent failure, was anybody inclined to believe them. When their father presented to the Dayton newspaper the telegram from his two sons in which they unequivocally declared their success, the dubious editors ignored it. Skepticism reigned in the aftermath of Langley's failure. The Dayton newspaper thus failed to capitalize on what would have been one of the greatest news scoops in history. If Langley with all his support and credentials couldn't fly, nobody could.

HISTORY HAD BEEN made; an entirely new era in human life was beginning. But popular realization of the Wright brothers' triumph came slowly, for not until about five years later did the general public acknowledge that flight indeed had been accomplished and that it could become a significant part of the future. A few were quicker than others to jump on the bandwagon.

Frank McCarroll of Dallas was said to have built in 1904 the area's first airplane, and, although documentation is lacking, he is also said to have made one or more successful flights that year. He took out patents on a number of forward-looking ideas, including a forerunner to the retractable landing gear and another that would permit a pilot to alter the shape of his plane's wings while in flight.

Samuel Franklin Cody, born in 1861 in Birdville, just east of Fort Worth, had a bizarre career that included work as a cowhand on the Chisholm Trail and as a performer in Wild West shows that toured Europe and North Africa. Although illiterate, he became fascinated with flying and the principles of flying, joined the British army as an aeronautical researcher, and in 1908 made the first powered airplane flight in Great Britain. He died in 1913 while testing a float-equipped plane that he intended to fly across the Atlantic. Britain honored this Tarrant County native by burying him with full military honors in a military cemetery after a funeral procession witnessed by 50,000 Britons.

By 1910 flight exhibitions were occurring regularly across the nation before spellbound crowds. After the first international air meet was held in Los Angeles in January 1910, the ambitious Dallas Chamber of Commerce immediately arranged for what they billed as the state's first exhibition of "heavier-than-air" flying machines. (Actually, it was not the first. The first recorded flight in the state already had occurred in Houston on February 18, 1910, when a Frenchman, Louis Paulhan, took to the air.) The Chamber's three-day program, March 4-6, featured a solitary pilot, Otto Brodie. Dallas merchants took advantage of the expected crowds from throughout the area with special advertisements in the newspapers. "Make your Easter purchases at Sangers and save the cost of your railroad fare," suggested Sanger Bros. A. Harris & Co. declared "aviation prices" for Friday, the first day of the meet. Brodie arrived by train from Chicago, accompanied by his disassembled Curtiss biplane, and a curious crowd gathered on the evening before opening day to see him put it together. Brodie announced a show that would include swallow swoops, figure eights, dips, rapid curves, fast ascents, and attempts to set world records in speed and altitude. Just twenty-three years of age and the nephew of Steve Brodie (the daredevil who jumped from the Brooklyn Bridge), Brodie boasted that he had a "national reputation for recklessness."

High winds nearly spoiled this introduction to flight for Dallas spectators. Brodie was able to lift his biplane only fifteen to twenty feet off the ground, flying about two-thirds the length of the infield at Fair Park. Spectators who had paid $1 admission were told to return next day, free of charge. On Saturday, with irregular gusts of wind, Brodie managed to climb thirty-five feet above the ground, then smashed into the ground. "That's what I get for trying to fly in this wind," Brodie said as he crawled from the wreckage and wiped blood from his nose and mouth. The meet was over. The Chamber of Commerce issued an apology for Brodie's failures. Their contract with him had stipulated that he must give at least one successful flying exhibition to earn his pay. Since he had not accomplished this, he was paid nothing. Spectators were refunded their admission fees. But the enthusiastic crowds, totaling more than 20,000, strongly indicated that they wanted more.

Despite this somewhat lack-luster program, the Dallas Chamber of Commerce and its "aviation meet committee," headed by J.E. Farnsworth, remained no less determined to bring to the city an international flying event. And before the year ended the committee had arranged to sponsor a visit by some of the world's most famous "birdmen," traveling as a part of International Aviators, Inc. The meet, scheduled for the first week of January 1911, was described by International Aviators as the "biggest airship tournament ever held in the world, with the one exception of the meet at Belmont Park, New York, last October."

International Aviators featured seven to eight pilots from throughout the world who were touring the nation's cities and giving dazzling displays of heights, speeds, and dives as they competed for prizes in their biplanes, monoplanes, a Blériot monoplane, and a tiny French-built "Demoiselle." Dallas Mayor Stephen J. Hay received a formal invitation to take a "complimentary ascension" in one of the airplanes. He was assured that the flight would be at a height of at least 2,000 feet so that if an accident should occur "a gradual descent may be made and a suitable spot selected to alight in order that the machine may not be injured." For his own part, the mayor would have to assure International Aviators that under no conditions would he make any movement whatsoever during the flight, nor would he offer any suggestions to the aviator as to how to manage the machine. Finally, the mayor "must not be subject to heart failure." The mayor declined the offer.

The organizer and star of International Aviators was John B. Moisant, who just recently had won a major prize for circling the Statue of Liberty and who was being highly touted for the Dallas appearance. (A young boy in Brooklyn named J. Erik Jonsson— many decades later a key founder of DFW International Airport— first became fascinated with aviation as he watched these planes circling the Statue of Liberty.) On the last day of December, in a New Orleans meet just prior to Dallas, Moisant was in an unfamiliar airplane which suddenly inclined and threw him to his death. This occurred on the same day that another famous birdman, Arch Hoxsey, who not long before had given President Theodore Roosevelt an airplane ride, crashed to his death in California. The perils of flying were clear. For audiences that was part of the attraction.

Undaunted, the Dallas meet went on as scheduled. American pilots Charles K. Hamilton and Joe Seymour, Irish aviator John G. Frisbie, Edmound Audemars of Switzerland, and three Frenchmen, Roland G. Garros, Rene Barrier, and Rene Simon, demonstrated their derring-do at Fair Park before crowds of as many as 20,000 within the fair grounds and another 30,000 or more on the sidewalks and on the roofs of every building in downtown Dallas. Garros, attempting one day to reach an altitude of 10,000 feet, got lost and had to land in a field near the new White Rock Lake. A couple out on a carriage ride saw him and gave him a ride back to Fair Park.

So well-received was the event that the Chamber of Commerce persuaded the aviators to extend the meet for three extra days. Thus, a meet that had been planned to be held January 4-8 lasted until January 11. Dallas glowed with pride.

FORT WORTH, thirty-five miles to the west, was watching these events with great interest and not a little envy. "Fort Worth Wants

Aviators," said a newspaper headline, succinctly summarizing the situation. Even before its residents had seen their first airplane the city had manifested a distinct interest in aviation when in 1909 a group of businessmen organized themselves as the Southwestern Aviation Conference (soon renamed the Southwestern Aero Club). This group joined Fort Worth's Board of Trade in an effort to bring the International Aviators to Fort Worth immediately after their Dallas event. An ad hoc committee, chaired by W.G. Turner and including among its members a bright young newspaper executive who one day would become known to symbolize Fort Worth and to dominate its civic and aviation enterprises, Amon G. Carter, conferred with the manager of International Aviation both in Fort Worth and in Dallas and struck a deal. For $7,000 the aviators would put on a two-day meet in Fort Worth immediately after leaving Dallas.

It was proposed and briefly considered that in a spectacular display of modern technology all the "machines" would be flown to Fort Worth from Dallas. But this did not occur; the thirty-five miles between the two cities was too great. The planes were shipped to Fort Worth in the customary way—by rail.

Prior to the airmen's departure a blue-ribbon committee worked frantically to ensure a successful show. Committee assignments suggested clearly the planning required. W.G. Turner served as general chairman. Other Fort Worth businessmen headed committees responsible for grounds and police protection, preparation of the grounds and grandstand, tickets, contract preparation, finances, music, advertising; and arrangements for school holidays to permit students to attend. Identified as the best site for the meet was the Driving Club just west of downtown (later a familiar location for Montgomery-Ward). A new grandstand had to be improvised to replace the one which recently had burned down. The contract between Fort Worth and International Aviators stipulated clearly that if there could be no flying for any reason—such as high winds or wet grounds—there would be no pay.

As it turned out, the winds were dangerously high, but on the first day, Friday, January 13; Roland Garros managed to get into the air to satisfy the terms of the contract. The French pilot looked warily at the tree limbs whipping about in the brisk breeze, eyed the awaiting crowd in the grandstand, and declared, "I'm going to fly." And he did, barely missing telephone wires strung out across one end of the field. He was the first man to fly in Fort Worth. On Saturday, the winds again an obstacle to the light aircraft, Rene Simon managed to make a ten-minute flight in the late Moisant's Statue of Liberty airplane. Next day, the aviators were off to Oklahoma City for another meet.

But their legacy remained in both cities, for they had inspired many. Two of the spectators at the Fort Worth event, Frank and Robert King, decided to make their own airplane in their father's barn. Alarmed at what he considered his sons' foolishness in building their own flying machine, Mr. King sent off to New York for a factory-made plane. When it arrived the King brothers assembled it as well as they could. A great puzzlement, though, was a bronze shaft that seemed to fit nowhere. They wrote the factory and got the answer: the piece had been included erroneously; it belonged to a motorboat. With their newly constructed airplane the King brothers taught themselves to fly, hopping from pasture to pasture on the southern edge of the city as curious on-lookers watched.

The same sort of thing had happened in Dallas. Local youths did their best to emulate the birdmen who had flown at Fair Park. Harry L. Peyton, a 19-year-old youth, built his own flying machine and successfully got it into the air in March 1912, probably flying from Caruth field, a cotton patch leveled for take-offs and landings in the Trinity River bottom. Peyton soon met Steve "Texas" Hicks, an expert rifle shot. They formed a partnership and started putting on unforgettable air shows. They flew in a 26-foot, 600-pound airplane that could be disassembled and fitted into two small packing cases for traveling. From the air Hicks would shoot at targets on the ground and also at odd objects tossed from a seat behind the pilot.

GOOD WEATHER, mountainless terrain, and blue skies made both Dallas and Fort Worth ideal locations for the activities of these early aviators. These were the days dominated by "birdmen," daredevil pilots in slight aircraft made of canvas, wires, and bamboo—very often of their own constructions—who seemed to have lost all fear of death now that they had been freed like birds from the earth. It was a world-wide phenomenon, for the French, Germans, Spaniards, Italians, and South Americans were also fascinated with aviation. They developed their own birdmen. Touring birdmen survived smash after smash, often climbing out of wreckage with a smile. Plenty of times they did not survive. They were, no doubt, a bit foolhardy, but crowds gathered not just to see them fly but to see how close to death these daredevils could come. And as the pilots increased in number and became more daring in their exploits, more and more were killed. The first American fatality in aviation had occurred in 1908. Five aviators were killed in 1908 and 1909, and in the year 1910 alone thirty aviators lost their lives.

On October 17, 1911, aviation history touched Fort Worth when an outside aviator flew in for the first time. He was Calbraith P. Rodgers, who landed his airplane at a pasture in the Ryan Place Addition just south of where Elizabeth Boulevard later would be. Rodgers, who had soloed earlier that year for the first time after only an hour and a half of instruction, was attempting to fly across the United States in thirty days to claim a $50,000 prize offered by publisher William Randolph Hearst. As many as ten thousand spectators screamed and shouted hysterically as Rodgers appeared in the sky and then put down his plane. He was greeted on landing by Amon Carter, and he handed to the *Star-Telegram's* editor, J.M. North Jr., a letter from Oklahoma. It was the first piece of air mail ever delivered to Fort Worth. Dallas, also eager for a look at this extraordinary endurance pilot, managed to persuade him to make a stop there after J.A.C. McCurdy, their featured pilot at the State Fair of Texas air show, damaged his plane in a landing cartwheel.

Rodgers, flying in a Wright-EX biplane, did manage to cross the continent. He was the first airman to do so. By the time Rodgers reached Long Beach, California, he had crashed fifteen times and had replaced so many parts of his airplane that only a strut and the rudder remained from the original. But since the trip took eighty-four days instead of thirty, he failed to qualify for the prize. Four months after he finished this epic journey Rodgers was killed in a crash in California.

In Dallas in 1912 Miss Mathilde Moisant, the late John Moisant's sister, became the first woman in the state to fly a heavier-than-air machine, doing so in a March flying meet. Also on the program, sponsored by the Moisant International Aviators, were altitude flights, fancy flying, speed racing, and an exhibition of bomb-throwing intended to display the usefulness of the monoplane in times of war.

Flying exhibitions became a staple at the State Fair of Texas each October. The most famous birdman of all, Lincoln Beachey, the first pilot ever to do a loop-the-loop, flew on four days in the 1914 State Fair. He earned $1,000 at the conclusion of each day's work, payable daily as his contract spelled out clearly. He would perform three flights a day of at least ten minutes' duration. He would "loop the loop, fly upside-down, and make his vertical drop each day." As an advertisement described his act, Beachey would be seen making a "skyward flight to a distance of 3600 feet, then making a vertical drop of 1500 feet at a speed of 240 m.p.h." He was, the advertisement continued, the "most intrepid aerialist the world has ever seen!" And Beachey proved it. His most spectacular stunt was to climb to a record altitude of 8,000 feet, then kill the engine and plunge straight down before pulling out at the last possible second. Attendance was reported at over 100,000 people. The year after his State Fair of Texas appearance Beachey drowned in San Francisco Bay when his plane broke up during an exhibition flight and he was unable to climb out of the wreckage.

With Beachey dead, the 1915 State Fair of Texas negotiated with aviator Art Smith, one of the developers of skywriting, to make two flights daily on all sixteen days of the October event. This included six night "illuminated flights" involving the use of pyrotechnics. Smith's pay for each flight was $263.16, to be tendered after the last flight of each day. Mayor Henry Lindsley expressed a wish to fly with Smith, and Smith invited him to do so, but the Dallas Commissioners passed a resolution forbidding it. The resolution, introduced by Commissioner A.C. Cason, said that the mayor was not entitled to engage in such a "precarious escapade" without permission of the board.

In Decatur, Texas, immediately northwest of Fort Worth in Wise County, the Ingram family became aviation enthusiasts and introduced the wonders of flight to large numbers of people throughout the area. John J. Ingram, a doctor, and his three sons, Jay, Aubrey and Selma, became addicted to flying after Jay, who had a Ford dealership and garages in Decatur, visited Dallas and met Charles A. Foster. Foster was an early aviator who held License No. 41 in the Aero Club of America. So fascinated was Jay Ingram with Foster's stories of flying that he invited him to come to Decatur and build a flying machine in his shop. Foster, encouraged by Ingram's support, agreed. For Foster's first airplane Jay Ingram bought a six-cylinder open Port Roberts motor for $2,500 and gave Foster the run of his shop. Six months later, with no blueprints or model, Foster had built a flying machine which managed flights of up to ten miles. Ingram and Foster, now partners, billed themselves as the Pioneer Aeroplane Exhibition Company, and their first flight from a pasture nine miles south of the city represented the first flying machine Wise County had ever seen. Foster taught Ingram to fly, and soon all the Ingrams were flying in five airplanes which they and Foster manufactured by hand in 1914 and 1915. Soon they were visiting county fairs all over Texas, Oklahoma, and Arkansas.

In Fort Worth the first mass landing of airplanes occurred on November 20, 1915, when a squadron of Army planes en route from Fort Sill, Oklahoma, to Fort Sam Houston in San Antonio landed in 90-horsepower biplanes. A slight mishap marred the landing. The squadron's commander, Captain B.D. Foulois, bent an axle in his landing.

THE IDEA SOON arose that Dallas and Fort Worth, twin cities and sharing interests and aspirations, should be connected by an air route. A likely pilot was Lestere Miller, a young Dallas aviator whose first solo flight had been made in a plane with a motorcycle engine. Miller operated the Texas School of Aviation at a landing strip at the east end of present-day Columbia Avenue in East Dallas, where he gave flying lessons between 1914 and 1917. The

Daily Times Herald arranged for Miller to fly to Fort Worth bearing messages of goodwill and gifts. Then he would return to Dallas with greetings from Fort Worth.

On the day of the flight, January 1, 1917, Miller climbed out of his sick bed, where he had been recuperating from an inflamed throat and high fever, mounted his flying machine at the landing field in East Dallas, and flew to a site at the Oak Cliff Viaduct (now Houston Street Viaduct) in the bottoms of the Trinity River for his take-off for Fort Worth. There, a huge crowd of 15,000 awaited him. They were not disappointed. For thirty-five minutes Miller did aerial acrobatics in his machine, powered by a 100-horsepower engine, and sometimes skimming over the heads of the crowd. Once, he tilted his plane downward toward a party of automobilists, lifting up only when he was within ten feet of them. When finally he landed to prepare for his departure to Fort Worth, the enthusiastic crowd of thousands surged toward him in a scene that seemed to foreshadow Lindbergh in Paris in 1927. Only after twenty policemen cleared the crowd did Miller have the space needed to go aloft again, and he headed now for Fort Worth bearing gifts.

Engine trouble at Cement City on the western edge of Dallas forced him to turn back before reaching Fort Worth. A week later, this time departing from the aviation field near Lakewood Country Club at 11:03 a.m. on January 8, Miller successfully flew to Fort Worth. He landed there at 11:40 a.m. at a field on the end of the Evans Avenue streetcar line. "Faster than the fastest train, swifter than the swiftest interurban, speedier than the speediest automobile," Miller had gained the distinction of "pioneering the regions of the upper air between Dallas and Fort Worth." Since his bag contained letters for delivery to Fort Worth, some said he had made the first air-mail delivery in Texas, but they forgot the letter Calbraith P. Rodgers had delivered in 1911 from Oklahoma. He carried greetings from the Dallas Rotary Club to the Fort Worth Rotary Club, a message from the Dallas Yale Club to the Fort Worth Yale Club, a letter from the manager of the Goodyear Tire and Rubber company to the Marr Airplane Company and the Ratliff Airplane Company in Fort Worth, letters from *Times Herald* readers to friends in Fort Worth, and many other items. Then

Miller flew back to Dallas, bearing on his return trip gifts from Fort Worth. The return took only twenty-one minutes.

For the first time, Dallas and Fort Worth had been connected by air. It was not yet a partnership, just a sharing of a common enthusiasm.

THE FIRST WORLD WAR was a great stimulus to aviation. With the outbreak of hostilities it was evident right away that the airplane could play an important part in victory. A month after the United States declared war Congress appropriated $12 million for the purchase of aircraft; in July 1917, $43 million more was allocated for that purpose. In August Congress approved the largest appropriation ever for a specific purpose: $640 million for the aviation industry so that annual capacity would reach 17,000 airships a year. By the end of the war about $1.25 billion had been approved for the purchase of army aircraft.

During the nineteen months that the U.S. participated in the war, forty-eight training fields were created to teach military pilots. Texas played an important role, for the climate and terrain were considered by many to be ideal, and the state became central to the Air Service's training element. In fact, the War Department in late 1909 had chosen Fort Sam Houston in San Antonio as its first site for a flight training center, and that site became the heart of air service training not just for the state but for the entire nation, as well. Both Fort Worth and Dallas played an important role in the training of military pilots. Their interest, heightened by the airplanes and military activity they saw daily, would be lasting.

Even before the United States entered the war, the Fort Worth area, under a joint agreement with the U.S. Signal Corps, Aviation Section, became the site of three facilities to train pilots for the Royal Canadian Flying Corps. Seeking the bluer skies and milder climate of Texas, the Flying Corps trained aviators at fledgling facilities at three sites under the umbrella of Taliaferro Field. Taliaferro No. 1, Hicks Field, was about ten miles northwest of Fort Worth. Taliaferro No. 2, Benbrook, was west of the city, and Taliaferro No. 3, Barron Field near Everman, was located about ten miles south of the city. A number of those trained actually were Americans who had joined the Canadian forces. Then, with U.S. entry into the war, Americans assumed control of the three facilities, but the Canadians continued to train and they were joined soon by American cadets. By November 1917 the first class of 150 cadets of the Royal Flying Corps had completed their final instructions in aviation gunnery, had been commissioned as lieutenants, and had been given $300 to buy aerial equipment before being shipped overseas.

Airplanes flying over Fort Worth at high altitudes (generally between 3,000 and 5,000 feet) in battle formation had ceased being a novelty to Fort Worth residents by late 1917. One aviator in November reached the remarkable height of 12,000 feet. Airplanes—or "machines"—were being built at the sites as rapidly as possible. By December 1917 some 5,000 cadets—British, Canadian, and American—were at Fort Worth's training facilities.

Almost daily American and Canadian cadet pilots died in crashes. Within an eleven-month period when training was on-going in these three fields, a total of 106 aviators or would-be aviators died. On a single day in February 1918, six pilots were killed. One of the six was the internationally famous dancer, Captain Vernon Castle, a war-time aviation instructor. Castle, accompanied by a cadet student in a JN4D Jennie, was bringing in his plane for a landing when he collided with another aircraft and fell to his death. The cadet escaped with minor injuries. An elaborate funeral was given for Castle, and a monument in his memory now stands near the scene of the crash.

A worried mother gave the cadets at Taliaferro a good laugh when she wrote to her son with this advice: "Be careful, son. Do not be reckless. Fly very low and very slow."

Some 1,500 fliers earned their wings at the training facilities and served with distinction as fighter pilots during the war. Aviators were commissioned as officers, but a large number of enlisted men were learning the mechanics of airplanes and how to build and repair them. A contingent of 1,200 military mechanics, motorcycle and truck drivers, and "men of other trades" arrived at Taliaferro in late November from San Antonio, another Texas city that had become the nation's most important military aviation center.

Dallas' involvement in cadet aviation training also was intense, but not as widespread or of the same magnitude as Fort Worth's. It originated in June 1917 when the president of the Chamber of Commerce appointed a committee of leading Dallas businessmen, including Mayor Joe E. Lawther, to go to the War Department in Washington, D.C., and try to secure a military flying school for Dallas. (A similar visit to the capital in 1913 had ultimately brought about a coveted designation as regional headquarters for a Federal Reserve Bank.) Committee members obtained an agreement that an aviation school would be located in Dallas if they could arrange for a suitable landing field. A site was located adjacent to Bachman Lake at Maple Avenue and Denton Drive. A fund was raised to buy some of the land outright and to lease the rest. The War Department accepted the site as proper and agreed to lease it at $8 an acre with an option to buy.

By November the Army had constructed a fine facility—hangars, repair shops, tents, and "airdrome stretches" for landing and taking off. An engine repair shop was built just south of the flying field to repair damage from "smashes" occurring in military airplanes all over North Texas. Soon a restaurant, post exchange, and store were opened. The entire facility was given the name "Love Field" to honor Lt. Moss L. Love, who had been killed during a training flight at San Diego, California, in 1913. An additional Army facility, Camp Dick, was established as a cadet gunnery school at Fair Park in Dallas.

In mid-November the 126th Aero Squadron of the U.S. Signal Corp arrived at Love Field from San Antonio under the command of Major Douglas B. Netherwood, who was designated as camp commandant. With the arrival of the first contingent of officers on November 10, tight security went into effect around Love Field. No visitors were permitted. Armed sentinels marched around the boundaries. Major Netherwood explained that the War Department had issued stringent orders against the divulgence of any information that might be of value to the enemy. "Although we are very far from the front, people must realize that this country is at war and the aviation program must be as zealously guarded here as it is behind the lines," said the major in a public statement.

One of the first eight men to be stationed at the airfield, Roy Cowan, told a newspaper reporter years later that Love Field was "nothing but mud, weeds, tarantulas, toads and jackrabbits." Cowan recalled seeing a row of empty hangars and wondering where the airplanes were. Then he saw a railroad siding lined with boxcars containing wooden crates. The crates contained the parts and engines of aircraft that had to be assembled before flying.

The first flights from Love Field were made on Friday, November 23, with Major Netherwood himself taking to the air for about fifteen minutes in a machine assembled on the grounds of the flying school. On the next day a cadet from the Royal Flying Corps at Taliaferro Field in Fort Worth landed at Love Field to fill his plane with gasoline before returning to his home base.

Crowds began to gather near the Lemmon Avenue entrance to Love Field to watch the flights. An account in the *Times Herald* described the scene:

> Here and there are tents around which are clustered officers and flying cadets. The tents are for the use of the instructors and their pupils. The instructors, of whom there are between twenty and thirty, each has four pupils. Yesterday the students were going up for short circular flights with their instructors. A machine would half run, half hop up to one of the tents where a student would enter the car and be strapped down in the second seat. Then the giant propellers commenced to revolve faster and the craft darted out over the ground for fifty or sixty yards, where it would take the air. . . . Less than seven minutes passed before the machine had covered its course and landed again, discharged the cadet and started off with a second. At one time yesterday between twelve and eighteen airplanes were in the air at one time.

Dallas was enthralled with its new aviation school. On Thanksgiving, 1917, Dallas families invited every military man at Love Field to their homes for dinner, half for noon meals and half for evening. Citizens soon learned that very rarely was the term "airplane" used for the machines. Instead they were planes, boats, or ships. One referred to an airplane as she or her, never he or him. A special unit of Dallas enlisted men was formed at Love Field, the Dallas Aero Squadron, or 197th Aero Squadron. Twice a day in late November a motor bus departed from town, 9:30 a.m. and 2:30 p.m., to take prospective recruits to Love Field for testing. A few days after this special recruiting device was announced fifty-three out of sixty-five applicants had passed the test.

In mid-December 1917 Lt. Col. Roscoe of Fort Worth's Taliaferro and Major Netherwood of Love Field, with assistance from the Chambers of Commerce, were mapping out aviation routes from Fort Worth to Mineral Wells on the west and from Dallas to Lake Charles, Louisiana, on the east. The route to Mineral Wells was to be extended as far northwest as Wichita Falls, and other lines were planned to connect Dallas and Fort Worth with Houston, and San Antonio. First, the Fort Worth-Dallas route would be completed, and then those two cities would be connected with "all towns in Texas having aviation fields." Fort Worth would be the central station for these routes, according to Colonel Roscoe. These distances were manageable, for "birdmen" from Taliaferro Field already had flown as far west as Abilene, about 140 miles away.

"Mapping out" an aviation route consisted primarily of selecting and marking suitable landing places along the way. The route between Dallas and Fort Worth, with a midway landing place at Arlington, was said on December 4, 1917, to be ready "within a short time." Colonel Roscoe wanted routes established so that cross-country flights could become daily occurrences. Landing sites—large, open, and well-drained—would have to be provided every twenty-five miles for emergency landings and repairs. To be visible from the air, these sites were marked with white circles seventy-five feet in diameter. Colonel Roscoe declared Fort Worth in December 1917 to be on the verge of being the greatest aerial center in the United States. (An active pilot himself, the colonel was having a private hangar built on the polo grounds at River Crest Country Club in Fort Worth where he would keep a machine for his own private use.)

Some of the aviators trained at the fields in Dallas and Tarrant counties made notable contributions to the war effort. Lieutenant Charles Herring Ball, who completed his training at Love Field on April 11, 1918, was awarded a Silver Star medal for his heroic surveillance work. Flying through thick clouds on the European front on a reconnaissance mission, Ball ducked through a momentary hole and found himself flying over a large gathering of German forces in preparation for a major offensive against the Allies. Ball's timely information permitted the Allies to launch a pre-emptive blow against the Germans and spoil their surprise attack. A Fort Worth man, First Lieutenant H.R. Clay Jr., shot down eight enemy aircraft, winning official recognition as an Ace.

By late summer, 1918, it was evident that the Allies were on the verge of victory. Captain Eddie Rickenbacker had shot down twenty-six enemy planes; Colonel William Mitchell developed his belief that the next war would be won by bombing from the air alone; and more than 20,000 military aviators had been trained.

Even before the Armistice was signed on November 11, plans for gigantic celebrations were being made. In Dallas a huge two-day "Flying Frolic" was held November 12-13, 1918, at Love Field in conjunction with a celebratory downtown parade. Thousands of local residents ventured to the facility to see the aviators (soon to be out of work) put on a splendid show which included bomb and gunnery demonstrations, aerial dogfights, formation flying, and parachute jumps. Railroads operated special trains from Union Station to Love Field on an hourly schedule, and for the Flying Frolic's opening on November 12 some 7,000 spectators were on hand. A highlight of that first day was a world record set by Lt. William T. Campbell, the officer in charge of flying at Love Field, who did 151 successive loop-the-loops. Next day another world's record was set when Lieutenant Bottrell did a parachute jump from a plane 7,900 feet above the ground. He landed in front of the spectators.

THE WAR WAS over. Cessation of hostilities brought a sudden crash to the burgeoning aviation industry. Lucrative government contracts to airplane manufacturers ended. Contracts were canceled. Airplane builders went into bankruptcy. But a key legacy existed. About forty flying fields to train military aviators had been established across the nation, many of them in Texas. Air mail routes had been developed. The 20,000 or so aviators trained by the military had developed not only skills but enthusiasm for flying. About 175,000 more men had learned the skills of aviation mechanics and supporting ground work. Their energies were not to be denied in the coming years. And luckily for them, a huge number of Air Service planes were designated as surplus property and sold at bargain-basement prices. A large number of newly released aviators were able to buy their own airplanes and use them and their new skills as the basis for civilian careers in flying.

Military flight training soon ceased in both cities, but the invigorating recollection of aircraft activity over once-empty skies could not be forgotten. The military lease of Love Field extended until September 13, 1920, although it appeared briefly that the government operations would continue there indefinitely. "Love Field Chosen as Permanent Post," read one optimistic headline less than two months after the Armistice. It would be, according to a report from Love Field, one of just eight flying fields in the nation to be continued, with cadets from other locations transferring right away to Dallas. But less than two months later it became clear that with the exception of the Aviation Repair Depot, the military would close its flying operations at Love Field. The physical improvements would remain, and the property would revert to the Dallas Chamber of Commerce and Manufacturers Association. (The Repair Depot would continue functioning at Love Field until March 1921 when it was transferred to Kelly Field in San Antonio.)

The Dallas Chamber found itself holding improved property with buildings, hangars, streets, public utilities, sewage plants, and landing fields that had been sodded and tile-drained. Portions of the land had been leased, not bought, and those portions, according to the agreement, were to be returned in "arable" conditions conducive to the resumption of agricultural activities. But the costs of tearing down buildings and removing all improvements would have required more money than purchasing the property outright, so the Chamber bought the land with the idea of developing an industrial district at the site.

Thus was formed in 1921 the Love Field Improvement District. Development was slow, but when it appeared that the flying activities still occurring there might be endangered, the Chamber of Commerce and the Dallas Flying Club arranged for the City of Dallas to lease eighty acres of the property as a municipal flying field.

Indeed, Love Field had become a haven for those who scraped together a living doing what they loved best—flying. These were the people who became known to the world as "barnstormers," so-named because of their frequent emergency landings near barns. Those operating out of Love Field called themselves the "Love Field Lunatics." They bought and sold airplanes, offered rides to tourists for small fees, gave lessons, or carried passengers to outlying towns. William Francis "Bill" Long, later billed as the "Godfather of Love Field," was one of them. Long offered free flying lessons with each purchase of one of the surplus trainers he had bought, declaring his customers to be ready to fly on their own after two hours of ground school and one hour in the air. For thirty-five years Long would operate the Dallas Aviation School at Love Field. One of the regular customers at his aircraft maintenance facility was a pilot nicknamed "Slim" who occasionally passed through—Charles A. Lindbergh.

A rowdy barnstormer named "Slats" Rodgers once flew his Jenny down Akard Street at the level of the Adolphus Hotel's eighth floor. Another time he wrecked his airplane while trying to clip a soft drink sign from the top of a Love Field building. On May 27, 1922, with a huge crowd of spectators, another daredevil performer fell head-first from the top wing of a looping plane into the cockpit, jamming the controls and causing the plane to plummet 1,300 feet before the pilot finally gained control and leveled off just before crashing.

C.G. Killingsworth, who became Love Field's first civilian operator in 1919, hired Troy Vencill and Art Spaulding to help him. Vencill and his wife lived on the site, and Mrs. Vencill became known as the "mother of Love Field." Killingsworth became manager of the Dallas Aeroplane Company, which had a number of airplanes used for taxi service to cities such as Houston and Muskogee, Oklahoma. Fees for flights were charged on a mileage basis.

On July 15, 1922, the Curtiss Flying School and Curtiss Aeroplane Company opened at Love Field under the direction of Captain S.C. Coon as part of a nation-wide network. Five pilots gave both elementary and advanced flying instructions for the school. Curtiss had five hangars at Love Field for storage of planes, and an additional hanger which offered complete repairs and services. Curtiss provided flying services to all points in Texas and Oklahoma. Two men who had been part of the military ground crew at Love Field, Byron Good and Clint Foster, leased Hangar No. 1 and began selling gasoline and oil and making aircraft repairs from this "aerial garage." In their shop in the early 1920s the two repaired airplanes bearing such names as "Pup," "Black Cat," and "Fire Fly." The two offered passenger service as well. Their motto was, "We go wherever there is air." Yet another early tenant was the southwestern headquarters for Fairchild Aerial Camera Corporation which specialized in aerial surveying for business and industry. Aerial photographs offered exciting, birds' eye views of properties never before available. Under local manager Lloyd M. Long, Fairchild would be responsible for many unique aerial views of the Southwest in the decades to come.

And the Army itself returned as a tenant, agreeing in November 1923 to lease space at Love Field. By 1926 Lieutenant William Morris was in charge of eight men, operating out of two hangars, who were providing meteorological and radio service to pilots concerning wind and weather conditions.

BY THE MID-1920s Love Field, basking in praise for its development, could boast of eleven modern hangars offering complete flying services. The Chamber of Commerce declared its facility to be "The Flying Center of Texas." Very few cities in the entire nation possessed such an accessible and fully equipped flying field, the Chamber pointed out. "Whether it be wings, motors, fuselages or tail skids a concern handling them can be found at the field."

When Colonel Billy Mitchell came through Dallas in 1925 shortly before his celebrated court-martial, he declared Love Field to be one of the "best flying fields in the country." Its repairing and refueling capabilities, he added, were "excellent." Mitchell predicted a striking aerial development for the city within the next two years.

Captain Coon of Curtiss Aeroplane declared Dallas the leading commercial airport in the nation. In the previous eighty-five days 315 Army planes and 175 commercial planes had been serviced. Coon's own company was doing booming business at Love Field. In August 1925 the Chamber of Commerce reported that since the previous June, Curtiss had sold and delivered from its Love Field facility 360 airplanes and 400 engines. The company was virtually building airplanes from the ground up. It carried a complete stock of parts for all makes of planes, and in a recent month had made shipments to forty states and four foreign countries.

The enthusiasm of Dallas citizens for aviation continued to be reinforced at special events. In September 1924, Love Field hosted the government-sponsored "World Cruisers," a group of three pilots and navigators in Douglas biplanes making the world's first-ever trip around the globe. As they neared the end of their journey their only stops in Texas were at Dallas, Sweetwater, and El Paso. When the aviators—among them a crew member from Dallas, Jack Harding—arrived they were greeted by a crowd of 10,000 or more who had waited for hours to greet them. So eager were the spectators that they broke through police lines and stampeded the pilots upon their arrival. Two years later when Floyd Bennett landed at Love Field in the same monoplane he flew to the North Pole with Commander Richard E. Byrd, thousands cheered him at Love Field.

FORT WORTH thought of itself in no less terms as a center for aviation, for enthusiasm for flying continued at a high level there, too, despite the loss of military support for the three fields. Other landing fields developed—a pasture at the end of Evans Avenue, the Jubilee field in the Ridglea area, and Aviation Garden at the end of Lake Worth Road. One could find surplus Jennies bought from the government for $200 tied to barbed-wire fences at the pasture at Evans Avenue. Scores of pilots who had been taught to fly in the military now were teaching others to fly, putting on exhibitions, buying and selling aircraft, walking on wings, and making parachute jumps as they tried to earn a living through what had become their passion.

A hardy and accomplished corps of "Flying Gypsies," as they came to be described in these post-war days, developed their skills on these fields. Henry Woods, who had acquired his enthusiasm for flying when he saw Roland Garros defy the high winds to fly in 1911 on West 7th Street, began his long-time association with aviation with his own company, Woods Flying Service. Seth Barwise, who went on to organize Texas Airways Corporation in 1927, one of the predecessor companies to American Airlines, was another.

The most legendary and colorful of all Fort Worth aviators, though, was Ormer Locklear, who gained credit for being the first person to make wing-walking a daredevil stunt that brought thousands to air shows in small towns and county fairs across the nation. Locklear had learned to fly at Barron Field, and his daring antics had begun there when—as legend has it—he climbed out of a cockpit in mid-air to replace a radiator cap. On another occasion he crawled out to the engine to tighten a loose plug wire. After barnstorming around Fort Worth for several months after the war, Locklear signed with a noted promoter, William H. Pickens, and began earning fees between $1,000 and $3,000 for thirty-minute shows in which he cavorted across the wings of a JN-4, hanging by his knees from the struts, and even transferring in mid-air from one airplane to another. Inevitably, he went to Hollywood, appearing in "The Great Air Robbery" in 1919 and starring in "The Skywayman" in 1920. He became a fixture at celebrated Hollywood parties at the homes of such luminaries as Charlie Chaplin, Cecil B. DeMille, and Douglas Fairbanks and Mary Pickford. "The Skywayman" was his last film, for while attempting a stunt his airplane failed to come out of a dive and he fell to his death. The actual incident was included in the movie. When his body was returned to Fort Worth for burial more than 50,000 people showed up. Years later a popular movie based on

Locklear's life, "The Great Waldo Pepper," starred Robert Redford.

One of the earliest airlines to be organized in the nation was formed in Fort Worth in 1919 when three ex-military pilots, Russell H. Pearson, K.C. Braymen, and D.H. McClure, purchased thirteen Curtiss JN4s and formed the Fort Worth Aerial Transportation Company. The first flight departed from the River Crest Country Club to deliver a package of candy from a Fort Worth firm to a mayor of another city. The company evidently was ahead of its time. Few customers or passengers materialized. Upkeep on the large fleet of Jennies was too expensive. The company folded in the same year it began.

Barron Field and Love Field became part of the federal government's Air Services Model Airways System, a system which extended from Bolling Field in Washington, D.C., to St. Louis and Kansas City, then south to San Antonio. In Texas, in addition to Dallas and Fort Worth, it included Waco and San Antonio. At these designated fields Army Air Service planes stopped for refueling, supplies, and repairs. The program, which lasted until 1924, was coordinated from Kelly Field in San Antonio.

At Kelly Field a staff sergeant named W.G. (Bill) Fuller was assigned to help maintain Model Airways sites in the southwest. Fuller recalled years later that providing regular personnel at Barron proved to be particularly difficult. Six or seven sergeants had been assigned to the field, but all in short order had been brought back to Kelly to either stand court-martial or be released from the Service because of their failures—selling government supplies, not being at the field to meet arriving aircraft, drunkenness, and other problems. The commanding officer at Kelly, Colonel H. S. Burwell, decided to close Barron, and he sent Fuller to Barron to take care of the details.

Arriving in Fort Worth, Fuller proceeded to take inventory and begin placing equipment in crates to be returned to San Antonio. Fort Worth Mayor H.C. Meacham, alarmed at this development, visited Fuller at Barron Field to see what he could do to maintain the facility. After hearing Fuller's report, Mayor Meacham called Colonel Burwell himself and evidently persuaded him to have second thoughts. Burwell instructed Fuller to store all the supplies and equipment in Fort Worth rather than bringing them with him to San Antonio.

"One night, several weeks later," Fuller recalled, "Colonel Burwell called me to his quarters and to my surprise, there sat Mr. Meacham, the mayor of Fort Worth. He had come to Kelly Field in an effort to re-establish an Airways Stop at Fort Worth." Meacham said that the City of Fort Worth was negotiating a lease for a hundred acres of land north of the courthouse for an air field. He requested Colonel Burwell to assign Fuller to Fort Worth to establish this new facility as an acceptable field that would meet Air Service needs. Meacham said that he personally would build a home there for Fuller, drill a water well for the facility, provide a place for the storage of government equipment, and build a shop for him to work in.

On July 3, 1925, the Fort Worth City Council adopted a resolution accepting the site, and on August 27 the Air Service assigned Fuller to Fort Worth to be in charge of developing the new Airways Station. Supplies as well as Fuller's household goods were packed onto an Army truck for his move to Fort Worth. Unfortunately, the truck's engine exploded at San Marcos not long after leaving San Antonio. Fuller lost all his personal possessions as well as a large amount of the government supplies, but he continued to Fort Worth and began a connection with aviation there that would endure for the remainder of his life.

Fuller had become intrigued with aviation as a boy in 1912 when he paid $25 to take his first flight in Trenton, New Jersey, with a pilot named Charles F. Walsh. Walsh was killed in a crash the next day. Four years later Fuller enlisted in the Signal Corps' Aviation Section. His first assignment was in San Antonio, where he helped set up Kelly Field No. 1. On November 16, 1917, he was shipped to Love Field in Dallas, where he was in charge of maintenance and repair of airplanes, and in fact became one of the early enlisted pilots in the Service. Then he had returned to San Antonio.

Fuller's enthusiasm for flying found a ready reception in Fort Worth. "I believe I have convinced the City of Fort Worth that a municipal Air Port is a necessity," he wrote to Colonel Burwell in December 1926. Fort Worth's City Council members appropriated

$35,000 for the construction of a steel hangar at the airport, and they also equipped the field for night flying. When Fuller completed his enlistment in 1927 he was hired as the civilian head of the airfield, and in that same year on June 28 the name of the Municipal Airport was changed to honor the man who had been most responsible for it, Mayor H.C. Meacham.

THE WAR HAD given the first major boost to aviation. Now, in the mid-1920s, the awarding of air-mail contracts provided another boost. The U.S. government had been experimenting with mail delivery by air since 1918, using the military's Air Service, but the Air Mail Act of 1925 began transferring mail delivery to private interests. A number of commercial carriers were organized to compete for these contracts. The largest and most impressive among the bidders was National Air Transport (N.A.T.), whose top officials included financiers, former government officials and private industrialists.

Here was an opportunity for energetic, civic-minded leaders who might be intent on furthering the interests of their cities. Dallas leaders determined to persuade N.A.T. to select Love Field as the southern hub for a feeder route going to Chicago and from there to New York City. Mail from Dallas would be concentrated from other points of Texas.

Dallas Postmaster John W. Philp was joined by a special Chamber of Commerce committee chaired by Arthur L. Kramer, by the Love Field Industrial District, and by the Dallas Flying Club in lobbying for Love Field. Their arguments and their work were persuasive. A first step was to enlarge Love Field from 80 to 117 acres, a size suggested by the government as necessary for mail service. In bargaining to win the daily flight the Chamber guaranteed National Air Transport at least a hundred pounds of mail every day for the first six months of operation. (Government compensation to N.A.T. would be $3 per pound.)

On May 6, 1926, in a special ceremony at Love Field, a pretty Dallas woman broke a bottle of ginger ale on the propeller of a "Carrier Pigeon" open cockpit biplane, christening it as "Miss Dallas." Six days later on May 12, 1926, regular air-mail service began for the first time in Texas when N.A.T. pilot Herbert L.

Kindred headed north with a batch of mail. The Carrier Pigeon was one of ten such planes owned by N.A.T. that had been designed especially for mail service.

This day was hardly less noteworthy for Fort Worth, for the N.A.T. schedule included a first stop there to pick up additional mail before flying toward Chicago. Then, on the return trip south, Fort Worth was the last stop before the final destination of Dallas. One of the Carrier Pigeons was christened "Miss Fort Worth" in a ceremony at Meacham. Fort Worth touted its role by pointing out that it would be the first city in Texas to receive mail from the north, and the last city in Texas to place mail on the north-bound airplanes. For that reason, the city expected to be the concentration point for air mail from all parts of the state. (In 1937 a Meacham Field promotional piece declared that "Fort Worth [is] definitely established as [the] third largest air mail center in U.S.; exceeded only by New York and Chicago.") Love Field's advantage was its designation as the Southern-most terminal for N.A.T., which leased hangar and office space there, and which already was the world's largest private air transportation company.

Planes departed from Dallas each day at 7:30 a.m., stopping at Fort Worth, Oklahoma City, Wichita, Kansas City, St. Joseph, and Moline before arriving at Chicago at 7:20 p.m. There, mail was transferred to the overnight plane to New York for delivery next morning at 6:15 a.m. Kansas City was a mid-way terminal. Two of N.A.T.'s airplanes were based in Dallas, four in Kansas City, two in Chicago, one in Oklahoma City, and one in the Tri-Cities area (presumably Moline, Illinois). The flight reduced by two days the amount of time normally required by ground mail to reach New York City. The Carrier Pigeons, built by Curtiss Aeroplane & Motor Co., had a top speed of 126 miles per hour. Each could carry 1,000 pounds of mail at an average cruising speed of 100 miles per hour, reducing by two days the amount of time normally required for mail to reach New York City from Dallas.

Two weeks prior to the inauguration of the service, about a dozen Dallas businessmen, eager to promote this new air mail service and achieve the 100-pound per day guarantee, made what they believed was the nation's first "Aerial Good Will Tour." It was a three-day trip in six airplanes covering 1,500 miles with stops in Houston, San Antonio, Austin, Waco, Brownwood, San Angelo, Abilene, Cisco, Mineral Wells, and Fort Worth. Official representatives from those cities as well as throngs of curious onlookers greeted them at each stop. The enterprising feat was a natural progression from rail to air, it seemed, for since just after the turn of the century Dallas businessmen had been conducting annual tours each spring by train in an effort to expand the city's trade territory. This tour, sponsored by the Southwestern Retailers, was supported by a large number of organizations—the Chamber of Commerce, the Dallas Flying Club, the Dallas Post Office, National Air Transport, and others.

During the first year of operation N.A.T. pilots on the Dallas and Fort Worth-Chicago route flew 776,000 miles without an accident or the loss of a single letter. N.A.T.'s traffic manager, Charles B. Braun, used a number of illustrations to explain the significance of air mail which applied not just to Dallas but to Fort Worth and much of the state as well.

> The city which was formerly two or three days from the centers of industry, commerce and finance is now only twelve hours from Chicago, twenty-four hours from New York. . . . Dallas banks sending items by air mail save one to two days interest. Cotton firms and oil companies make money the same way. Loan companies are enabled to communicate with the home office, push a loan through in three to four days as against the former seven. Wholesale houses use the air mail for fast communication with buyers in the East and the sending of samples from the East. The events of yesterday in the North, the East and other sections are rushed by news reel companies by air mail and flashed on Dallas theater screens today. The traveling salesman sends in his orders by air mail, and goods are shipped one to three days sooner. A part of a machine must be replaced, it is sent by air mail or air express, work goes on and no time is lost.

IF DALLAS AND Fort Worth had shown great enthusiasm for aviation to this point, now that enthusiasm became almost an obsession. Reports about fliers, airports, and airplanes from around the world and particularly in Texas, Love Field, and Meacham Field filled the newspapers.

When in May 1927 Charles Augustus Lindbergh became the first man to fly solo across the Atlantic Ocean, the obsession with aviation reached virtual hysteria, not just in Dallas and Fort Worth but throughout the nation. The future, long awaited, had arrived. Those cities who were not prepared to anticipate the future and be ready to take advantage of it would pay a price. Merely leasing an air field, as the City of Dallas was doing at Love Field, no longer was deemed sufficient. The city must *own* an airport.

One month after Lindbergh's flight, Dallas was designated as divisional headquarters of the U.S. Bureau of Air Commerce, an office established to inspect airplanes used for commercial purposes and ensure safety standards. Officials based in the Dallas headquarters would be in charge of Texas, Oklahoma, Louisiana, and Arkansas.

One day after this designation the *Daily Times Herald* printed a front-page editorial, "Dallas Must Have a Permanent Air Depot." The time had come, the newspaper declared, to make the city truly "the center of aviation in the Southwest." Indeed, the editorial declared, "the nation is watching Dallas and it is up to the citizens of this city to get into action without delay." The necessary land had to be found that would meet "all the requirements of the government and be adequate to aviation needs for years to come."

Before the week was over Mayor R.E. Burt began negotiating with trustees of the Love Field Industrial District Corporation about purchasing Love Field. Some believed that Love Field was not the best site for future growth. Burt, unconvinced himself, obtained the help of the Dallas Flying Club and Lloyd Long of Fairchild Aerial Service to examine several additional sites for a municipal field—a field in the Trinity River bottom, a site on the east side of White Rock Lake (which had the advantage of permitting flight by hydroplanes), and a place in Oak Cliff at

Stevens Park. Finally, it was determined that Love Field, with its existing improvements, was the best choice. On July 13, 1927, city commissioners adopted a formal resolution to buy the facility.

"The establishment of this airport will be one of the mile-posts in the progress of Dallas," wrote the *Times Herald* in a follow-up front-page editorial. "The purchase of this airport lays the foundation for making Dallas one of the national centers of aviation. We are now prepared to announce to the world that Dallas is in the forefront of progress with facilities to meet the demands of the new age of transportation."

Not to be left behind, just three days after the city's announced plan to buy Love Field, Fort Worth held a formal dedication of its Meacham Field. Mayor William Bryce spoke as the former mayor for whom it was named, H.C. Meacham, looked on.

Other developments were rapidly occurring during these exciting times. One fortuitous event was a national tour by Charles Lindbergh himself in the same monoplane he had used to cross the Atlantic, *The Spirit of St. Louis*. He would make stops in Fort Worth and Dallas in September in the midst of his three-month tour. In Dallas he would dedicate Love Field as the city's new municipal airport.

Dallas' "chewing gum king," William E. Easterwood Jr., who had made a fortune with Orbit Listerated Gum and who been one of the foremost boosters in promoting the city as an aviation center, saw another opportunity to put the city on the national map. Lindbergh himself had won a prize for flying solo to Paris, and now Easterwood made another dramatic offer—$25,000 to the first pilot who flew from Dallas to Hong Kong. Easterwood's prize overreached the $25,000 Dole prize already being offered to the first aviator to fly from San Francisco to Hawaii.

A Dallas pilot named William P. Erwin immediately declared that he would try to win the double prize of $50,000, and a number of prominent businessmen stepped forward to finance an airplane for him. These included George B. Dealey of *The Dallas Morning News*, movie mogul Karl Hoblitzelle, banker Fred Florence, and John W. Carpenter of Texas Power & Light Co. They donated enough money to build a suitable plane, similar to

Lindbergh's *Spirit of St. Louis*. When on August 6, 1927, the green and silver monoplane was unveiled and christened as the *Dallas Spirit*, some 10,000 spectators were on hand for the festivities. The program was broadcast live across the state by radio station WFAA. Mayor Burt declared the moment one of the greatest in Dallas history. The governor of Texas, Dan Moody, was a prominent presence, too.

Erwin, a former World War I pilot, successfully flew the first leg of Easterwood's requirements from Dallas to San Francisco, where he joined fifteen other entrants poised for take-off to Hawaii. There, only seven of them were declared fit to lift off. Tragedy awaited. Two of the contestants, laden with heavy loads of fuel, crashed on the runway. A third airplane, piloted by a woman, disappeared into the ocean, and so did another. Before Erwin could take off in the *Dallas Spirit* word came that two aircraft had successfully arrived in Hawaii, claiming both first and second of the Dole prizes. Erwin insisted on departing anyway, saying he wanted to search for the two missing airplanes. Some 400 nautical miles out, Erwin's navigator and radio operator reported an encounter with a storm that caused a tailspin from which they barely had recovered. Then came another frantic message: "We're in another tailspin." No further word was heard. The *Dallas Spirit* vanished, never to be heard from again.

THE ARRIVAL of Colonel Lindbergh a month later shortened the period of mourning. On September 26, 1927, thousands of festive spectators, gathered at Meacham Field hours ahead of time, saw the Lone Eagle circle downtown two times before swooping down at Meacham, then climbing up into the clouds once more before finally landing at 1:59 p.m. Governor Dan Moody was there to greet him as were former Mayor Meacham, other dignitaries, and military friends from his training days at Brooks Field in San Antonio. W.G. Fuller, who had been at Brooks, recalled having seen Lindbergh make his first forced parachute jump there after he had collided with another plane at an altitude of 5,000 feet. Also on hand were Dallas representatives—Mayor Burt, Col. Easterwood, B.B. Owen, Drury Roberson ("Miss Dallas"), and others—who extended a formal invitation to the colonel to come the next day to Dallas. After a festive ceremonial parade through downtown Fort Worth, Lindbergh and the official party stopped at Panther Park, where he spoke to 20,000 school children who had been given an afternoon holiday for the occasion.

Next day at Love Field Governor Moody and Mayor Burt greeted Lindbergh after he landed in the *Spirit of St. Louis* before a crowd of 10,000. An estimated 100,000 people, the largest crowd in the city's history, stood along the streets and cheered the newly commissioned colonel—the same pilot once called "Slim" who sometimes stopped at Love Field—as his open car shuttled up and down Main, Elm and Commerce streets. At a press conference in the Adolphus a group of reporters, who seemed intimidated, asked inane questions. "How does it feel to fly, colonel?" "What makes that little paddle go round?" "How long will it be until Fords have wings?" At the banquet that evening Lindbergh's remarks were broadcast over KRLD. "Keep your airport—it will place you among the commercial leaders of the world."

How ironic that, actually, the city had not yet purchased Love Field. Even though city commissioners had voted to purchase the facility and the owners had agreed to a price of $400,000, a number of serious questions had arisen to delay the purchase. Was Love Field really big enough, and if not, could additional acreage be purchased? Could the $400,000 price be reduced so that additional acreage could be bought? Were other sites better?

By the spring of 1928 these matters were receiving almost daily attention in the city's newspapers. Estimates of additional acreage needed to make Love Field big enough ranged from seven to fifty acres. What was desired was a runway of 2,500 feet for every prevailing wind direction. But payment of $400,000 would exhaust available funds and make it impossible to buy the needed acreage. Mayor Burt was one of the harshest critics. Love Field was too small, he believed, and the surrounding neighborhoods too well-developed to achieve "Class A" status.

Once again, other possible sites arose for a municipal airfield. Water Commissioner S.E. Moss favored two sites west of town, both of which he said were "beautifully laid out for airports."

One would have been virtually a mid-city airport, twelve miles west of town on the Fort Worth pike near Mountain Creek, available for as little as $300 an acre. The other, a site near Dalworth, already had been graded as an automobile speedway and could readily be adapted for an airport. B.B. Owen, former president of the Dallas Flying Club, spoke in behalf of many aviators when he contended that it would take five years to condition another landing field to be as good as Love Field, which often was touted as one of the best in the nation. Postmaster Philp and Mayor Burt believed that the city needed two sites, the second to be used as a training site.

As Dallas quibbled, fears arose that it might lose its still tentative position as the center of aviation activity in the Southwest. Fort Worth already had purchased its airport, and so had Houston, San Antonio, Tulsa, and Oklahoma City. All of them were working to attract air lines and airplane factories. (Across the nation, by 1930 municipalities owned 448 of the 1,527 existing airports in the nation.) By late March Postmaster Philp, Chamber of Commerce officials, and flyers were urging Mayor Burt and the city commissioners to "make up their minds on something—either Love Field or some other site." Nothing was being accomplished to advance aviation while officials wrangled with indecision, they warned. The *Times Herald* reported that already "Fort Worth has offered inducements to a number of Love Field operators in an effort to get them to locate at Meacham Field.

Finally, on March 30, 1928, the Love Field Improvement District agreed to lower its asking price from $400,000 to $325,000. The price was acceptable to the city commissioners, and the deal was done. The reduction in price would permit Dallas to pay $75,000 for yet another airfield in Grand Prairie. This was Hensley Field, which was dedicated to military usage and would continue over the years to be used for military flying. As to the stated need for additional acreage at Love Field, Mayor Burt said now that the city would not purchase more land. Love Field should be big enough for "several years," he said. The city declared April 21 and 22 to be "Aviation Day," to be celebrated at Love Field with air races, exhibition flying, and a free-for-all race. By mid-May one of the city's commissioners, Arthur J. Reinhart, completed flying instructions from Lt. Harry Weddington, and District Attorney William McCraw had announced that he would purchase an airplane for his office.

BESIDES THE air mail route tying Texas to Chicago and other cities, there remained the matter of creating air mail routes within the state of Texas, particularly to connect other cities in the state with N.A.T.'s link to Chicago. One line would connect Houston and Galveston, and the other Austin, San Antonio, and Brownsville. It was determined that Dallas, not Fort Worth, would be the logical point for connecting these lines to N.A.T., but it was a Fort Worth company, Texas Air Transport (T.A.T.), that won the contracts and began the air mail service on February 6, 1928. T.A.T. was formed by Temple Bowen, who was in the bus transportation business, and his brother Chester. Their initial five airplanes were christened by Amon G. Carter, who also served as master of ceremonies for the February 5 afternoon festivities.

The Bowen tenure was short-lived, for controlling interest in T.A.T. was taken over by A.P. Barrett, whose broad visions for aviation did not at all seem ordained by the casual manner in which he became involved with it. This occurred in the summer of 1928 when Barrett was in the garden of his Fort Worth home with his 3-year-old son, Hunter. An airplane with the T.A.T. insignia flew overhead. "Daddy," the boy cried, "buy us a plane." Barrett, thus prodded, took his son to Meacham Field and told a pilot standing next to a T.A.T. airplane that he was interested in buying it. "That plane can't be bought," the pilot laughed. "It belongs to Texas Air Transport of the Bowen Line." Barrett responded that he would simply buy Texas Air Transport, which he did, purchasing in October that year 288 of T.A.T.'s 300 shares with the backing of Amon Carter of the *Fort Worth Star-Telegram* and five other investors.

Barrett immediately began an expansion of the airlines and the recruitment of top-flight executives, among them Robert Smith, who had been aviation secretary of the Dallas Chamber of Commerce, and Cyrus R. Smith, then assistant treasurer of one of his subsidiary utility companies. C.R. Smith later would become a legend in the aviation business after he became president of American Airlines. Robert Smith would become president of Pioneer Airlines. Almost immediately Barrett offered a two-day guest aviation course for Texas newspapermen and city officials, with resulting favorable news stories being printed all over the state. He broadened T.A.T.'s activities to include far more than flying the mail by creating five separate units: the original mail service, T.A.T. Flying School, T.A.T. Flying Service (charter and passenger), Texas Aeromotive Service, and the Texas Air Transport Broadcasting Company. Flying classes were taught by the same veteran pilots who flew the air mail. The broadcasting company, originally operating as KFQB and renamed KTAT, provided the latest weather information and ground-to-air communication. "Once the Training Center of Military Aviation and Now the Commercial Aviation Training Center of the Universe," boasted a brochure published in 1928. "There are but few training schools, if any, in the world, which offer you the opportunity to learn aviation as thoroughly, as professionally and as scientifically as you may learn it here," the brochure boasted.

In addition to the hangar at Meacham Field, others were built in Dallas, Houston, and San Antonio. From all of these hangars flying classes were offered, and one could also buy airplanes, engines and parts.

Barrett's vision was large. He aspired for Fort Worth to become the aviation hub of the nation and also to Central and South America as well as Europe, for he prophesied a rapid increase in the speed of aircraft which would shrink distances in a manner not yet realized by others. As part of that dream, he began drawing up plans for an ultra-modern skyscraper, the Aviation Building, where executives representing the airlines that would be flying soon to Fort Worth would have their offices. Barrett came to believe that the "Texas" in his company's title was too limiting; before the decade ended he changed it to Southern Air Transport. Southern Air Transport became the most important airline in the South, a key progenitor to the eventual American Airlines.

Barrett's vision and the success of T.A.T. were not the only reasons for Fort Worth to glory in its aviation prowess despite

Dallas' selection as the terminus for all three air mail routes. On July 6, 1928, a pilot at Meacham Field, S.W. Ruff of Austin, managed to get his aircraft off the landing field while towing a glider with Earl Akin of Breckenridge at its helm. This was the first airplane-towed glider flight in the world. The next year two Fort Worth pilots, James Kelly and Reginald L. Robbins, set the world's endurance record when they kept their Ryan brougham monoplane aloft for 72 hours and 32 minutes. This was not easy, for the aircraft had to be refueled in mid-air three times each day from another aircraft. The pilots cleverly devised a very narrow catwalk to the engine so that they could service it in mid-air. In this day of record-breaking the duo held their title only briefly. The next month a pair of fliers in Cleveland surpassed them.

Delivering air mail was more profitable than carrying passengers, and at first N.A.T. and T.A.T. concentrated on their letter-carrying. But April 1927 N.A.T. obtained several new "cabin-type" planes which had three passenger seats. On September 1, 1927, passenger service to Chicago began at Love Field when R.B. Kuteman climbed into the N.A.T. Travelair monoplane piloted by Herb Kindred. A one-way fare from Dallas was $100.30, and a Dallas passenger could take the fifteen-minute flight to Fort Worth for just $3.50. The trip from Fort Worth to Chicago was $96.80. Passengers sat in three small wicker chairs fastened to the floor, with optional safety belts available ("to hold you in if it makes you feel safer") that were proclaimed by one passenger as "just a nuisance." Less than a year later, on June 8, 1928, T.A.T. began passenger service.

As the decade ended both Dallas and Fort Worth were thoroughly committed to aviation and to their own municipal air fields. Mail routes were expanding, passengers were beginning to take advantage of the flights, airlines operating out of the airports were getting stronger, aircraft were being assembled and available for purchase, all kinds of auxiliary services were being offered, and flying schools were teaching people to be pilots out of both airports. The range of the newer, sleeker and more powerful airplanes was being extended, but not yet to the point that the existence of two excellent airports, thirty miles apart, was a problem instead of a blessing.

THREE

Rivals in Aviation

✈

*Usually, the rivalry was good-natured, but on the subject
of aviation, in which economic benefits seemed substantial,
the competition became heated even in the earliest days.*

With the glowing promise of aviation high on the agenda of
those cities aspiring to future growth and progress, it was only
natural that Dallas and Fort Worth would be consumed with the
notion of building up their own separate municipal airports.
Uniting in a single mid-cities facility simply was not practical, nor
was it seriously considered. With the limited power and short
ranges of early airplanes and their need for frequent repairs and
service, the nearness of the two cities had been a convenience.
Publications directed toward municipal planning such as *American
City* touted the advantages for cities to have their own airports. A
widely cited study appearing in that publication stated that
municipal airports should be "not more than 10 miles from the
business center of the city."

Virtually every city in the nation had its own municipal
airport. By 1931 half of the nation's 1,114 airports were owned by
municipalities. The state with the most municipal airports was
Texas, which by 1935 had fifty-eight. These municipal fields

usually were bigger and better equipped than privately owned facilities.

With Texas a hotbed of aviation activity, Dallas and Fort Worth were in the heart of it. The state ranked second in the nation in the number of airfields, trailing only California, and it had the third largest number of transport and industrial pilots. In 1930 the Dallas Chamber of Commerce's aviation committee reported—perhaps with exaggeration—that in regard to passenger service, Love Field was the third busiest airport in the nation. The city's annual payroll in aviation was said to be $750,000.

Even at this early date the idea of building a single airport between Dallas and Fort Worth had occurred, however briefly, at least to a few. As early as 1927 A.K. Kilgore of Dallas began writing letters to officials, including U.S. Senator Morris Sheppard, advocating a midway airport. The U.S. Post Office, sometimes bothered with the duty of transporting air mail from one city to the other, itself evidently suggested the possibility of a midway airport in 1930.

Most of the commercial air routes included stops at both Dallas and Fort Worth, a fact that ultimately would seem a nuisance rather than a convenience as far as the airlines were concerned. Certainly the two major routes stopped at both cities. N.A.T.'s Dallas-to-Chicago mail route often was described as the Chicago to Dallas *and* Fort Worth line. American Airlines' New York and Washington route to Los Angeles also stopped at both Dallas and Fort Worth. Not all of the routes did. Long & Harmon's service over much of Texas stopped at Fort Worth but not Dallas. To get its air mail on Long & Harmon's airplanes Dallas had to send accumulations of mail daily on a 5:30 a.m. train to Fort Worth.

The greatest profits for these newly formed airlines came from carrying mail, not people. Air mail service had expanded rapidly since its introduction. Air mail routes in 1926 had totaled 2,800 miles; by 1930 the figure had jumped to 30,000 miles. Passengers continued to be occasional only, for airplanes were not primarily equipped to handle them. Moreover, the general public lacked confidence in the safety of airplanes to use them with any degree of regularity. Too many barnstormers had crashed.

But all this was on the verge of changing in the new decade, as figures for passengers on flights from Meacham Field indicate. In 1929 Meacham averaged just 1.2 passengers per airplane—5,446 passengers flying in 4,511 planes. By 1932 the number of passengers there had jumped to 34,285 with 9,964 flights, and in 1936 the number of passengers climbed to 75,173 with 11,053 flights.

Passengers were increasingly comfortable because technology was developing bigger, more powerful, more comfortable and safer airplanes. The all-metal aircraft had been developed; "hooded" cockpits replaced open ones; instrument flying became a reality; the two-way radio enhanced safety; and landing fields were more numerous and better developed. The new Lockheed Vega monoplane, introduced in 1927, could carry a pilot and six passengers for a distance of up to 900 miles at 135 miles per hour. The first truly modern airliner, the all-metal Boeing 247, was brought into service in 1933. It carried ten passengers and was powered by two Wasp radial engines. United purchased a fleet of these Boeing 247s, hired stewardesses for each plane, and boasted that Chicago now could be reached in six hours from Dallas. Shortly afterwards, Douglas offered its own twin-engined passenger plane, the DC-1 (DC: Douglas Commercial), which in 1934 was modified into the DC-2 and then in 1936 was enlarged into the very popular and efficient DC-3, an airplane which catered to passengers by offering reclining seats, soundproofing, air-conditioning, and a galley to produce hot foods. By 1939 the DC-3 was carrying about three-fourths of the nation's growing domestic air traffic. It would continue to be built until 1946.

One of the early and key turning points in directing these airlines' attention toward passengers occurred in June 1929 when Postmaster Walter Brown eliminated the former method of payments based on pounds of mail carried per mile and replaced it with the amount of cargo space made available. The effect of this, deliberate on Brown's part, was to encourage airlines to purchase larger airplanes. Rather than fly them half-empty, they began to encourage passengers to fill up the remaining space.

Big business saw that money could be made in commercial flying. The nation's many smaller airlines began to be consolidated into a handful of large ones. Their names would dominate the industry for years to come.

The airlines serving Dallas and Fort Worth were significant parts of these mergers, as were the individuals who had been involved. A complicated series of mergers in 1928 saw N.A.T., which had initiated air-mail service for Dallas and Fort Worth, became a part of United Air Lines. United now became a coast-to-coast carrier, and in 1931 the company constructed a modern steel and brick hangar at Love Field with offices, waiting rooms for passengers, rest rooms, and baggage rooms. T.A.T., its name having been broadened to Southern Air Transport, became in 1930 a part of American Airways (soon to change its name to American Airlines). Fort Worth's Amon Carter, who had helped finance A.P. Barrett in taking over T.A.T., became the largest shareholder in the company and began his long-time service on American's board of directors. In 1935 Cyrus R. Smith, who had got his start in aviation with T.A.T., became American's influential and long-time president. American also took over in 1930 another airline which had been operating out of Dallas with significant success, Erle P. Halliburton's Southwest Air Fast Express (SAFE), which primarily carried passengers in Texas and Oklahoma.

Delta Air Lines had its beginning in June 1929 when C.E. Woolman gave up crop-dusting to begin flying passengers from Birmingham, Alabama, to Dallas. Without a mail contract, the line lost money, and Woolman sold his company to American. Then in 1934 Woolman won the mail route from Charleston, South Carolina, to Dallas, and began a profitable operation, again under the name Delta. Braniff Airways started in 1930 when the Braniff brothers, Paul and Tom (both of whom had been inspired to enter aviation with Lindbergh's 1927 flight), began transporting passengers between Tulsa and Oklahoma City. When the government canceled all existing air mail contracts and awarded new ones in 1934, Braniff won the Dallas and Fort Worth route to Chicago. Braniff relocated its operations and maintenance facilities to Love Field, and in 1942 the company moved its corporate headquarters to Dallas.

By 1936 there were ten airlines flying passengers out of Dallas daily; Fort Worth had two airlines operating thirty-four schedules daily. The two cities were not far apart in the amount of activity. Precise comparisons are not available, but Fort Worth reported that Meacham Field accommodated 75,173 passengers in 1937 with 11,053 takeoffs and landings. A year earlier Dallas' Love Field boasted of 48,625 passengers with 13,178 takeoffs or landings. Both Love and Meacham had four runways of approximately the same length. Both cities, too, were losing money on their municipal airfield, but so was virtually every city in the nation because of their eagerness to provide the best facilities. Fort Worth's enthusiasm for aviation, led now by publisher Amon G. Carter, continued to be undimmed despite the fact that Meacham was being operated at a small loss each year between 1934 and 1938. This was not unusual, for a 1939 survey of eighty-four municipal airports showed seventy-eight of them to be operating in the red. Dallas' operations at Love Field would lose money until 1951. The willingness to absorb losses suggested the value that Fort Worth and Dallas and the nation's cities placed on providing the best possible facilities for airlines.

IT WAS CLEAR that a certain degree of competition in aviation—even animosity—already had arisen between the two cities during the 1930s. An incident concerning flight training for reserve officers indicated in 1931 that Amon Carter was especially mindful of competing with Dallas. Dallas' establishment of Hensley Field in Grand Prairie had been a signal achievement, for it was said to be the only field in the world devoted exclusively to reserve officers' training. The facility had 232 acres, an administration building, a large hangar, officers' quarters, and barracks for enlisted men. In the late 1920s Amon Carter importuned the field's commanding officer, Lt. Harry Weddington, to come to Meacham Field to give flight training there to Fort Worth's reserve officers. Told that no government funds were available to buy gasoline for training flights in Fort Worth, Carter agreed to pay for the fuel himself if the government would reimburse him when funds became available. In 1931 Carter sent a note to Weddington requesting reimbursement for $138. Weddington responded that he was under the impression that since the training had been conducted in Fort Worth rather than at Hensley Field, no reimbursement was required.

Carter, furious, sent a fiery letter telling him that he had a "hell of a lot of nerve" in avoiding payment. "I realize that you have never been very friendly to Fort Worth and this has been shown conclusively in your efforts in behalf of Dallas in the past and I do not mind passing the word along to you that we would be just as happy over here if you never came back," Carter wrote.

On Dallas' part, it could quietly resent the fact that Fort Worth had been designated as the regional office for the government's chief regulatory body for aviation, the Department of Commerce's Aeronautics Bureau, to be re-established in 1938 as the Southwest regional office for the Civil Aeronautics Board. This office provided important aviation services throughout the Southwest—maintaining airfields, licensing aircraft and pilots, prescribing traffic rules, and operating a radio service for pilots. As early as 1930 some twenty mechanics, radio operators, maintenance men, and clerks were working out of the office at Meacham Field under the direction of George Miller. A fleet of twenty trucks was on hand for crews who maintained fields in several states. They carried camping gear with them, so that if darkness halted their work, they could spend the night on the spot and resume work next morning exactly where they had left off. One of the important services provided by this office was the operation of a radio station which emitted broadcast signals to permit pilots to stay on course even in darkness or fog. Over a series of beacons the station emitted a series of dots and dashes which alerted the pilot if he got off course and even directed him to get back on course. Weather broadcasts also were sent out over the air waves.

The influential hand of Amon Carter was seen by many to be the key to Fort Worth's designation as headquarters for this important regional office. Its existence in Fort Worth, especially in coming decades, would be a sore point for Dallas, whose leaders believed that it unduly favored Fort Worth over Dallas in its actions and policies.

Outspoken and extroverted, Carter took special delight over the years in chiding Dallas. Born in Wise County in 1879 in a log cabin, he quit school at the age of eleven to help his family. In 1905 he had helped found the *Fort Worth Star*, and in 1908 he and his partners acquired the rival *Telegram*. In 1923 Carter gained control of the newspaper. His expert salesmanship expanded from newspaper advertising to civic affairs. He became the youngest president ever of the Fort Worth Chamber of Commerce, and it became his primary goal in life to advance the interests of Fort Worth. "That man wants the whole government of the United States to be run for the exclusive benefit of Fort Worth," exclaimed Vice President John Nance Garner. He not only was the publisher of the dominant newspaper in Fort Worth with a huge circulation throughout West Texas, he established Fort Worth's first radio and television stations, WBAP and WBAP-TV. His investments in oil paid off hugely, and he persuaded many noted oil men to move to his city in the 1920s. Once, when chewing out one of his reporters, Carter exclaimed in serious exasperation, "By God! I speak for Fort Worth!" And this was undeniably true, no matter who the mayor of the city happened to be. In 1950, when Carter received the Frank M. Hawkes Memorial Award for his contributions to American aviation, he was praised as "one of the true pioneers of American aviation."

It was largely because of Carter's efforts that in 1937 Fort Worth opened a new $150,000 air-conditioned terminal building at Meacham Field, three years before Dallas managed to do the same. The terminal was dedicated to Carter. Deferential remarks made toward him by the several speakers showed how powerful a presence he had become. The dedication, printed on a plaque, read in breathless terms: "Dedicated to the Matchless Texan, Amon G. Carter, Range-Rider of the Air. In Appreciation of His Effective Activity in the Advancement of Aviation Thru-Out the World." The nation's assistant postmaster general, Harllee Branch, flew to Fort Worth and declared that the new terminal was the most complete and most modern in the nation. It was "a monument to the vision of a progressive city, and much of the credit for it is due to your distinguished citizen, Mr. Carter."

Carter, master of ceremonies, proclaimed the terminal to be "far better" than the one at Los Angeles, "better" than Chicago's terminal, and he "wouldn't trade it for the one at Newark." (At this time Newark was said to have the busiest airport in the entire world.)

Among those present were a number from Dallas, including City Manager Hal Moseley. Speaker after speaker referred to the rivalry between the two cities. Carter said that the mutual work of the two cities toward canalizing the Trinity River was "the only thing we ever found we could trust the other on." Moseley responded that "there's quite a little rivalry between Fort Worth and Dallas, but it makes us fight a little harder." C.R. Smith of American Airlines said he had seen "Mr. Carter erupt for a week" after American Airlines moved its operations to Dallas, but that now Fort Worth had the outstanding administration building in the country and the only air-cooled one in the nation.

A card printed soon afterwards by the Fort Worth Chamber of Commerce described Meacham Field as being "the third largest air mail center in the U.S." with 624,179 pounds of mail sent out during 1937. There were four runways—the longest 4,000 feet— and the overall field had 320 acres. Meacham was headquarters for an Air Mail District, U.S. Weather Bureau, U.S. Department of Commerce Communications (radio), the Fourth Airways Navigations District of the Department of Commerce; and a Department of Commerce's Airline and Maintenance Inspection office.

In 1939 the Civil Aeronautics Authority added to Fort Worth's aviation prowess by opening at Meacham a new airway traffic control center that directed traffic on all airways within a radius of 200 miles of Fort Worth. An elaborate system was installed on the second floor of the Administration Building to achieve this purpose.

Dallas, not to be outdone in its terminal facilities, in 1939 broke ground at Love Field for a modern terminal. In October 1940, the $225,000 building opened on the east side of Love Field on Lemmon Avenue. The two-story building, crescent-shaped and air-conditioned, was declared to be "the finest airport terminal west of New York."

Love Field boasted of numerous government activities connected with aviation, including a weather forecasting bureau and the office of the supervising inspector of the Seventh District,

Bureau of Air Commerce. The Dallas School of Aviation continued to thrive, and a total of forty-eight air mail and passenger planes were arriving and departing daily in 1940. In that same year the facility handled 102,045 incoming and outgoing passengers. Love Field proclaimed itself to be one of the five most active municipal airports in the nation. It had 278 acres with thirteen hangars.

BY THE END OF the decade, then, these two Texas cities, thirty-five miles apart, had every right to be proud of their aviation facilities and the civic effort and foresight that had been required to achieve them. Yet, airplanes had continued to grow bigger and more powerful. The need for frequent stops no longer existed. The popular DC-3 now was about to be superseded by the huge DC-4, requiring longer runways which would be expensive for both Meacham and Love. Dual stops only thirty-five miles apart in the new and larger aircraft were becoming economically impractical for the airlines. Additionally, the automobile and improved highways also had shrunk the distance between the two cities. The possibility of a single midway airport to serve both cities had become far more realistic and practical, although the fact that Dallas, with a population of 294,734, was rapidly picking up more passengers than Fort Worth, with its population of 177,662, complicated the issue. Should such an airport be midway, or should it be closer to the larger city where more activity was occurring?

On September 26, 1940, the CAA's director of airports, A.B. McMullen, sent from his Washington office a letter to the CAA's airport engineer in Fort Worth, Hester Smith. Both Dallas and Fort Worth had requested federal aid for further expansion of their airports, he wrote, and the way out of this dilemma very well could be a midway airport to serve both cities as well as surrounding areas.

Texas Governor W. Lee O'Daniel already had appointed a Texas Aeronautics Advisory Committee (TAAC) to consider such matters. In the fall of 1940, the body held a public hearing in Wichita Falls, the highlight of which was TAAC's discussion over whether or not it should encourage the Civil Aeronautics

Authority recommendation and ask Dallas and Fort Worth to unite in a single airport.

The ensuing debate, sometimes heated, lasted an hour and a half. Dallas spokesmen agreed that a joint airport would be appropriate, but that if such a facility were built, it should be in Dallas County because of Love Field's greater passenger volume. Fort Worth spokesmen quickly protested. Finally, TAAC decided not to endorse the idea of a joint airport but turn the matter over to the two cities. "Fort Worth Delegates Win Joint Airport Argument," recorded the *Fort Worth Star-Telegram* headline.

It was understood that the CAA was prepared to allot $1,895,318 toward the construction of such an airport, an amount that would include appropriations toward the installation of superhighways connecting both cities to the site. Dallas and Fort Worth would furnish the land and buildings, while the federal funds—in addition to the highways—would provide runways, drainage, and lighting.

An Associated Press reporter who covered the meeting wrote this suggestive sentence: "Discussions so far have indicated the Dallas-Fort Worth airport would be a field of international importance, providing facilities for the largest transport planes in transcontinental service and also as a base for Pan-American Airways planes between New York and Latin America."

Dallas Mayor Woodall Rodgers seemed immediately agreeable to the idea. If Fort Worth objected too much to a Dallas County site for the airport, he said, then the field could be placed astride the Dallas and Tarrant county line! Whether or not Fort Worth cooperated, Dallas would work for this great new airport, said Dallas Chamber of Commerce executive C.J. Crampton. "If no cooperative arrangement is possible with Fort Worth, Dallas will give full consideration to working out arrangements for a well-located intermediate field under Dallas' ownership and management," he said, pointing out that more than 600,000 people lived within a thirty-mile radius of the proposed midway field.

Looking to the future, Crampton observed that transcontinental flights soon would make only one mid-continent stop, and that a combined Dallas-Fort Worth airport would be that logical stop. Eleven east-west airlines already were stopping at Dallas and seven at Fort Worth. For those flights that stopped at only one city—usually Dallas now—passengers were being carted back and forth by limousine. A mid-cities airport would end that inconvenience. Moreover, Fort Worth's Meacham Field needed an expensive fifty-foot dirt fill to extend its runways to meet Class 4 requirements of future airports, while improvements under way at Love Field soon would make it eligible for a Class 4 designation, Crampton said. All these things seem to mitigate toward agreement at a mid-cities location.

Fort Worth, after some deliberation, agreed before the month was over to co-sponsor the joint airport, but with an important qualifier. The mid-cities airport would be used for military purposes only. This was fine with Mayor Rodgers of Dallas, who said that his city preferred to retain the commercial traffic at Love Field anyway. But the CAA, when notified of this new understanding, said it would not participate in an airport to be used solely for military purposes.

With the ensuing reluctance of these two cities to go further with their talks, the mid-cities town of Arlington, population 4,000, saw its own opportunity. Its city officials won agreement from American Airlines and Braniff Airways to participate with it in a mid-cities airport. The airlines would purchase the land, deed it to the City of Arlington, then lease it back so that they could operate and maintain the facility. The CAA would allot $490,000 to Arlington to build a Class 3 airport with runways of from 3,500 to 4,500 feet.

The announcement came as a shock to both Dallas and Fort Worth, who saw themselves as being pre-empted. With their own interest now rekindled in this abrupt way, they began to try to persuade Arlington to yield to them. Dallas' Fred Florence pleaded with Arlington's City Council to let Fort Worth and Dallas handle the new airport. Florence, a highly respected banker and behind-the-scenes power broker in Dallas, told council members that Arlington was simply too small to assume the financial obligations of the project. The Chambers of Commerce of both Dallas and Fort Worth now agreed to participate in the same sort of arrangement that Arlington had made, except that the airlines would purchase 1,000 acres instead of 640 acres to turn over to the two cities. The CAA would construct the landing fields, and the two airlines would operate a terminal. The terminal, or the administration building, would be built precisely mid-way between the Baker Hotel in downtown Dallas and the Texas Hotel in downtown Fort Worth.

Arlington's City Council was unpersuaded. At a closed meeting members voted to continue negotiations with the CAA and the airlines, and later to invite Fort Worth and Dallas to join them if they wished. Dallas and Fort Worth responded by sending spokesmen to Washington, D.C., and pleading their case before CAA Assistant Administrator Lucius Clay. Clay's response was to encourage representatives from all three cities and the airports to meet and work out a new agreement.

Thus was held an eight-hour meeting on October 16, 1941, at the Fort Worth Club. The parties agreed that all three cities would build a 1,000-acre airport midway between the cities, to be used first for pressing national defense needs during this time of war and later for commercial operations.

"Midway Airport," as it now was being called, would be located near Euless in Tarrant County virtually midway between Dallas and Fort Worth. A Midway Airport Corporation would be created by the three cities to administer policies and collect fees as determined by the municipalities. Four of the corporation's seven members would represent the airlines, two each from American and Braniff. Each of the three cities would have one member. The corporation's capital stock of $200,000 would be provided entirely by American Airlines and Braniff Airways. American and Braniff would purchase the 1,000 acres and deed the property to the cities. Once the airport became available for commercial purposes, the airlines would be given fifty-year leases. American and Braniff would build the terminal building and the CAA would construct the landing field. Signing of a contract was delayed until the CAA had time to draw up plans for the new facility.

AT THE MOMENT, other aviation matters seemed more immediate and pressing. In 1940, with war clouds increasingly dark, President Franklin Roosevelt had announced that the U.S. aircraft industry would be called upon to produce 50,000 aircraft as part of the nation's defense effort. This staggering number seemed impossible to achieve, just as the 20,475 quota in World War I had appeared mammoth. Aircraft manufacturers began searching for sites to produce large numbers of aircraft. Once again, Texas became a center of American military aviation, both in production of aircraft and in the training of pilots at military bases in Fort Worth and San Antonio.

North American Aviation, Inc. selected a site adjacent to Dallas-owned Hensley Field in Grand Prairie to begin mass production of military aircraft. On September 28, 1940, ground was broken for a main production building of 855,000 square feet, and on April 7, 1941, the building was dedicated. Between 1941 and 1945 more than 20,000 aircraft, including the P-51 *Mustang* fighters and T-6 *Texan* trainers, rolled off the assembly lines there. A work force of more than 39,000 employees had worked twenty-four hours a day in three eight-hour shifts to achieve that number.

Yet another airplane manufacturer, Consolidated Aircraft Corporation, desired a location in the Dallas-Fort Worth area. The first preferred site had been the same one North American chose near Hensley Field. Both the Dallas and Fort Worth chambers of commerce, anticipating the economic benefits of such a huge manufacturing enterprise, sought to persuade Consolidated to choose them. Initial studies by Consolidated indicated that a site adjacent to North America in Grand Prairie had many advantages, but Amon Carter and his *Fort Worth Star-Telegram* initiated a massive propaganda blitz to bring Consolidated to Fort Worth. Largely because of this, it was believed, in late 1940 the War Department proposed for Consolidated a site on the west side of Fort Worth, a suggestion that was backed up by a $10 million allocation for the plant's construction. Fort Worth added $3 million to that figure in the form of land purchase bonds. Consolidated could not resist, and groundbreaking ceremonies for the new plant were held on April 18, 1941. The production building was to be nearly a mile long. One day less than a year after groundbreaking, on April 17, 1942, the first B-24 *Liberator* bomber was completed. It was the first of more than

3,000 of the giant bombers to be produced there before the war ended.

Consolidated was adjacent to Tarrant Field, an Army Air Force Base later named Carswell Air Force Base. The Army initiated at Carswell one of the nation's first B-24 transition schools, and more than 4,000 students learned to fly the B-24 there.

Arrangements for the new Midway Airport—overshadowed now by these other significant developments—proceeded more quietly, but not for long. As planned, the Midway Airport Corporation had been formed. A Fort Worth man, Raymond Buck, was selected as its president. A 640-acre site approximately mid-way between the two cities near the town of Euless in Tarrant County, was located by the CAA, then purchased and optioned by American and Braniff. The deeds were handed over to Arlington. The site was immediately south of State Highway 183, then under construction as a northern link between Dallas and Fort Worth. Initial plans by the CAA showed the airport's terminal building facing north toward Highway 183 rather than east toward Dallas or west toward Fort Worth. (This site would turn out to be immediately south of the present DFW Airport.)

While all the acreage was just inside Tarrant County, the site was slightly closer to Dallas. Fort Worth officials, unhappy, suggested to the CAA another site a mile to the west. This proved to be too late and too impractical, and Fort Worth agreed reluctantly on the original site upon which runways already were being constructed. Now, however, evidently as a gesture to please Fort Worth and to make the terminal itself almost exactly at the mid-way point between the two cities, the CAA's new plans showed the terminal building on the west side of the property with its entrance pointing toward Fort Worth. A newspaper sketch in Fort Worth showed a proposed highway leading directly from the terminal to the downtown area. Dallas' access to the building, although equal in distance, would not be direct.

This change in plans, when revealed, drastically changed the situation. A series of heated exchanges between leaders of the two cities was filled with such hostility and mistrust that the enmity would not be overcome for decades. Mayor Rodgers charged in

Otto Brodie, surrounded here by admirers, in 1910 was first to fly in the North Texas area. In his exhibition at Fair Park in Dallas, Brodie was able to get only 35 feet above ground.

A traveling company of "birdmen" from International Aviators, Inc., in 1911 demonstrated their skills and bravery in both Dallas and Fort Worth, inspiring a burst of enthusiasm for aviation in both cities. This biplane is being pushed into position at the Dallas Fair Park show.

Dallas and Fort Worth were "united" in flight for the first time in January 1917 when Lestere Miller flew to Fort Worth from Dallas with a load of letters and gifts, then returned to Dallas bearing items from Fort Worth. With him on the right is a Pathe News cameraman.

National Air Transport became the most important early airline to take advantage of U.S. mail contracts which became so important and coveted by Dallas and Fort Worth and other cities.

aining military pilots for service in the first World War was an important activity in both allas and Fort Worth that greatly influenced their commitments to aviation. This is Love eld in November, 1918. Fort Worth had three such aviation training facilities.

:h Fort Worth and Dallas hosted Colonel Charles Lindbergh when he made his national r in 1927 after flying across the Atlantic. Enormous crowds greeted him. He arrived at both es in his *Spirit of St. Louis*. Here he is atop his airplane in a hangar at Love Field.

Opening ceremonies for the new Midway Airport—by now called Greater Fort Worth International Airport—took place in April, 1953. Praise for it was fulsome.

Amon Carter, foreground, and Thomas S.Byrne, during construction of Midway Airport.

Dallas' Love Field terminal, opened in 1940, faced Lemmon Avenue on the east side of the airport. It was declared "the finest airport terminal west of New York."

s Fort Worth sought to persuade Dallas to become a partner in developing a mid-cities irport, one of its arguments was that Love Field, shown above in the mid-1950s, was in a ongested area without sufficient space for further development.

For more than a year it was hard to discern progress on the airport that was understood to be the biggest in the world upon completion. By late 1971 the ultimate shape of the distinctive half-circle terminals could be vaguely discerned from the air.

A pilot's view of DFW and its runways as they appeared nearly thirty years later in 1998.

Pouring concrete for DFW's long runways was one of the largest jobs of its kind in the world. There was enough concrete to pave a four-lane highway between the airport and Oklahoma City; enough to cover all of Monaco with a layer three-feet thick.

Jpon completion in 1973 DFW's half-loop terminals spaced along a central spine and urrounded by runways made a very impressive and one-of-a-kind sight.

Ultimately there would be three modernistic control towers at DFW, more than any airport in the world. A topping-out ceremony marked the completion of the first one.

The graceful system of highways and loops connecting DFW's terminals and the central spine are clearly indicated in this overhead shot taken as the airport was nearing completion.

Terminals 2E, foreground, and 2W, background, are taking shape in December 1971.

When this photograph was taken in February 1969 at Western and Chapparal roads, the eleven airport board members from Fort Worth and Dallas were working together smoothly. Phase one, the lengthy process of grading and drainage of the site, was under way.

Photograph by Raff Frano

Former members of the DFW Airport Board, who represent a wide variety of business and civic endeavors, maintain their ties by belonging to the Friends of DFW Airport.

Dedication of the airport in September drew huge numbers of spectators who clogged the highways. The logistical problems created by the crowds did not dim their enthusiasm.

Many well-known persons attended the four-day, Texas-size celebration that marked the airport's dedication. Above, the president of Iran Air, center, presents a plaque to mark the occasion. Texas Governor John B. Connally is at left, and Thomas M. Sullivan, right.

Left to right, Thomas M. Sullivan, Henry Stuart (who in 1976 would succeed Erik Jonsson as chairman of the DFW Airport board), J.C. Pace Jr., Mrs. Pace, and comedian Jack Benny.

Thomas M. Sullivan, an airport veteran, was DFW's first executive director.

Erik Jonsson of Dallas provided important leadership as first airport board chair.

(Below) At dedication festivities in 1973 the mayors of Fort Worth and Dallas arrived in a festive mood. R.M. Stovall of Fort Worth is at left; Wes Wise of Dallas is on the right.

All photos on this page courtesy of Dallas-Fort Worth Airport Records Management

An American Airlines flight originating from New York with stops at Memphis and Little Rock made the first landing at DFW just after midnight on Sunday, January 14, 1973. Despite the late hour, a large crowd and many from the news media greeted the passengers. In the center is J. Lee Johnson III, and just behind him is Dallas Mayor Wes Wise.

Information desks were set up in the various terminals to assist passengers upon arrival.

Willard Barr, mayor of Fort Worth in the early days of DFW Airport, was honored as a recipient of the J. Erik Jonsson Award.

Vernell Sturns brought stability when he was named interim executive director in 1986 at a critical time.

All photos on this page courtesy of Dallas-Fort Worth Airport Records Management

R.M. (Sharkey) Stovall of Fort Worth, left, and Bob Folsom of Dallas were joint recipients of the Jonsson Award in September 1990. Both were former mayors of their cities.

Bayard Friedman, left, an original DFW board member, won the Jonsson Award in 1993. Presenting the award was Jack Evans, former Dallas mayor and former board member.

Oris W. Dunham Jr., was executive director at DFW from 1986 to 1990.

Bob Crandall of American Airlines, whic became the largest tenant at DFW Airport

wo Concordes landed simultaneously at DFW in January 1979 to introduce Concorde
ervice. Under a unique plan, Braniff pilots flew the airplane to Washington, D.C.,
nd pilots for British Airways and Air France continued the flight to London and Paris.

rench and British Concorde pilots surround Jack Downey (third from left), deputy executive
irector of DFW, and Harding Lawrence, center, Braniff's chief executive..

U.S. Senator Kay Bailey Hutchison
and Jan Collmer, board member and
stunt flier, at the 1989 Erik Jonsson
Awards luncheon.

Congressman Jim Wright, author of the
Wright Amendment, at the airport's
dedication in 1973.

All photos o
this pag
courtesy c
Dallas-Fo
Worth Airpo
Record
Managemer

Congressman Dale Milford, left, and Ernest Dean, who later would succeed
Tom Sullivan as executive director, at dedication ceremonies in1973.

When the new runway opened in October 1996 it was celebrated with a 5-K event entitled "Run the Runway." More than 4,500 participants came for the occasion.

In 1997 Betty Culbreath was elected DFW's second woman board chair.

Erma Johnson in 1987 became the first woman to chair the DFW board.

Jeffrey P. Fegan was named the airport's executive director in 1994.

essence that Amon Carter had secretly persuaded the CAA's regional director, L.C. Elliott, to move the location of the administration building to favor Fort Worth. The direct thoroughfare proposed between downtown Fort Worth and the building would inevitably prompt along it the greatest development, Rodgers and others in Dallas believed.

"Dallas, as a city, can't take this thing without fighting back," Rodgers said. If Dallas loses, he emphasized, its future would definitely be impacted.

"Fort Worth has city-slicked Dallas and is bragging about it," said *The Dallas Morning News'* Felix McKnight in the opening sentence of one in a series of stories on the issue. "If the fraud is permitted to stand, Fort Worth is destined to become the air transportation capital of the Southwest. . . . [Dallas] woke up one foggy morning to find Fort Worth bragging that the terminal would be on the west side of the field, not, as originally planned, on the north side. The new plan placed the terminal where it would not be accessible from any road now reaching Dallas," he continued.

Carter, acting largely as a one-person team in behalf of his city, would not be outdone in the debate. In a telegram to Rodgers he charged him with making "some fantastic statements frankly not in keeping with the facts. I am sorry you have worked yourself into a frenzy just because Fort Worth has the temerity to merely ask for a square deal or an even break regarding the location of the new airport." The airport itself was still a mile closer to Dallas than to Fort Worth, and the location of the terminal not only was not that important, it was the CAA's plan, not his.

Carter absolutely denied having lobbied secretly for the change, explaining that Fort Worth had merely asked for a "fair deal on the distance between the two cities" and that the change in the building's location achieved that goal. Never, he said, had there been a specific agreement as to where the administration buildings would be located. Elliott, pressed to explain the change, acknowledged that he had made the change to appease Carter, but he did not say that Carter had requested the change.

· The argument raged for days. Dallas spokesmen referred to the far greater amount of aviation activity in Dallas, with approximately 75 percent of the area's air passengers now represented at Love Field, not just because of the city's larger population but because runway limitations at Meacham had brought additional flights to Dallas. Even agreeing to go to the mid-point for an airport was a compromise on their part, they said.

Dallas leaders requested a hearing before CAA Administrator C.I. Stanton in Washington to protest the terminal's location. Fort Worth quickly responded. It wanted to be heard as well. When the meeting was held on March 22, 1943, Secretary of Commerce Jesse Jones, Stanton's superior, had decided to be there as well. Dallas brought to the capital a group of fifteen top leaders, headed by Mayor Rodgers, Nathan Adams, and Dallas Congressman Hatton Sumners. Fort Worth's delegation was headed by Amon G. Carter, whose supporting cast included Mayor Newt McCreary and City Manager S.H. Bothwell.

The meeting sparkled with fireworks. Hostility was open. Nathan Adams said that if the terminal remained on the west side of the property Dallas would not join as a partner. Dallas' flights would remain at Love Field. Rodgers claimed that American Airlines, of which Carter was chief stockholder and an influential board member, was the behind-the-scenes force who caused the removal of the terminal to the west side. Carter, free-swinging as was his custom, charged that Rodgers had stirred up the present controversy because of an approaching re-election campaign. Carter especially raised the ire and suspicions of Dallas' delegation when he referred to the disputed terminal as "our building." "These Dallas men come up here to tell the CAA that you're going to do things their way or not at all," he said. "Why, they're going to take their ball and bat and go home if you don't."

After the seven-hour meeting Carter appeared willing to make a concession. He acknowledged that Fort Worth might agree to the original location on the north side if it could be placed half way between the two cities. CAA Administrator Stanton had said earlier that the CAA would accept the north side location "provided we do not have to spend any money to change existing runways."

Secretary of Commerce Jones, however, was in no hurry. A decision might take months. "There is no need for an immediate decision because the building cannot be constructed until after the war," he reminded. Meanwhile, the Army would use the new runways at Midway to train pilots.

Still suspicious and irritated, Rodgers afterwards said that "if on our honeymoon this is the best we can get, God forbid what would happen to us over in Tarrant County in after-married life." Carter was in a taunting mood. "So somebody stole your airport? Some big bully is carrying it away on his shoulders. We usually answer when Dallas talks about us, but their argument this time is so amazing, so fantastic, so amusing, we just don't have the answers."

Rodgers and Adams announced that they would file a formal request with the Civil Aeronautics Board to leave Love Field as a commercial airport if their request for a terminal relocation was denied. Adams' ad hoc aviation committee would continue its meetings, and its goal would be to "cement" the city's position as "air capital of the Southwest." A new master plan for Dallas, to be prepared by Harland Bartholomew, was pending, and Rodgers said he would ask that aviation facilities be considered in his planning. "If we don't get our request for neutral location of the building we shall go right ahead for the protection of our patrons," he said.

Conversations with knowledgeable sources in Washington and with competent engineers, they said, had led to a concern that by the war's end even the new Midway Airport might be entirely outmoded because of short runways and other structural features such as State Highway 183 on its north side and a railroad track on the southern border. "That information was disappointing and discouraging for us, for we had genuinely hoped for a super airport that would anticipate needs for the next twenty-five years," a committee member said. The City of Dallas property at Love Field extended to Bachman Lake, and surveys showed that the present runways, 4,700 feet long, could be lengthened to 6,500 or 7,000 feet. Even so, the progress of aviation might require the construction of two or three new airports in Dallas County, the committee members reported.

Within a week the Dallas officials' position became uncompromising. No matter what ruling the CAB gave—whenever that might occur—the city would not be a partner in the Midway Airport. The aviation committee had decided unanimously that the city's own "close-in" airports were needed to maintain postwar air development. Dallas already was examining new sites for additional airports in Dallas County. A new "superairport" or several airports would need to have 1,500 to 3,000 acres on the property and the runways should be 8,000 feet long to meet federal recommendations for handling the new four-engine airplanes. Neither Love Field nor Midway had space for that, the officials declared. Expansion of Love Field continued as a possibility, but acting City Manager V.R. Smitham said it would be cheaper to develop a new site than to raze seventy-two residences required to enlarge Love Field to that size. (In 1944 the City of Dallas purchased 1,026 acres of land south of town at Hampton Road and U.S. Highway 67 to build an airport for private planes, but it was not envisioned as a replacement for Love Field. Named Redbird Airport, it became active and self-supporting after the war.)

R.L. Thornton, the banker who soon would become known as "Mr. Dallas" because of his aggressive civic leadership, said that the Midway Airport had been conceived to cut expenses for the airlines, not for the convenience of Dallas or its patrons. "They kidded the government into spending $980,000 for an airport in the scrub oaks eighteen miles from Dallas that never will be used. Who wants to ride eighteen miles to an airport just to help the airlines pay expenses? With Arlington as the sponsor, and Fort Worth as the dictator, Dallas never could get a fair deal at Midway. We can't afford to trade 77 percent of the patronage for only 50 percent of the benefits."

Three months later the Midway runways—without a terminal or supporting structures—were ready. They would be used throughout the remainder of the war as a military installation with little attention paid to it.

Harlan Bartholomew's master plan report for Dallas' future seemed to strike a final blow against cooperating with Fort Worth on further developing Midway for commercial purposes. It was, he reported, too remote, too inaccessible, and too small. "It just doesn't fit into any comprehensive plan of airports to serve the future needs of Dallas." He recommended instead a 5,300-acre site for an airport on the east side of Dallas, opposite of Fort Worth, north of U.S. Highway 175. He envisioned it as replacing Love Field as the city's primary airport. Love Field would be dedicated to private flying, non-scheduled commercial flights, and industrial and service activities. Beyond these two airports, Bartholomew envisioned a system of twenty-one airports spread throughout Dallas County to accommodate the anticipated post-war boom in aviation.

This recommendation for an east-side airport soon seemed entirely forgotten. Instead, the city quickly began a series of further investments into the more accessible Love Field site that would make abandoning it less and less likely as the years passed. The first in a series of enlargements to the terminal was made in 1944 to accommodate the rapidly growing number of passengers. A master plan was commissioned and adopted in 1945 for its long-term development and enlargement, and a $5 million bond package was passed for its improvement. Land was purchased for runway extensions that would continue into the 1960s. Civic pride in the facility heightened as business boomed and provisions were made to accommodate the growing number of passengers. A Civil Aeronautics Bureau survey in 1942 showed Love Field to be indisputably the leading airport in the state in terms of passenger activity, followed by Houston, San Antonio, and Fort Worth.

Fort Worth, bolstered by $2.5 million in aviation bonds, similarly gave up any notion of a midway airport operated by the two cities. The city located a new site for a bigger municipal airport six miles south of downtown. The CAA approved the plan and allotted $340,000 toward its early stage development. By 1947 the city had spent $676,637 to obtain 2,172 acres at the site.

THE POST-WAR BOOM in aviation far surpassed what most people had anticipated. Not only was the American public starved for consumer goods that had been scarce or missing during the war, they were ready to travel. Their old fear of flying seemed to have evaporated. The DC-4's, originally intended for passenger service, had been flying across the Atlantic routinely and on a daily basis during the war. Now they were returned to commercial transportation uses. In 1948 major airlines began offering reduced "coach" fares to attract even more customers. Airplane manufacturers competed fiercely to build newer, bigger and faster aircraft, and in 1948 in England the first turboprop airplane, a compromise between the piston engine and the jet, appeared. The jet age was just around the corner.

Quietly, Fort Worth officials began to re-think the possibility of a midway airport. Such a site seemed more and more logical, even inevitable. An airport south of the city had almost no chance of ever becoming the area's dominant facility since Dallas patrons certainly would not go that far. A midway airport, even if owned by Fort Worth alone without Dallas participation, could become the area's dominant facility, especially with an approving nod from the CAA and its authority in approving new flights, in classifying airports, and in authorizing federal funds to assist in developing the airports. The previous arguments in favor of a midway airport not only persisted, their logic became even more pronounced. Such a site would offer clear economic advantages to the airlines. Moreover, with the CAA favoring a location between the two cities the agency almost certainly would shift flights from Love Field to a newer and bigger midway location. With these things in mind, Fort Worth began secret negotiations with Arlington, the CAA, and leading airlines to take over the midway site and build a modern, jet-age facility that could handle the next generation of aircraft.

The negotiations proved successful. On October 29, 1947, Fort Worth Mayor Edgar Deen and City Manager W.O. Jones announced that Fort Worth would build at the Midway site an $11.5 million super airport. Its grandiloquent name, the Fort Worth Transcontinental and International Passenger Airport Terminal, suggested clearly its ambitions, although that fancy title soon was forgotten. The City of Arlington and the Midway Airport Corporation—jointly owned by American, Braniff, and now a third party, Delta—would transfer the property to Fort Worth. The facility would be enlarged from 966 acres to 1,344 acres, its boundaries extended to Highway 183 on the north and adjacent to the Burlington Rock Island Railroad on the south.

Fort Worth spokesmen declared the CAA to be "enthusiastic" in its support for an airport that would be as "strategically located as this one is for serving the requirements of international, transcontinental and area travel." The City of Arlington expressed equal pleasure because the arrangement would permit "a greater airport facility for this area than otherwise could be hoped for." Allocations from the CAA would assist in funding the project.

Dallas was shocked. The threat of such a facility to its own aviation interests was immediately obvious. The CAA could shift flights from Love Field to the Fort Worth airport, and it was clear that a major facility such as this would prove to be a powerful attraction for the airlines, many of whom were on record as preferring a single stop in the area instead of two.

Dallas Mayor Jimmy Temple, who had succeeded Rodgers after four terms in office, and City Manager Roderic B. Thomas learned of the plan only one day before its announcement in Fort Worth when Tom Braniff, president of Braniff Airways; E.P. Simmons, president of the Dallas Citizens Council; and D.A. Hulcy, president of the Dallas Chamber of Commerce, paid them a special visit to inform them. Braniff reportedly urged that Dallas try to work out a deal with Fort Worth so that it could participate as a partner in the airport. Otherwise, he reportedly warned, Dallas would lose its international and transcontinental flights to Midway.

Civic leaders and city officials quickly sought reassurance from the airlines that they would not desert Love Field. Braniff, despite his recommendation to cooperate with Fort Worth, pledged continuation of large-scale service for Dallas. M.D. Miller, vice president of American, gave similar assurances. "Dallas is an extremely important part on our transcontinental routes and service to Dallas will not suffer," he said. "As far as we are concerned, Fort Worth merely has acquired itself an airport on the east side of Fort Worth."

However, one unidentified airline official told a newspaper that it certainly was reasonable to expect that transcontinental lines would stop at only one of the two cities, and they might reasonably prefer a midway terminal to one located in one city or the other. As to the future, if the new midway field should be classified by the CAA as an international airport, Miller of American had "no doubt" but that his airline would apply for landing rights there. Such an eventuality posed a definite threat to Love Field's already ambitious plans to develop international flights. Braniff's much promoted non-stop to Mexico City from Love Field had turned out to be non-stop only en route to Mexico City. Return flights were forced to stop at San Antonio for customs clearance because the government, pleading insufficient funds, would not place customs agents at Love Field despite the fact that the city had recently opened a $300,000 international building adjacent to the terminal for that purpose. If customs officials should be placed at Midway, that's where international flights would land.

The Dallas City Council passed a carefully worded resolution, or "policy statement," concerning the dilemma at its next weekly meeting. The new project, the resolution said, once again had raised "the possibility of discrimination" against Dallas residents in their transportation needs. "Efforts of the city of Fort Worth to obtain a new airport and the location of that airport are not subjects for comment by the City Council of Dallas," the resolution tactfully continued. But, it emphasized, if commercial airlines should attempt to move their passenger and air freight loading points to locations farther removed than Love Field, an act that would be an inconvenience and financial burden to Dallas residents, it would be contested "with every means available to us."

Next day's Dallas newspapers carried a story in which the Aircraft Owners and Pilots Association in Washington, D.C., had given a "superior" rating to Love Field, the only facility in the state of Texas to earn such a rating. But far down in the *Times Herald* story was an alarming sentence for Dallas' Love Field supporters: "There was some indication that commercial airlines may seek to move their terminals and loading points to the projected Midway Airport." Certainly, if Amon Carter had his way, American Airlines would be likely to do so.

The president of the Dallas Aviation Association, E.J. Reeves, was more candid. He was certain that commercial airlines would move their flights to the new Midway airport as soon as it was ready. "A boy in the third grade at school could figure that out," he declared. He reported that the directors of his association would consider asking Dallas to join Fort Worth in its development of the new airport.

The president of Dallas' powerful Citizens Council, an organization of chief executive officers whose authority superseded even the City Council in its influence on city affairs, took note by forming a committee composed of Dallas' most powerful citizens to examine the matter. E.P. Simmons named R.L. Thornton as chairman, and Arthur Kramer, Nathan Adams, Fred Florence, John W. Carpenter, Karl Hoblitzelle, S.J. Hay, E.M. Dealey and Tom C. Gooch as members.

"Dallas has been outmaneuvered," an editorial in *The Dallas Morning News* lamented. But, it observed, with Dallas providing three-fourths of the airline business in the area, it would be "unthinkable" for the big airlines to abandon Love Field.

A large and generally unspoken fear in Dallas continued to be Amon Carter's influence with American Airlines. Not only was he its biggest shareholder and an original member of its board of directors, but as a single individual who seemed to rule over an entire city, he also exercised considerable political influence. And, of course, the logic in building a mid-cities airport could not be denied, no matter how inconvenient it might be for Dallas citizens. With aviation continuing to develop larger, more powerful airplanes, a single midway stopping point undeniably was appealing to aviation management. The *News* warned that Dallas' civic leadership must either go ahead with far-sighted developments in the immediate environs of Dallas, or it must work out an equitable agreement for Midway Airport. "Our leadership should do this now, not after sitting back and waiting a while to see what developments will be.

Soon the prospects for Love Field's future darkened at the same time prospects for Midway grew brighter. In its 1948 National Airport plan, subject to Congressional approval, the CAA recommended that Midway would become the primary airport for Dallas and Fort Worth. Love and Meacham fields would become "feeder" or auxiliary facilities. Midway's runways would be lengthened to 6,500 to 7,500 feet, and its overall size doubled. Love Field, would be upgraded but not to the same extent, its runway lengths increased to between 5,500 and 6,500 feet.

"Love Field is enveloped by above-average residential development, and it is evident that it cannot continue to be expanded at a rate to keep up with the rapid development of aviation at Dallas," the CAA stated.

The agency listed five reasons for making Midway the primary field for North Texas: (1) Through passengers not terminating at either Fort Worth or Dallas would save time through the elimination of a stop; (2) passengers destined for Fort Worth from the East would save time by eliminating the Dallas stop; (3) passengers destined for Dallas from the West would save time by eliminating the Fort Worth stop; (4) the airlines would effect a "great saving" by eliminating a stop; and (5) both Fort Worth and Dallas would receive the benefit of all airlines stops at Midway.

An interesting part of the CAA plan was to construct at White Rock Lake in Dallas a seaplane base. It would open a new phase of flying for Dallas, the CAA noted, and "it should be the most popular improvement proposed." Dallas Mayor Pro Tem Wallace Savage was skeptical. Why hadn't Dallas been consulted on this? "I don't think the people would be agreeable to changing a public park into a seaplane base," he commented.

If Congress approved the 1948 airport plan as recommended, the government would provide approximately 50 percent of the funding required to expand Midway. Dallas would receive only enough federal funds to reach the level recommended by the CAA.

Fort Worth Congressman Wingate Lucas declared that he would do all he could to secure Congressional approval of the CAA plan. Dallas Congressman J. Frank Wilson vowed that he would do everything he could "to protect Love Field and to stop the plan from being carried out."

In this battle Fort Worth and CAA clearly were partners. A CAA spokesman, Ralph Lee Jr., said that his agency would prefer that Dallas help Fort Worth on the project, but if not, his agency would continue to assist Fort Worth . The $340,000 in federal funds already earmarked by the CAA toward Fort Worth's now abandoned airport project south of town, was being shifted to the Midway project.

Dallas quickly developed a strategy to protect its own airport and—inevitably—to hold back the Midway airport so that it would not become superior to Love Field. City Manager Roderic B. Thomas prepared an appeal that would by-pass the CAA regional office in Fort Worth, where the suggestions undoubtedly had originated, and go directly to the national CAA headquarters in Washington, D.C. CAA officials halted this effort; any such hearing would have to originate before the regional CAA office, and at the ensuing hearing held in Austin, Dallas was unsuccessful.

Dallas' Congressman J. Frank Wilson took another approach— to cut off federal funding for the airport, which now was expected to be given $11 million in federal funds to match local funding of $11 million. Yet another direction lay in seeking to remove all limitations by the CAA on Love Field expansion. Love Field's master plan, already filed with the CAA, contained provisions that could make the facility superior to that envisioned for the midway airport.

Dallas City Manager Thomas said plans for the new Midway Airport gave new urgency to Dallas' long-range aviation plans for making Love Field a super airport. The city already had invested $3.6 million in Love Field and the terminal already had been enlarged to three times its original size since being completed in 1940.

Thus was set the stage for a battle that would consume so much of both cities' energies for many years. In his fight in the House to reduce CAA appropriations for Midway, Wilson succeeded. But the U.S. Senate restored the funds after a determined delegation of Fort Worth went to the nation's capital and lobbied their case. The CAA retreated from its notion to relegate Love Field a secondary role compared to Midway, acknowledging that they could more or less be equal. Improvements to Love Field would continue with CAA approval, for the constantly growing volume of activity there could not be denied. Customers had to be served. In June 1948 Fort Worth strengthened its hold by reaching eastward to annex the property on which Midway—now being described frequently by the Dallas press because of its distance to downtown as the "19-Mile Airport"—was being developed.

Dallas in 1949 launched its own initiative to improve its standing with the CAA, and by December the manager of the Chamber of Commerce's Aviation Department reported that CAA officials, "from the top down," had impressed the Chamber with its sincere considerations of improvements for Love Field.

DISPUTES OVER the Midway Airport overshadowed other aviation activities in the two cities, but a great deal was happening. For one thing, Tarrant Field, the military airfield adjacent to Consolidated Vultee Aircraft Corporation plant (which in 1954 would become part of General Dynamics Corporation's Convair Division), in 1948 had acquired a new and lasting name—Carswell Air Force Base. It was named for Horace S. Carswell, Jr., a Fort Worth native who won the Medal of Honor and other military honors for having given his life heroically in 1944 as the pilot of a B-24 on a mission over the South China Sea. Carswell Air Force Base had gained international attention in 1949 when a crew stationed there flew a huge B-50 airplane, the *Lucky Lady*, around the world on a non-stop flight that covered 23,308 miles in ninety-four hours and one minute. Mid-air fueling at various points around the world kept the huge aircraft aloft. Besides the pride and triumphant that Fort Worth and the military felt about this accomplishment, there was tragedy. Captain William Gardner Fuller Jr., son of the veteran military man who had kept Meacham Field open in the 1920s (and who would spend almost all his career there and later at Fort Worth's new mid-cities airport), lost his life on one of the re-fueling missions. Captain Fuller's B-29, the last plane to refuel *Lucky Lady*, disappeared on its way back to Luzon after completing the refueling.

In 1950 another major aircraft manufacturer, Bell Helicopter, moved to the mid-cities area, settling in Hurst east of Fort Worth. Workers in a new multi-million dollar facility began producing large numbers of helicopters, their numbers increasing markedly with the advent of the Korean war. These choppers were used especially for airlifting wounded servicemen from the front to medical facilities behind lines. The Bell Model 47, a major component of the MASH units, later would be immortalized in the movie and television series, M*A*S*H*. Bell's helicopters also served civilian purposes such as herding cattle, ferrying city executives, traffic reports by news stations, and patrolling high-tension wires.

Not until June 1950 was ground broken for Midway's terminal building. Amon Carter, of course, handled the shovel for Fort Worth. He was assisted by a most unlikely and surprising partner, the prominent utility and insurance executive, rancher and civic leader from Dallas, John W. Carpenter. Carpenter, serving his first of two terms as president of the Dallas Chamber of Commerce, was defying conventional wisdom for Dallas' civic leaders by his support of the project. "Come on, John. Let's dig a little dirt today instead of throwing it," Carter said playfully, as he handed over the commemorative spade.

A few months later, Carpenter, in his year-end report to members of the Chamber, recommended that Dallas cooperate with Fort Worth in developing the "Midway International Airport." At the same time, he assured the likely Dallas skeptics who would emerge, that planned expansion and improvement of Love Field should be carried out as soon as possible. "The great Dallas-Fort Worth metropolitan area, already with nearly one million population, needs both of these airport facilities. We must plan now for the time when this area will have twice this many people to serve."

As Carpenter noted, the two cities had been cooperating fully on other projects of mutual interest, particularly in the long-time goal to make the Trinity River navigable. He saw no reason why they should not unite to promote the entire "Dallas-Fort Worth Metropolitan Area" as the largest single metropolitan area in the South.

"Most of our problems and troubles today have been caused by lack of foresight in the past and our failure to envision the possibilities of our great city," Carpenter observed. In an indirect reference to the Midway airport controversy, he summed up: "No individual, no group, and no community can expect to accomplish much if it bases its plans and progress to pacify its fears of anything."

City of Dallas Aviation Director George Coker seemed to agree in comments made at the same time. It appeared to him that there was ample need for both airports. He cited an example: When LaGuardia had opened in New York City many had assumed that the Newark Airport would be diminished, but this did not prove to be the case. "We'll lose some flights to Midway," Coker said, "but we took them from Fort Worth in the first place, when Meacham Field got inadequate to handle the DC-6s. Now Fort Worth will take those flights back. But this area is always going to be a tremendous air traffic center. I think we'll laugh in the years to come, to think we were afraid of Love Field's future. There's room enough for both."

An unidentified person cited in a newspaper account as an aviation expert, believed that Love Field indeed would find itself relegated to secondary status compared to Midway. Love Field would retain the "milk runs" to Houston and San Antonio, and perhaps a few major flights, but he believed that the bulk of the cross-country and intercontinental traffic would go to Midway.

Inspired no doubt by what appeared to be a more flexible mood in Dallas, Fort Worth now offered an olive branch. A *Dallas Morning News* reporter, in a behind-the-scenes report on the nature of the initial approach, put an interesting twist to it. It was said that two American Airlines officials, acting at the behest of Fort Worth interests who were beginning to feel that their city had over-extended its resources in its commitment to Midway Airport, believed it essential to gain Dallas' participation. "Amon Carter is getting old and soft," they reportedly said, and he "might be willing" to let Dallas come in on the airport.

The offer, made to Mayor J.B. Adoue Jr., was for Dallas to become a full and equal partner in Midway. There would be no penalty for not having been a partner from its inception. Adoue, a plain-spoken banker who often took independent and controversial stands, rejected the offer outright.

"It is no secret," the *Dallas Times Herald* acknowledged, "that some of the city's most influential businessmen have changed their thinking about the 19-Mile Airport and are now ready to negotiate with Fort Worth on any basis. They contend that Love Field will be outmoded in a few years and that it cannot be expanded enough to take care of traffic in the next 10 years." If such leaders existed, though, outside of Carpenter himself they remained anonymous, and Adoue as mayor of the city flatly rejected the Fort Worth offer.

Love Field's future—no matter that it was among the busiest airports in the nation—still was dependent to a large degree on CAA policies if it were to maintain its dominance. The CAA's 1951 National Airport plan, despite Dallas' intense lobbying, still placed Love Field at a disadvantage relative to Midway, although by now both airports were labeled as "class five." The CAA appeared to be poised to give Midway and not Love Field an intercontinental classification. The CAA had "corrected" the length of Love Field's primary 5,200-foot runway to just 4,400 feet because of adjustments for altitude. The city's planned extension of this runway to 6,200 feet (the contract was due to be awarded right away) would actually amount to a "corrected" length of only 5,100 feet, short of the mark for an airport designated as "intercontinental." Midway's longest runway was projected to be 6,400 feet before its correction, but the CAA plan would allow Fort Worth to seek federal grants to expand its runway to qualify for the more desired intercontinental classification. Adding to Dallas' unrest, the CAA also planned to allow Houston to expand to intercontinental status, too. Further salt in the wound for Dallas were the 1950 passenger statistics that gave Love Field a huge advantage over all Texas competitors: Dallas, 442,450; Houston, 229,250; and Fort Worth, 50,375.

Another continuing thorn for Dallas was the fact that its international building, open since 1947, still had no U.S. customs agents assigned to it. Although the government had not discouraged Dallas from erecting the building, it could not fulfill its central purpose until the federal government declared Dallas a port of entry. Only American Airlines used the international building, but American's allegiance still seemed tilted strongly to Midway, where it already was building a fine new structure that would become its training center for flight attendants. It was understood that many of its operations as well as flights would be transferred to Midway upon its completion.

In August, Mayor Adoue, City Manager Charles Ford, and Chamber of Commerce General Manager Ben Critz once more urged federal designation of Love Field as a port of entry. Houston and San Antonio already were ahead of Dallas in intercontinental flights. Without port of entry designation it appeared that Fort Worth with its possible upgrade to intercontinental classification soon would be ahead, too.

IN APRIL 1951 CAA's chairman, Delos W. Rentzel, visiting unofficially with business executives in Dallas, suggested another approach to the airport situation. The two cities might create a joint non-political airport board to oversee aviation development. Its duties would include the operation of all their airports. "Dallas and Fort Worth need to forget their horse-and-buggy feud and get some overall control of all the airports around here," Rentzel said, referring not only to Love Field, Midway, and Meacham, but also to Dallas' Redbird in Oak Cliff and Hensley Field in Grand Prairie. He pointed to the success of similar airport boards elsewhere—in New York City and surrounding towns, in New Orleans with a three-airport authority, and in Akron and Canton, Ohio, where a joint authority existed.

John W. Carpenter, whose large property holdings in the area between Dallas and Fort Worth surely heightened his disposition to cooperate with Fort Worth, liked the idea. In an open letter that summer to members of the Dallas Chamber of Commerce, he followed up on Rentzel's suggestion by urging that Fort Worth and Dallas unite in the creation of a Dallas County-Tarrant County airport authority to oversee and complete the development of Midway Airport and Love Field. He repeated his conviction that Midway posed no threat to Love Field. Even after Midway was in operation, Love Field would be essential, he insisted.

No one in Dallas arose to support Carpenter, although Fort Worth Mayor J.B. Edwards declared that the suggestion made "good sense." Dallas' response to Carpenter's proposal was hostile. Mayor Adoue thought the idea was "ridiculous." Citizens Council president T.E. Jackson said that the thought of most of his members was that "we should stay away from controversy and develop Love Field." Most of Carpenter's fellow board members tactfully withheld public comments; others openly disagreed with him.

The Chamber's aviation committee, responding to Carpenter's call to resist the status quo, undertook another study of aviation needs for the entire area. James W. Aston, a former Dallas city manager and now a bank executive at Republic National, headed the committee. His group worked in conjunction with a similar committee from the powerful Dallas Citizens Council that was chaired by retailer Stanley Marcus. Carpenter refrained from issuing any ultimatum to his committee, and he had little or no authority with the Citizens Council. He said, "Whatever action the Citizens Council and the Chamber of Commerce take will be a constructive move for the city of Dallas."

The *Dallas Times Herald* viewed a possible partnership as not economically justified. Fort Worth had invested more than $4 million of its own money into the Midway Airport, and the federal government had contributed another $4 million. Yet another $4 million appeared to be needed. Dallas was seen as an easy source for those funds, the newspaper conjectured. "Dallas has already spent more money on Love Field to develop it into a major port than Fort Worth apparently intends to expend on the 19-Mile airport. Why should Dallas sacrifice its own investment in a close-in airfield to help Fort Worth complete a field that will not be convenient to either city?" The very fact that transcontinental flights were landing in the Dallas-Fort Worth area at all was due, the newspaper contended, to the development of Love Field, toward which Fort Worth had contributed nothing.

Midway's longer runways, its greater capacity to make them even longer, and the CAA's obvious inclination toward Midway continued to weigh heavily on the minds of Dallas officials and civic leaders as they pondered their next step. Concerned about the limitations of Love Field as contrasted to Midway's touted potential, the directors of the Dallas Citizens Council once more asked Dallas aviation director George Coker for some answers. Coker told the group that it would be absolutely feasible to double Love Field's size from its then 600 acres to 1,280 acres, and that

Dallas already owned and was holding in reserve more than 400 acres around the airport in anticipation of the Master Plan expansion. It also was possible, he said, to lengthen Love Field's main runway to 8,500 feet and to build yet another runway that was 8,500 feet long on the other side of the field (a goal that would be achieved in 1963).

In August the *Times Herald*, emboldened surely by Coker's favorable assessment, waxed even firmer in its support of Love Field. Civic leadership must "dismiss once and for all the theory that the possibilities of the airport are limited," the newspaper stressed. "The master plan for Love Field was adopted almost a decade ago and will be carried out if there is no interference. Fort Worth, meanwhile, should be able to achieve its own airport goals without hampering those of Dallas.

The City of Dallas and the Chamber of Commerce, still pondering Coker's favorable assessment but thinking that an outside evaluation was needed, hired a New York City consultant, James C. Buckley, to analyze the situation for them. Buckley's report to City Council came first, and when he appeared before that body in March 1952, his findings upset Mayor Adoue. "You are employed by Dallas, but it looks like you are working for Fort Worth," Adoue declared. Not only did Buckley think that Dallas should enter into a regional airport plan with Fort Worth, in his opinion Love Field inevitably would have to yield some of its flights to Midway. While Love Field now had about 80 percent of the area's air traffic, he believed that once Midway opened Dallas should expect to retain no more than 65 percent of that traffic.

The Dallas Chamber of Commerce's new president, Ben Wooten, found Buckley's report to be "economically sound" and practical, an opinion shared by W.W. Overton of the Chamber's aviation committee. Their assessment also infuriated Adoue, who said the two Chamber officials were wanting to give Dallas' aviation business to Fort Worth.

Buckley's written report to the Chamber of Commerce, seventy-five pages long, provided statistics that reinforced the case for Love Field. It had, he found, a larger percentage of traffic originating or terminating within the city than any airport in the nation. Additional costs of Love Field's users to go to Midway would be approximately $1 million a year. Love Field operations provided 3,650 jobs and a payroll of $14.5 million. Buckley's recommendations also detailed improvements needed for Love Field that were in general accord with its master plan.

The way seemed clear for an even larger commitment to Love Field. As a result of Buckley's report, the Chamber of Commerce requested City Council—half a year before Midway was to open—to call a bond election for massive improvements to Love Field. City Council complied, and a $12.5 million bond program was presented to the city's voters for approval in January 1953. Projects before the voters included an entirely new terminal at a new location, a relocation of Lemmon Avenue to provide for expansion and relocation of other airport activities, extension of the 6,200-foot runway to 8,500 feet, and building on the other side of the airport a new 8,500-foot runway. The program also called for improvements for the city's airport in Oak Cliff, Red Bird. Voter turnout was the largest for any election of any kind in Dallas history. The final outcome was 19,481 for and 15,194 against. Opposition had been led by a persistent group of homeowners in the Love Field area.

CAA officials expressed their pleasure at the outcome, but with Midway scheduled to open five months later their enthusiasm for that facility was undimmed. Nor did the plans for Love Field's improvements alter American Airlines in its announced plans to divert some of its flights to Midway as soon as it was ready, and also to move there its regional headquarters and sales office from Dallas.

George Coker was philosophical about losing flights to Midway. The advent of the DC-6 and its requirements for longer runways earlier had caused some of American's transcontinental flights to transfer to Love Field from Fort Worth's Meacham Field, he said, because runways there were too short for take offs bearing full loads. Those flights, understandably, would return to Midway, he said. During a certain twenty-minute period at Love Field these days there were three New York-to-Los Angeles flights on the ground at the same time. One of these flights easily could be moved to Midway without affecting Dallas' air service at all, he observed.

FOUR

Partners at Last

✈

On the last day of September [1964] the CAB
announced its decision. The two cities
would have to be served by a single regional airport.

When Midway Airport was dedicated on a Saturday
afternoon, April 25, 1953, it had a new name—Greater Fort Worth
International Airport. It also had a secondary but equally official
designation—Amon Carter Field—to honor the man who had been
the moving force behind it. It would become commonly known not
by its longer first title but the simpler one, Amon Carter Field.

C.R. Smith, American Airline's chief, had tried in vain to
persuade Carter to refuse the honor of having his name placed on
the airport, arguing that it would certainly foreclose the possibility
of Dallas' participation, at least for a while. In these heady days
of optimism, though, any reluctance on Dallas' part—if it even
was considered—might have appeared to be of little consequence.

Carter was president of a new private corporation that
actually had control of the airport. The company, the Fort Worth
Air Terminal Corporation, had taken out a thirty-six year lease
on the property from the City of Fort Worth. Fears in Fort Worth
about financing and operating such a large modern and expensive
facility—as evidenced by the very narrow 1961 bond election and

given the record of municipal airports throughout the nation for operating in the red—had been ameliorated by this special arrangement. Carter had put together a group of twenty-three Fort Worth businessmen who subscribed $250,000 in capital stock to form the corporation. Amon Carter now, in a real sense, had his own airport.

Carter, however, was not present for the gala festivities that Saturday afternoon of the dedication. In fact, he would fly only once more in his life, for he had but two years to live. Carter lay this day in bed in a Fort Worth hospital, recovering from two heart attacks. But he was not too ill to review carefully the *Star-Telegram*'s coverage of the dedication by reporter Irv Farman, just as a few months earlier he had dictated changes in an advance story to make certain that the superlatives were sufficient. Looking at Farman's story now and seeing that the article contained—as Farman knew his publisher would insist—an inordinate amount of glowing descriptions that defied all normal reportorial standards for objectivity, Carter handed the copy back to him. "I hope you wore a bow tie when you wrote this," said Carter. "Why?" asked Farman. "I'd hate for all this stuff to splatter off the keys and stain your tie," the publisher replied.

In truth, there was great reason for superlatives, for the airport was a state-of-the-art facility, instantly declared as one of the world's finest by aviation experts who were there. "Marvelous," exclaimed Tom Braniff. "A grand piece of work, strategically located," said Charles Horne, former administrator of the CAA, adding that he was certain it would pay off "big dividends." The executive secretary of the American Association of Airport Executives called it "one of the finest airports" he had ever seen. "I think they looked far into the future in designing it," Horne said. The director of aviation for the Port of New York Authority, Fred M. Glass, said, "The combination of the building, airport and approaches makes it one of the outstanding airports in the world."

From Mexico came General Alberto Salinas-Carranza, chief of civilian aviation in that country. Ironically, he had been flown to the new facility from Love Field, arriving just in time to hear his name announced. "I'm very happy with the idea of such a wonderful, functional and modern international airport being so near in flying distance and time to Mexico City."

President Dwight Eisenhower could not attend, but he sent as his representative Air Force Secretary Harold E. Talbott, who officially dedicated the airport. Raymond Buck, president of the Fort Worth Chamber of Commerce, was master of ceremonies. A thirty-piece band from Carswell Air Force Base played music, and the Cowtown Posse, a group of about fifty western-clad riders on horseback, paraded past the speaker's stand.

Thirty thousand people were there for the dedication, including Carter's son, Amon Carter Jr., who read a statement from his father. Carter predicted that the airport would serve two million passengers and be a "dream come true."

The east side of the 1,780-acre property abutted the Dallas County line. Its main runway was 8,400 feet long—longer by far than Love Field's main runway—and a second runway was 6,400 feet long. A third one was 4,100 feet long. Once the jet age arrived, the longest runway was projected for extension to as long as 12,000 feet.

The terminal was situated at the point that had so irritated Dallas, on the west side nearer Fort Worth. Far larger than Dallas' still modest 1940 terminal, it contained 242,000 square feet with expansion possibilities planned for 500,000 square feet. The lobby, 60 feet wide, 180 feet long and 31 feet high, was decorated in a modern western style. There were three levels. The ground floor contained baggage areas, airline operations offices, air freight and cargo areas, and other facilities such as a barber and beauty shop. On the first floor were numerous concessions, a huge spectators gallery, and access to the seventeen airplane gate loading positions (as based on DC-6 spacing) that were five more than Love Field's twelve loading spaces. Restaurants as well as the Weather Bureau office, CAA safety operations offices, and others were located on the second floor. In the Amon Carter Suite, reserved for VIPs and corporation officials, a $100,000 collection of Frederic Remington and Charles Russell western paintings were on permanent display. In American Airlines' Admirals Club another collection of western art could be viewed. Its value was placed at $106,000.

There were, of course, hangars, shops, and office buildings on the grounds. The control tower, one of the largest in the nation, was equipped with the most modern safety devices.

The editor and publisher of *American Aviation* magazine, Wayne W. Parrish, declared the terminal to be the finest in the world, "a tremendous civic victory for Fort Worth." Dallas, he said, would have to take "a back seat."

Just after midnight the airport opened. The first scheduled arrival, American Airlines Flight No. 605, a New York-to-Los Angeles flight, landed at 12:01 a.m., April 26, with fifty-two passengers aboard. The cheers of more than 3,000 spectators greeted the passengers. The first one to step off the airplane was Mrs. Robert I. Ross. She was from Dallas. The next was Mrs. Frank Brandt. She was also from Dallas. Passengers three and four were Mr. and Mrs. E.L. Smith. They, too, were from Dallas. The fact that they were from Dallas hardly dimmed the enthusiasm at all; after all, the new airport must attract Dallas' passengers to be a success.

Now, of course, the goal for Greater Fort Worth—or Amon Carter Field—was to have enough flights to make this great facility successful. American Airlines had twenty-six flights at Amon Carter as opposed to the thirteen previously scheduled at Meacham. Love Field's former forty-three American flights now dropped to thirty-one. Some 550 American Airlines employees also were moving to the new airport as well as the regional headquarters offices.

The Dallas Chamber of Commerce reacted angrily to American Airlines' new schedule. A week after Carter's opening the Chamber's twenty-eight member aviation committee met to consider the matter. Also attending were the city's new mayor, the venerable Mayor Robert L. Thornton—"Mr. Dallas," members of the Dallas City Council, and Chamber President Ben Wooten. The committee adopted a report decrying the inconveniences they believed were being forced upon Dallas' travelers. They also denounced American Airlines as a monopoly and threatened to appeal its schedule changes to the CAB. Especially upsetting was the fact that passengers intending to come to Dallas between 5 and 6 p.m. from New York, Chicago, Atlanta, and Miami landed not at Love Field but at Carter Field, and that passengers departing between these hours for Los Angeles, San Francisco, and Mexico City had to go to Carter for departure. Moreover, the erratic schedules meant that many passengers departing from Love Field—perhaps even parking their cars there while away— might find themselves returning instead to Carter. American's ticket agencies in many cities, the committee claimed, were selling flights to Dallas that arrived at Carter Field instead of Love. In light of this, the Chamber said it would ask the CAB to authorize new flights to Dallas from a number of airlines, including United, Eastern, Braniff, and Delta. The committee's ire was directed primarily at American because of the number of its flights. None of the five other airlines serving the area had diverted such a large number of flights to the new facility.

Adding further concern for Dallas was a CAB decision on July 31, 1953, granting new routes for Central Airlines into Oklahoma. The agency specified that both Dallas and Fort Worth must be served on these routes from Carter Field. This decision, the Chamber believed "threatened the very foundation of Dallas' position as an air transportation center." The Aviation Committee's announced strategy now was "holding the line" to prevent further attrition at Love Field and continuing to push for the improvement of Love Field according to its far-reaching master plan.

By May 1954 income at Love Field had dropped $11,000 in the past seven months because of Carter Field's competition, but in October a happy surprise awaited Dallas. For the previous fiscal year Love Field showed a profit of $5,237. Modest though this sum seemed, it was the airport's greatest annual profit ever. It represented the third consecutive year that Love Field had shown a profit, and it came even after paying $665,770 in interest and principal on airport bonds. Perhaps even more surprising was the fact that for the fiscal year Love Field had shown a 3 percent gain in scheduled airplane traffic. Customers clearly continued to be attracted to Love Field because of its closeness to a majority of travelers and the greater number of flight offerings there.

Carter Field had yet to establish itself, and the continuing preponderance of traffic at Love Field indicated that this would be more difficult than thought, if even possible. According to the CAA's own figures, in the third quarter of 1953 Love Field had boarded 79 percent of all passengers in the Dallas-Fort Worth area; in the second quarter of 1954 that percentage climbed to 81.7 percent. Even American Airlines, with a reduced number of flights, gained 31 percent more passengers at Love Field during the second quarter of 1954 than in the same quarter a year earlier.

As to the argument that a new midway airport would be more economical for the airlines, the CAA report for the first full year after Carter's opening showed that the cost of enplaning passengers there was far higher than at Love Field. Expenses for American Airlines were running $40.08 per passenger at Carter as compared to $6.17 at Love. For Delta-C&S Air Lines, the cost at Carter per passenger was $43.48 as compared to $4.25 at Love.

The trends continued in the CAA's third-quarter figures. Carter Fort Worth enplaned 34,103 passengers on 5,101 flights. Carter, clearly, needed more passengers.

Fort Worth was especially proud in early December 1954 when a thick fog closed Love Field from 6:30 a.m. to shortly before noon. Amon Carter remained open, handling 128 flights that day which had been diverted from Love Field. This was approximately ninety-four more flights than ordinarily were handled during that time. "Amon Carter Field had its biggest test Saturday and passed with plenty to spare," the *Star-Telegram* recorded.

A different kind of problem for the CAA was the now more complicated air-traffic pattern over the skies of Dallas and Fort Worth. Carter and Love Field were only twelve miles apart, and there was also the matter of airplanes at Hensley, Carswell, and Meacham fields. Control towers at the individual airports handled their own flights at altitudes below 5,000 feet, but above that level all flights in the area were handled by the CAB's air route traffic control center in Fort Worth. In a study of this problem, prepared by the CAA's technical development and evaluation center at Indianapolis, Indiana, blame was laid at the feet of Dallas' "civic pride" for having failed to cooperate with Fort Worth in developing the mid-cities airport. ("Civic pride" was a phrase destined to be emphasized and enlarged upon a few years later by FAA Administrator Najeeb Halaby in a criticism of Dallas.)

Dallas Chamber of Commerce President Jerome K. Crossman countered the CAB's charge by claiming that Amon Carter Field itself was the mistake. In fact, he said, within the past ten days some Fort Worth citizens had admitted their error in building the airport and "pleaded that we [in Dallas] should do everything possible to help them sustain their present white elephant."

Indeed, the financial figures from Carter Field were not encouraging. For the fiscal year ending September 30, 1954, Airport Manager W.G. Fuller's figures showed a net loss of $48,668, a loss which would have been a profit of $187,063 except for a debt service payment of $235,731.

A FEW MONTHS later on November 5, 1954, CAB Chairman Chan Gurney again sought to reopen the question of Dallas' participation in Carter Field. In a letter to Fort Worth City Manager W.O. Jones, he asked his city to consider selling a half interest in Carter Field to Dallas.

"We are always disturbed by any situation which tends to hinder in any way continued progress toward the achievement of the finest obtainable airline service for the United States traveler and shipper," Gurney wrote. Elaborating, he said:

> The Board has felt for some time that the continuation of the controversy which has existed between the cities of Fort Worth and Dallas concerning the use of what is presently named the Greater Fort Worth International Airport, and Love Field, is not consistent with the best interests of commercial aviation generally, and can only result in handicapping the continued growth and development of air transportation in the area involved.
>
> While the Board greatly admires the spirit of enterprise and aggressiveness which both Dallas and Fort Worth have shown in the development of civil aviation and in which both are truly outstanding, it would appear that continued progress depends to a considerable degree upon a satisfactory resolution of the question of the

relative use of the Fort Worth Greater International Airport.

Accordingly, Gurney offered these suggestions: (1) sell a portion of the airport to the City of Dallas at the original cost to Fort Worth; (2) change the name of the airport to something indicating its true position of serving both Dallas and Fort Worth, such as Dallas-Fort Worth or Fort Worth-Dallas; and (3) explore the possible formation of a joint port authority administered by a board of directors composed of leading citizens of the communities. In the latter event, Gurney wrote, the board might operate other airports in the system as well. Such an organization, with appointments made by the governor of Texas, conceivably could purchase the assets of the airport and operate it as a business enterprise.

> If end results such as these can be obtained, we are sure that improved service will result to both cities consistent with their growth requirements, and unquestionably better service than can be rendered to each community on a competitive basis as at present. We are, we feel, justifiably concerned by the continuation of this dispute at unnecessary cost to the taxpayer in payments to the carriers having subsidy requirements, to the larger, self-sufficient airlines in higher operating costs, and to the traveling public in terms of conveniently available air transportation service.

Gurney then signed off with the final word, "Your consideration of these suggestions and early comment thereon will be greatly appreciated."

Fort Worth's leaders immediately were agreeable. Mayor Edgar Deen; Amon Carter, president of the Fort Worth Air Terminal, Inc.; and J.M. Leonard, chairman of the terminal company; quickly sent a letter to Mayor R.L. Thornton and the Dallas City Council, offering half interest in the Fort Worth Air Terminal, Inc., for $4 million. The offer included a change in name that would put Dallas first: "Dallas-Fort Worth Airport; Carter Field." The name of the Fort Worth Air Terminal, Inc., would be changed to Dallas-Fort Worth Air Terminal, Inc. Dallas would be given equal representation on its official staff and board of directors, and all rights and facilities of that corporation would be transferred to an appropriate authority when and if one was established.

"We will be glad to discuss further details at your convenience. Will you please advise us of your views?" the Fort Worth officials concluded.

Dallas' unofficial reaction, issued by the Chamber of Commerce, was quick and somewhat contemptuous. Chamber President Crossman and the chairman of the Chamber's aviation committee, Angus G. Wynne Jr., declared in a joint statement that the offer amounted to an effort by Fort Worth to bail itself out of financial problems. "What it boils down to is this: Fort Worth is offering to sell Dallas a detour—a detour which the air travelers and shippers of Dallas would then have to use." The only thing new in Fort Worth's letter, they claimed, was the offer to add Dallas' name to the airport. "We have been accused of having civic pride, and Dallas does have civic pride. But we don't think the citizens of Dallas have the kind of civic pride which would lead them to pay $4,000,000 for the right to change the name of another city's airport from 'Greater Fort Worth International Airport, Amon G. Carter Field,' to Dallas-Fort Worth Airport, Carter Field,' " they said.

In the joint statement the two men pointed out that Fort Worth had less than 125,000 originating and terminating air passengers a year compared to Dallas' 750,000. "The inconvenience and unnecessary expense involved in a Dallas passenger's use of the Fort Worth airport, multiplied by 750,000, amounts to staggering totals. These are the basic reasons Dallas insists on continuing the use of Love Field."

They contended that CAA Chairman Gurney's reference to the "controversy" and "dispute" between the two cities reflected "an amazing lack of knowledge" of the facts and the economics involved in Dallas' effort to secure for Love Field the air service required by Dallas' own traffic. "Mr. Gurney is completely in error if he thinks Dallas has initiated or is waging any dispute or controversy with Fort Worth. . . . We sincerely hope Fort Worth will continue to grow and prosper, and we also hope that it can make a financial success of its airport."

Even if Dallas purchased a half interest in the airport, they argued, the combined requirements to handle the air traffic from both cities would be more than Carter Field could accommodate without further expensive improvements, the statement continued. Nothing, they believed, should be permitted to interfere with the new $5 million terminal being constructed at Love Field or with the other planned improvements. Within the week, the Chamber's board of directors asked the City Council to reject the offer and to expedite the program expanding Love Field.

Fort Worth continued to maintain a calm demeanor. Crossman's counterpart as president of Fort Worth's Chamber of Commerce, Charles S. Nash, appealed to him in a 1,000-word letter sent by special messenger to drop all bias or bitterness in considering the offer. "The compelling reason for the Fort Worth offer is a sincere desire to work out an arrangement which will result in the best possible air service for all the people of Tarrant and Dallas Counties and the entire North Texas area," he wrote.

The arguments for a united mid-cities airport were even more compelling now than in 1941 when the two cities had agreed to one, Nash said. There had been a near doubling of population with the most rapid growth occurring between the two cities, highway access had been improved, and far more industrial development had occurred. Few companies would want to move to an area "where neighbor is pitted against neighbor," he wrote.

Crossman remained unmoved. "We would be recreant in our duty to Dallas, just by the stroke of the pen, to agree to go off to an airport many miles distant, and not contiguous to the city, and spend millions a year in extra cost and inconvenience to suit the whim and fancy of a group in another city," he responded. Crossman also went a step further. He sent telegrams to CAB members demanding that because of the CAA-inspired offer they disqualify themselves in future Dallas air service cases because of their demonstrated prejudice in favor of Fort Worth.

Communications between the mayors of the two cities concerning the offer were cordial. Mayor Deen of Fort Worth sent Mayor Thornton of Dallas a copy of Nash's letter to Crossman as a courtesy with a note expressing "a spirit of friendliness and with a feeling of sincere belief that the municipal governments of our two great cities can work out this situation to the satisfaction of all concerned." Thornton replied in a far more cordial fashion than had Crossman. "I have read it [the offer] with great interest, and please let me assure you personally, that whatever may happen to the airport controversy my friendship and respect for you, your city council, and the people of your great city will be as it has always been—my best."

The actual decision lay not with the Chamber of Commerce but with the Dallas City Council. City Manager Elgin Crull, following instructions of City Council members, asked Fort Worth's city manager, Jones, for specifics about financial commitments and the city's lease agreement with Fort Worth Air Terminals.

Jones' response contained yet another surprise. Fort Worth now was lowering the price for a half share in the airport to $2.7 million, a reduction of $1.3 million.

As Dallas' City Council pondered this sweetened offer, a Dallas group of citizens who were in the midst of a legal struggle to halt Love Field's runway expansion plan, spoke out with another opinion. Jack Gillespie Jr., president of a Love Field homeowners association, told the CAB's Gurney that he should feel confident that his suggestion was "appreciated by thousands of Dallas citizens as being in the public interest." His organization also wanted to apologize for the "disgraceful" treatment of Gurney and the CAB by Crossman. "He does not speak for the people of Dallas or for their elected representatives," Gillespie wrote. Home owners around Love Field would continue to be a thorn in plans for expansion of the facility in the years ahead as they protested against the overhead noise.

Just more than two weeks after Fort Worth's initial offer, the Dallas City Council, on a roll-call vote, unanimously adopted a polite, moderately worded letter of rejection. Mayor Thornton said the City Council had been studying the matter for two weeks, "almost night and day," before coming to its conclusions. The Council's letter assured Fort Worth that its decision was made "solely on the merits of the proposition without regard to any bias

or prejudice which may have arisen in the past."
   It continued:

> We believe the air transportation needs of Dallas and Fort
> Worth, as well as the needs of other communities in the
> respective areas served by our two cities, require both your
> airport and ours. Certainly the reasonable projection of
> growth of our two cities, and of the respective areas to
> which they provide primary service, indicate that both
> airports will be needed even more tomorrow.
>
> Furthermore, our studies convince us that a partnership in
> Greater Fort Worth International Airport would mean a
> greater annual cost to the taxpayers of Dallas than will the
> continued use of Love Field and its further development to
> meet our present and anticipated future needs.
>
> On the one hand we have weighed the expenditures which
> will be required to complete the Love Field master plan.
> On the other hand we [have] taken into account the money
> which would have to be spent to provide facilities at the
> Fort Worth airport adequate for the total traffic which
> now is being handled separately at Love Field and at your
> airport. We have also recognized the recurring annual cost
> to Dallas travelers and shippers if they were put to the
> additional expense involved in ground travel to and from
> the Fort Worth airport.
>
> Even if you gave us a half interest in your field, and we
> transferred our traffic there, we would still have to
> participate in the very sizable capital investment required
> to make your airport adequate for our combined traffic.
>
> For all these reasons it is the unanimous and unreserved
> opinion of the City Council of Dallas that the acceptance
> of your proposal is not to the best interests of the City of
> Dallas, to the area it has long served, nor to the future of
> air transportation needs of the broad areas which look to
> Dallas or Fort Worth for basic services.
>
> We therefore, respectfully decline your offer.

It is our sincere hope that the citizens of each of our cities will recognize that the Fort Worth airport and Dallas' Love Field are here to stay. We would like to move ahead with you in parallel progress.

We certainly have no quarrel with the people of Fort Worth. You have our friendship, and we want yours. We believe that we should have a great common interest in working to bring the benefits of competitive air service to our respective cities.

With this rejection, hope for Carter Field's future success seemed to rest to a large extent on the Civil Aeronautics Board. It appeared for a while that Fort Worth's influence with that agency might be bolstered. Wingate H. Lucas, the Fort Worth Congressman supported by Amon Carter but recently upset in his Congressional bid for re-election by Jim Wright of Weatherford, a town west of Fort Worth, now became mentioned prominently for an appointment to the CAB.

The possibility of a Fort Worth man in that position—a man widely identified as having been supported by Amon Carter— especially alarmed Dallas Chamber President Crossman and Aviation Committee Chairman Angus G. Wynne Jr. The two mounted a campaign to halt his appointment on the grounds that Lucas could not be impartial in considerations involving the two cities. Wynne advised his committee members that Fort Worth was exerting all possible political pressure to secure his appointment, and "in view of his long and close association with the interrelated interests which seek to capture Dallas' air transportation business and move it to another city, I have grave doubt that he could, as a member of CAB, be open minded regarding Dallas air service needs." Wynne urged that telegrams of protest be sent to President Eisenhower and other prominent public officials. Crossman sent a telegram to the President notifying him that Dallas was a party to eight proceedings then pending before the CAB. It would be impossible for Lucas to be impartial in these matters, Crossman said in the telegraph, and even if he disqualified himself he would inevitably influence fellow board members.

The anti-Lucas campaign succeeded. Dallas' Republican Congressman Bruce Alger, after contacting White House officials, reported that the appointment would not be forthcoming. The fact that Dallas County voted heavily for President Eisenhower in 1952 and sent the state's sole Republican to Congress—Alger—was said by some to have weighed heavily in Eisenhower's decision to support Dallas' wishes.

In June 1955 Amon Carter, his health having been in decline for some time, died at the age of 75. Surely no city in the nation had ever had its fortunes so closely identified with one man. Nor had any city's fortunes in aviation been tied so closely to a single individual. One Fort Worth terminal had been dedicated to him and the next had been named for him.

The airfield that was named for him clearly was in trouble. Any expectation that passengers from Dallas, despite the city's initial opposition, would recognize the value of this finer airport and begin to patronize it now seemed hopeless. Dallas' new terminal at Love Field would be even bigger than Carter Field's terminal. Its twenty-one loading gates would outnumber by four those at Carter. Its lengthened runway and the new runway both would be longer than those at Carter. Since Carter had begun service, passenger loads had remained virtually at a stand-still. In fact, the month of June 1953, two months after its opening, remained a year later its busiest month to date.

In March 1955 Fort Worth's R.L. Bowen, chairman of the Chamber of Commerce aviation committee, wrote a lengthy letter to area newspapers in which he complained about distortions in Dallas' news coverage and expressed hope for a better future. "The time will come, within less than the next 10 years, when there will be over 2,000,000 people in Dallas and Tarrant Counties, and we wonder just how they are going to be handled by the present facilities, some of which can not be adequately enlarged. However, we do know that the Greater Fort Worth International Airport can be doubled in capacity without the acquisition of any additional land and at a very reasonable figure. So, time, patience and facts will tell the story and Fort Worth is adequately supplied with all of these requisites." He recalled the quote, "You can fool some of the people all of the time, and all of the people some of the time, but you can not fool all of the people all of the time." In conclusion, he wrote, "Self-sufficient people and dictators have usually paid the penalty in the long run."

IN JANUARY 1955 Mayor Thornton presided over the opening of Love Field's new 7,750-foot runway. Ten months later he poured the first barrel of concrete for the foundation for the new $6.5 million airport terminal. Two years later in October 1957 Love Field's new terminal opened. It was six times the size of the old terminal on Lemmon Avenue, and it was bigger and grander than Carter Field's terminal that not long before had been proclaimed as the best in the world. The new Love Field terminal had 375,000 square feet of floor space (compared to Carter's 242,000 square feet). Its lobby was 150 by 185 feet (compared to Carter's 60 by 180 feet). Its final price tag was $7.7 million. Gil Robb, publisher of *Flying* magazine, called it "the finest air terminal in the world." That same year at Love Field American got a new $1.5 million building; Delta, a $1 million building. Braniff opened a new headquarters at Love Field at a cost of $6.5 million. Southwest Airmotive, an aviation service company, opened a new $1.5 million facility.

The dearth of passengers and the steadily decreasing number of flights at Carter Field prompted rising concerns. A 1957 news story in the *Fort Worth Press* summarized the situation: "Unless you time your visit during one of the peak hours, you'll still find the glamorous giant lobby of the Carter Field terminal building almost empty of customers." With the airline industry on the verge of a full-scale conversion to jet carriers, a new strategy emerged at Carter Field to take advantage of that fact. The powerful new jet airliners would make only one stop on their coast-to-coast flights, and that likely would be either at Chicago or Dallas or Fort Worth. Fort Worth officials began a $445,000 project to extend the main runway by 2,050 feet. "If Carter Field can offer longer runways, more safety features and better ground maintenance the jets are bound to choose it over hemmed-in and overcrowded Love Field," the *Press* reported.

Also lending hope for a brighter future was the opening in 1957 at Carter Field of the American Airlines Stewardess College, a $1 million facility built in a country club-like setting of beautiful scenery and natural stones, and with a large swimming pool. Many luminaries attended American's dedication services: Sam Rayburn, speaker of the U.S. House of Representatives; Tom McCann, mayor of Fort Worth; Robert L. Thornton, mayor of Dallas; and C.R. Smith, president of American. At this new facility prospective flight attendants would attend a five-week training session before being assigned to American's various bases. Central Airlines also lent encouragement to prospects. In the fall of 1957 Central began building a new headquarters at Carter. American's stewardess college and Central's new headquarters were expected to bring in enough income so that the city no longer would have to subsidize utility bills at the airport of $2,500 a month.

By 1960, though, Carter's problems had intensified. On June 1 the City of Fort Worth took over operations from the Fort Worth Air Terminal and instituted salary cuts for many of the personnel because of the annual losses. Airport revenue for the fiscal year 1960-61 was estimated to be $832,716; expenditures were predicted to exceed that figure by $44,000. City Manager L.P. Cookingham proposed raising the price of gasoline sold at Carter by 4 cents a gallon, upping hangar rental space by 50 percent, and increasing office space rental by 10 percent. New parking fees and the addition of a "kiddy" ride concession might produce some other revenue, he reported.

Concerned about Braniff's service to Carter and inspired by complaints from Fort Worth Mayor Tom McCann, the city's Aviation Board summoned the Braniff district sales manager, George F. Scott, to respond. Instead of soothing Fort Worth's wounded feelings, Scott poured salt into the wounds. He chose this moment to announce that Braniff was canceling two of its East Coast flights at Carter. The airplanes were carrying about as many crew members as passengers, Scott said.

Board members, shocked, lashed out. The CAB should "compel" airlines to land one-third of the flights coming to the Dallas-Fort Worth area at Carter Field without making a stop at Love Field, said Marion Hicks. The board directed City Manager Cookingham to invite Trans World Airlines to provide direct and exclusive service at Carter. "If we can't do this, then I think we have lost our battle to save Carter Field," said City Councilman Gene Cagle.

Two days later Cookingham sent a sharply worded letter to Braniff's president, Charles E. Beard, to advise him that Braniff no longer could use Carter Field free of charge to train its jet crews. "Need I remind you that it has been your policy not to operate any jet flights to or from this airport?" Cookingham wrote.

Carter Field, these days, was looking over the edge of a steep cliff. The 24,350 departures there in 1960 would drop in just five years to 7,059. The number of enplaned passengers in 1960, 148,615, would further fall in 1965 to a disastrous 29,131 passengers. By this time the airport was virtually abandoned.

The picture at Love Field was just the opposite. For the same time intervals, Love Field's 61,027 departures in 1960 would increase to 72,106 in 1965. Its 1,313,158 enplaned passengers in 1960 would more than double in 1965 to 2,782,010.

But Love Field supporters had their own concerns, only slightly different although of far less magnitude. In April 1962 the Chamber of Commerce's Aviation Committee stressed to CAB Examiner William J. Madden that Dallas desperately needed a direct, one-stop Europe-Dallas flight. The flight, proposed by Braniff and Pan-American, would stop in Chicago and then fly to London and Frankfurt. Houston, which was below Dallas in almost all flight categories, already had two direct European flights daily.

American Airlines, seen for years by Dallas as Fort Worth's advocate, announced in April 1962 that it was moving a major part of its maintenance and flight supervisory personnel from Carter back to Dallas. The move was expected to save the airline about $500,000 a year by avoiding duplication.

The precipitous decline at Carter caused great alarm in Fort Worth, not just for the sake of its investment there and civic pride, but because the quality of air service for its citizens was suffering. For the flights they needed for travel and business, more and more Fort Worth residents were having to drive past Carter Field to get to Love Field. The city's hope for gaining a higher quality of service now was possible only if the CAB could be persuaded to follow its long-term inclination and designate Carter Field— Greater Southwest—as the regional airport for Dallas and Fort Worth.

In such a mode of thought, on May 10, 1962, the president of Fort Worth's Chamber of Commerce, Raymond Buck, and City Attorney S.G. Johndroe Jr., sent without any publicity a letter to the CAB asking that it investigate the possibility of specifying a single regional airport to serve both cities. The Fort Worth leaders blamed the major carriers, now including American as well as Braniff and Delta, for seeking in effect to create a regional airport at Love Field by concentrating flights and activities there without sanction of the CAB or FAA. This, they contended, was in clear violation of the Federal Aviation Act. "Our situation is acute," Buck and Johndroe wrote. "We are rapidly losing services because the above-mentioned carriers are transferring and centralizing their schedules at Love Field, Dallas."

THE FAA's administrator, Najeeb Halaby, in May 1961 had urged in a press conference in Dallas that the two cities create a joint airport authority. Getting no significant reaction at the time, the next year he soon began making a series of statements that fanned the simmering airport controversy once more into a raging fire. Halaby, a Dallas native, had concluded that a regional airport was necessary to serve the area, and he was seeking some way to achieve that goal.

On August 9, 1962, Halaby declared to a Senate appropriations subcommittee that the FAA did not intend to spend "another penny" at Love Field. "Childish civic pride" in Dallas, he said, enlarging on the phrase first used by the CAB in 1954, was costing American taxpayers millions of dollars even though "a darn good jet airport" sat idly nearby. His comments were like a torch to Dallas' civic, business, and governmental leaders. They reacted angrily.

Just over a week later, Avery Mays, now the Dallas Chamber of Commerce president, made a conciliatory gesture. Dallas was ready to discuss future regional airport needs with Fort Worth. However, Mays stressed, any "arbitrary assumption" that Carter

Field would be the ultimate answer to the question was out. "We are willing to meet with the Fort Worth Chamber of Commerce any time to consider objectively and factually any matter regarding the mutual interests, convenience and economics of the two metropolitan communities," he said.

Fort Worth responded quickly and positively. Raymond Buck, Chamber of Commerce president, said his organization was "anxious to discuss" with Dallas leadership the present and future airport needs of the area. "To be productive," he said, "such a conference would have to be free of prejudice and bias." He could not resist observing that the advantages of using the site or locality of "what is now presently Carter Field are obvious and many." Still, he acknowledged, Fort Worth would be willing to study another site. Fort Worth's city manager, Cookingham, pointed out that in the final analysis the city governments would have to make decisions of this nature.

Mays said that his offer was in no way intended to curtail progress on Love Field's ongoing improvements. Mayor Earle Cabell said that while he supported the idea of long-range aviation planning, he was even more interested in completing Love Field's new $8 million parallel runway. Fort Worth Mayor John Justin appointed a group of three, including himself as chairman, to work with him on a committee to represent Fort Worth in examining the matter. The other two were Amon Carter Jr., chairman of the Chamber's aviation board, and J. Lee Johnson III, chairman of the City Council's aviation board and a *Star-Telegram* executive. Carter, of course, was Amon Carter's son; Johnson was Amon Carter's son-in-law.

Three days after Mays' conciliatory offer, the CAB officially ordered hearings to be held on whether Dallas and Fort Worth should be served by a single regional airport. Parties to the hearings would be the two municipal governments, their chambers of commerce, American Airlines, Braniff Airways, Central Airlines, Continental Air Lines, Delta Air Lines, Eastern Air Lines and Trans-Texas Airways. The announcement brought optimistic and grateful expressions from Fort Worth, but touched in Dallas feelings of resentment and determined opposition.

Mayor Cabell said the hearing order scotched any chance of talks between Dallas and Fort Worth. "Such talks now would be nothing but a mockery," he declared. "I will not stand idly by as a citizen nor as an officer of the city and see a debt of $32 million saddled on the taxpayers of Dallas, the loss of $35 million annually in payrolls and the possible bankruptcy of several fine firms. . . just to pull Fort Worth's and the FAA's chestnuts out of the fire and save them from further financial loss in the operation of an airport that should never have been built in the first place." Mays agreed. "A federal agency has injected itself into Dallas' affairs," he said. "Under the circumstances, since the Dallas case must be presented to the CAB, such talks would be fruitless."

Mayor Justin of Fort Worth said there was no reason to think that Carter would profit from such a hearing any more than Love Field. He revealed now that he and City Attorney Johndroe had requested the hearing in the spring. Congressman Jim Wright separately had asked for a hearing. Dallas' own M. J. Pellillo, who headed the homeowners' group fighting the new runway at Love Field, also had petitioned for such a hearing.

Dallas' reaction seemed pre-ordained—to cancel the hearing. Fort Worth's strategy also was predictable—it saw no reason at all for canceling. Dallas, it claimed, was practicing "narrow partisanship" in its request to vacate the order. "In Fort Worth's view, the important and controlling consideration is the future development of the North Texas area." One thing seemed certain: such hearings normally lasted two years or longer before finally being decided. Beyond that was the possibility of appeals in the federal courts.

With Najeeb Halaby away on vacation, one of his top aides backed up his boss' position about spending not another nickel at Love Field. He wrote to Dallas Congressman Bruce Alger and informed him that it would not be proper to "make additional capital expenditures" at Love Field while the hearing was pending. Installation of an instrument landing system there would be irresponsible prior to that time.

Back on the job at the end of August, Najeeb Halaby held a press conference in Washington attended by some fifty reporters. He urged Dallas and Fort Worth to exert local initiative and create a mutual long-range aviation plan. Air traffic was expanding so rapidly over the country, he stressed, that the area would need Love Field, Amon Carter, and several other general aviation airports.

Only the previous Sunday, Halaby told the reporters, he had flown over Love Field. Its limitations seemed obvious to him. "I wish all civic leaders of Dallas would take a helicopter and fly over Love Field and look at the way in which this runway is being placed there for heavy operation of jets," he said. It would be surrounded—just as Love Field already was surrounded—by Bachman Lake, factories, schools, and housing developments. An instrument landing system for this new runway would cost $400,000 instead of the usual $250,000 because of these problems, and there was no certainty it would work anyway in the face of so much area interference.

Congressman Jim Wright contended that if the two cities did not soon join forces, Houston likely would take over the role as regional leader in air service. But Dallas, led by Mayor Cabell, stiffened in its stance. If a regional airport has to be designated, the Dallas City Council declared in a resolution, it should be Love Field. The resolution also called for the city to employ all necessary counsel to develop and present pertinent data for the CAB hearing, and it emphasized that the city must go ahead with the work toward its new 8,800-foot runway. The earlier site that Fort Worth had chosen for a new airport, the one south of the city, had been a proper one, selected by experts and approved by the CAA, the resolution declared. Since that time "dominating influences" had forced its abandonment in favor of the Carter Field site in the center of "the most complex air-traffic pattern in the Southwest and only 12 miles from Love Field." Overtures by Fort Worth since that time, City Council members declared, had been based on "pure sophistry and brainwashing sessions to sell Carter Field as the regional airport."

Unperturbed, two days later Fort Worth's Justin urged creation of a Dallas-Tarrant County Airport Authority to take over all public airports in the two counties. "We must consider such things as congestion, length of runway and safety in planning for a regional airport," he said. "Love Field certainly has some space limitations, and, of course, the debt is a factor," he said. "A bi-county airport authority could take and assume the control and debt for all public airports in the two counties. A profitable regional airport could defray any bonded indebtedness at Love Field without costing the Dallas taxpayers anything."

In November 1962, figuring that the name of Amon Carter Field had been anathema to Dallas and an obstacle to cooperation between the two cities, J. Lee Johnson III recommended and the Fort Worth City Council agreed to rename it and to include Dallas in the title. Greater Fort Worth-Amon Carter Field thus became "Greater Southwest International Airport—Dallas-Fort Worth Airfield." The change was logical, Johnson said, "because of the board's view that the airport's ultimate destiny is to be the principal regional intercontinental airport for the Southwest part of the United States." If the move was intended to gain Dallas' favor, it backfired. Dallas City Council's response was to instruct its city attorney, Henry Kucera, to determine whether the use of "Dallas" in the title was legal. "This was pure presumption on their part," Mayor Earle Cabell said. "It's unethical to use the name of Dallas on any shanty in Fort Worth."

Earlier, when the name change was being considered, the city's aviation board had requested recommendations from citizens. The most popular name submitted had been Dalworth International Jet Air Terminal. Other suggestions had included Carter-Thornton International Airport and Truce Field.

Changing the code designation for the airport from ACF (Amon Carter Field) to DFW also caused protests. Braniff complained to the FAA's Halaby that the change would cost the airlines $250,000. Moreover, the company said, the FAA's "acquiescence" in the request might indicate to some observers "a seriously prejudicial and ethically unsupportable prejudgment" of the upcoming airport hearings.

Meanwhile, as the two cities prepared their arguments for CAB examiner Ross I. Newmann, CAB figures released in March 1962 showed that as many people were boarding planes at Love Field in nine days as did in nine months at the Fort Worth airport. Figured on a daily basis during that time, 4,924 persons boarded airplanes at Love Field while only 165 persons boarded airliners at Fort Worth's newly named Greater Southwest. For the entire nation during the full year of 1962, Dallas ranked seventh in the nation during 1962 in the number of persons boarding planes with a total of 1,800,000 passengers. And for the fiscal year of 1962 the airport tallied a record net income of $1,426,719.

The CAB hearings, which began in the spring of 1963 and were not completed until final pleadings in September 1964, produced a ponderous amount of material, estimated at one point to be 5,000 pages. Final briefs from all parties—the two cities and their chambers of commerce, the airlines, the FAA, the CAB's Bureau of Economic Regulation, and Dallas' Citizens Aviation Association—were filed on December 9. Most of them favored Fort Worth, although Braniff favored keeping Love Field in its present capacity. American and Delta preferred serving a single airport in the area, but did not specify which one. Newmann was unable to estimate when his decision could be expected.

THE LONG-AWAITED decision—actually more akin to a "non-decision"—came on April 7, 1964, from Washington, D.C. Newmann stated in his fifty-page long ruling that "it would not be in the public interest" to designate either Greater Southwest or Love Field as the regional airport. He criticized both cities and airports. Love Field, he said, was limited in size and its possibilities for future expansion. By the early 1970s, despite the new parallel runway under construction, he declared that Love Field's terminal and accompanying facilities would not be able to meet the needs of a booming city like Dallas. "While Love Field can meet the area's current needs and its needs for the immediate future, its expansion capability from a long-range standpoint presents an extremely serious problem. In short, Love Field's time is running out," his decision stated.

As for Fort Worth, Newmann pointed out that past voting records indicated that Tarrant County voters might not support a bond issue would be needed to enlarge Greater Southwest to meet the expansion demands of a regional airport. He also criticized the city's arguments to the CAB, for it had offered plans for enlarging their airport that merely duplicated service already available at Love Field.

A joint airport, Newmann said, had to satisfy two basic requirements, neither of them met by Dallas or Fort Worth. "First, there must be a true joint partnership entered into in good faith by the communities involved. In order for the project to be successful, the cities must be willing to cooperate in its planning, construction, operation and support. Second, the entire Dallas-Fort Worth area should be carefully scrutinized so the airport can be located at the best possible site."

Newmann pointed out that the ultimate goal indeed was to build a "supplemental airport" to serve the North Texas area at some time in the future. Both cities stood to benefit if a "fair and equitable solution to their problems" could be worked out. "One possible solution would be the creation of an airport authority (removed from the pressures of civic pride) which would assume full responsibility for the planning, development and operation of all airports in the Dallas-Fort Worth area."

Fort Worth especially expressed dissatisfaction. "The fight isn't over by any means," said Mayor Bayard Friedman, indicating that an appeal to the full Civil Aeronautics Board was certain. He believed that there was a "substantial chance" that the CAB would reverse Newmann's ruling. As to Newmann's idea that a joint airport authority be created, J. Lee Johnson III pointed out that such an authority had been proposed by Fort Worth for a long time but that Dallas had consistently rejected the idea. Johnson took some satisfaction in Newmann's sentence, "Love Field's time is running out," which he believed to be the most significant sentence in the report.

Congressman Jim Wright was the most plain-spoken of all. Newmann's report, he said, was "weak-kneed, mealy-mouthed and wishy-washy." He would support any Fort Worth effort to "appeal this frail and anemic recommendation in the hope that the board will have enough spine to carry out its glistening promise of a few months ago regarding the saving of federal funds through the creation of regional airports."

With an appeal pending, Dallas' new mayor, Erik Jonsson, a founder of Texas Instruments who had assumed the mayor's office in early 1964 when Earle Cabell resigned to run for Congress, and the new president of the Chamber of Commerce,

Robert B. Cullum, sent an offer to Fort Worth. They proposed meetings with Fort Worth to make long-range aviation planning for North Texas' airport needs beyond the year 1970—as Newmann had suggested. But they wanted Fort Worth to drop its appeal of Newmann's decision.

Fort Worth's Mayor Friedman and its Chamber of Commerce president, J. Lee Johnson III, said they remained committed to the idea of a regional airport. They would be happy, however, to sit down and discuss mutual aviation needs with Dallas officials. "We hope that our early meeting will finally culminate in a sound workable plan for a regional airport which will assure the vitality and continued growth of air transportation for the Dallas-Fort Worth area for years to come."

There were those who were skeptical of Dallas' motives and sincerity. The homeowners group which had been fighting Love Field's new runway, the Citizens Aviation Association, which had been given the right to file briefs with the CAB in the regional airport question, was especially critical. James P. Donovan, attorney for the group, said the offer was a "legal nullity" which contradicted the official resolutions of the City of Dallas. The requested meetings with Fort Worth were strictly to create a good image with the CAB, he contended.

When the CAB decided in June 1964 to review Newmann's decision, Dallas seemed unalarmed. "This was not unusual or unexpected," said Avery Mays, chairman of the Chamber of Commerce's aviation committee. Dallas' Mayor Jonsson agreed that the action did not seem to be unusual. "This is an important case," he said. "They do this every once in a while. All it means to us in Dallas is that we will have to submit more briefs. . . . Our case was carefully built and should stand up. We should come out all right."

Meanwhile, with this issue and possible talks between the two cities still pending, both prepared for the CAB appeal to be heard in September. At that hearing in Washington, D.C., both cities sent large contingents to argue once more their cases along the same lines as before. Afterwards, CAB Chairman Alan S. Boyd said a decision would be announced at an indefinite time in the future. "You can say within the next two years," he told reporters after oral arguments had been completed on September 15. A ruling was not expected before spring of 1965.

It came much sooner. On the last day of September the CAB announced its decision. The two cities would have to be served by a single regional airport. The agency issued an ultimatum: The two cities had 180 days to decide themselves on such a facility. Otherwise, the CAB itself would "proceed promptly" to issue its own decision on it. "We contemplate a voluntary arrangement for an orderly transfer that will be finally effected no later than sometime in 1968," the ruling stated. The field must "meet without limitation, the present and future requirements for transcontinental cargo and passenger services."

It did not dawn at first on Dallas or Fort Worth that the end of their long dispute over a mid-cities airport actually was over. Further appeals to the federal courts were possible, and past history indicated that such a move was likely.

However, in Dallas, certain doubts had arisen. The 8,800-foot runway, due to open soon, had been fiercely opposed by Love Field homeowners. Cost of the runway was $4.5 million, and it had been made possible only by moving several large buildings from its pathway. It was clear that further expansions of Love Field could not continue indefinitely.

Mayor Jonsson was certain that neither facility would serve the purpose of a regional airport. A compromise with Fort Worth on an entirely new airport seemed possible. "Probably, a joint airport at a mutually convenient location by the early 1970s will be the solution," he believed. Robert B. Cullum, the Chamber's president, continued to favor Love Field. "If there must be one airport, this well-established, well-equipped plant should be the one. I can't see anything that would disqualify Love Field down through the years." Avery Mays, chairman of the Chamber's aviation committee, acknowledged that "on first impression, the action looks unfavorable to Love Field." But it appeared to be no more favorable to Fort Worth, he believed.

Years later Jonsson said that he and other Dallas leaders realized that jumbo and supersonic jets then being developed for the future simply would not be able to use Love Field. They represented, he said, a "new ball game," not just an orderly continuation of past developments. "If you were heedless of what might be coming in a technical sense in the next few years, then you'd be building the second and third and maybe the fourth and fifth airports as experimental places." Such a situation, he knew, could not be tolerated by taxpayers.

Fort Worth was happy about the decision. "We are willing and will be happy to go into this matter with our Dallas counterparts. This suits us fine." Acceptance by the CAB of a regional airport concept, he said, was something which Fort Worth had been advocating all along. Chamber President Johnson was optimistic that the two cities could agree on a site. "I have no doubt we can get close, if not actually reach an agreement." If nothing else, he believed, the idea of Houston taking away aviation business should prompt the two to get together. "We have never said Greater Southwest has to be the airport—we have only said that Love Field cannot be it," he said.

Talks began almost immediately to see what might be achieved. Within a month six negotiators, three from each city, already had met three times behind closed doors at the Inn of the Six Flags at Arlington. Erik Jonsson, Robert B. Cullum, and Dallas Mayor Pro Tem Carie Welch represented Dallas. Bayard Friedman, J. Lee Johnson III and banker H.B. Fuqua represented Fort Worth.

In these meetings nerves often were on edge. One individual in particular emerged who seemed always to release the tension in the air with a well-timed witticism to keep the talks going on a productive basis. This was the diminutive Robert B. Cullum, head of the family-owned Tom Thumb food store chain in Dallas and a long-time Dallas civic leader. Years later, two of the Fort Worth representatives, Bayard Friedman and J. Lee Johnson III, both doubted that the negotiations could have been successful without Cullum's peace-making abilities and capabilities for seeing all sides of the questions.

Erik Jonsson recalled that when discussions became too pointed, Cullum sometimes would say to Fort Worth's Johnson, "Let's go out to the john. I've got something private I want to talk to you about." They inevitably would return in good spirits, and matters would proceed in a productive fashion.

Weekly meetings at the Inn of the Six Flags continued. Five days before Christmas, 1964, a reporter who walked close to an open door in a room where the representatives were meeting saw what appeared to be maps and plans spread across a bed. The negotiators quickly shut the door, and later acknowledged that airport sites were being discussed. Details could not be told, Friedman said to reporters afterwards, but "we have a lot more in common than otherwise." Both Friedman and Jonsson said they believed the cities would reach agreement before the CAB deadline.

On the last day of December, 1964, it appeared that no more than two or three meetings would be required before the negotiators would be ready with a recommendation. The CAB's 180-day deadline, which would be reached in March, posed no problem, said Friedman and Cullum in a press conference after their New Year's Eve meeting.

On May 28, 1965, the representatives from the two cities signed a memorandum of understanding that they would submit to their respective city councils for approval. Dallas and Fort Worth, by now it was clear, together would build a new airport, bigger and grander than the Midway Airport or Love Field.

FIVE

From Prairie
to Planes

✈

*We shall open up new avenues to people who do not know
the history and the quality of life here in the Southwest.*
Thomas M. Sullivan

With such a monumental, complex task ahead of them, Dallas'
and Fort Worth's airport representatives had no time for
dawdling—even if they were not yet an official airport board or
specific airport authority. Ultimately anticipated was an airport
authority with the power to levy taxes and to exercise the power
of eminent domain. But discussion over a permanent organization
would be complicated, and it had the potential to become
explosive. Now was the time for serious planning toward an
airport; its completion would require years of work. The City of
Houston already was far along in planning a new airport
scheduled to open before the end of the decade. It would have the
potential to achieve dominance in the Southwest before the new
combined Dallas and Fort Worth airport could even open—a
situation to be avoided at all costs.

To get the "dirt flying" the first objective was to hire an
architectural-engineering firm with high-level experience to do the
conceptual planning for the entire project. News stories referred to

this important decision as hiring a "consultant," but of course it was far more than that. Erik Jonsson, acting on behalf of Dallas, and J. Lee Johnson III, representing Fort Worth, took leading roles in this selection process. In early June 1965 they interviewed representatives of four potential firms. Joining them for several out-of-town interviews was Ross I. Newmann of the Civil Aeronautics Board. What they were looking for, Jonsson told the press in a deceptively simple statement, was a firm representing competency, the ability to start work immediately, and cost efficiency.

In late July they found who they were looking for—the prominent New York City firm of Tippetts-Abbett-McCarthy-Stratton, Engineers and Architects. The firm, soon to be identified in newspaper headlines as "TAMS," had headquarters on Park Avenue. Walther Prokosch, one of twelve partners in the firm, would be the general consultant for the project.

Prokosch had impeccable credentials. A graduate of the Yale School of Architecture and a full partner in the firm, he was in charge of all airport design and planning as well as all architectural work done by the firm. He had been involved in the planning and construction of major airport facilities throughout the world, and he was the co-author of a book, *Airport Planning*.

As stipulated, Prokosch and TAMS, working with the Dallas and Fort Worth negotiating teams, moved very quickly. The first important task before them was to identify somewhere a large expanse of land as the best site for the airport. Many important factors had to be considered, but the essential one was to find a site equally distant from the two cities. There had to be enough land not just to build an airport but to build one that could expand. Natural or man-made obstructions such as rivers or valleys or high-rise structures, future and present highway configurations, the location and amount of residential, commercial, and industrial properties, atmospheric conditions and prevailing wind directions, and composition of the soil were among the many factors to be considered. While the terrain in Northeast Texas was no worse than rolling in any location, in any area big enough to build a huge airport were creeks, valleys, floodplains, highways, industry, utility lines, communication towers, and residential developments.

Location—quite obviously—was the consideration of foremost interest. It was uncertain at this early stage as to precisely how much land would be required. The realization that the airport could be far more than a compromise that satisfied minimal requirements was gradually dawning. "We started out somewhere around five thousand to six thousand acres," recalled J. Lee Johnson III. "Erik or Bob [Cullum] or somebody finally bounced it up to about 18,000 acres." Board members began exploring with TAMS several prospective sites, often taking long automobile rides to check distances and times required to reach them from the two downtowns. Johnson recalled years later that the first popular choice to emerge was much farther south than the site ultimately chosen. Its topography was excellent, but a problem soon ended its consideration—insufficient highways.

The agreed-upon site had far superior highway access, a factor which accounted for the final decision. It was, somewhat ironically but quite logically, immediately north of the Greater Southwest Airport which had been the subject of so much controversy. Straddling the Dallas and Tarrant County border, it was about seventeen miles from each downtown area. The site, as originally conceived lay south of Grapevine, and west of Irving. The location was announced at a press conference in late September 1965 at the Inn of Six Flags in Arlington, where negotiations had occurred. As initially announced it would be approximately 11,000 acres, a figure that would later be increased to 18,000 acres. Even 11,000 acres seemed astonishingly huge. Erik Jonsson later said he "fought hard" for 25,000 acres, and considering the opposition that would arise in the 1990s to the construction of a new runway, he and others regretted not having achieved that enormous size and the insulation it would have brought from nearby communities.

Also announced at the press conference was another important milestone that was overshadowed by news of the site: the creation of an official although temporary governing body for the airport. In large part the previous negotiating team became the official if temporary governing body. It was a six-person board, three members from each city. This board would make the numerous and important decisions that previously had been done by the negotiating team members as surrogates for their two cities. As to the make-up of the new body, it consisted almost entirely of the same negotiating teams. Dallas members were Jonsson, Chamber of Commerce President Hobart D. Turman, and City Councilman Frank Hoke. Turman replaced Robert B. Cullum, and Hoke took Welch's position. Cullum, who had played such a critical role in the meetings between the two cities with his wit and ability to drive a hard bargain without creating animosity, was not permitted to serve. Jonsson explained that he was ineligible because he lived in Highland Park rather than Dallas. However, Jonsson added, he would sit in on board meetings as an observer. For Fort Worth, Mayor Willard Barr announced the selection of former mayor Bayard Friedman, J. Lee Johnson III, and H.B. Fuqua. Both city councils also agreed to furnish $10,000 each to the board for expenses.

Members had three-year terms of office or until a permanent authority was created. They were charged, as the contract between the two cities specified, with planning, acquiring, establishing, developing, constructing, enlarging, improving, maintaining, equipping, operating, regulating, protecting, and policing the new facility. It would have the power to apply for, receive and disburse any federal, state or other funds toward ownership, control and operation of the airport. It would not have taxing authority or a power of eminent domain.

Beaming with pride at the press conference was CAB Examiner Newmann, whose agency had sought for so long to force the two cities to come together and who in large degree had been responsible for it. He was visibly pleased. "There has been a very substantial change in the attitudes of the two cities," he said. This present occasion, Jonsson noted, represented the beginning of a new era of cooperation between the two cities, not just in aviation but for many ventures in the future. Fort Worth's Willard Barr agreed, calling the day "a momentous occasion for both Dallas and Fort Worth . . . . truly a new era."

As to the bigger news—the site selection—the community most directly affected was the small but growing town of Grapevine on the north side. The news prompted in this small community of 5,000 residents an overnight real-estate boom. One Grapevine real estate firm sold in just two days about $250,000 worth of property, more than its normal sales for a month.

But Grapevine had fears, too, as indeed did other nearby communities, especially Irving. The mayor of Grapevine expressed concern that the mammoth airport's property would create a permanent barrier to his town's growth. The town's school superintendent feared that his already-strained tax base would further deteriorate if the airport annexed large parcels of property. (This matter of the airport's impact on Grapevine would continue to be a matter of concern. Eventually, Grapevine city officials requested airport board members to hold land acquisition in the vicinity of Grapevine at a minimum. In return, Grapevine's mayor, Ira E. Woods, promised to provide appropriate zoning on the city's land adjacent to the airport. Board members agreed to acquire only land that was necessary.) This agreement ultimately would be reinforced by a recommendation by the North Central Texas Council of Governments that neighboring municipalities re-zone land adjacent to the airport to discourage construction of incompatible buildings such as residences, hospitals, and schools.

The sudden spurt by land speculators in Grapevine prompted Jonsson to issue a warning. Opportunists might find themselves "badly burned," he observed, because at this point the airport's boundaries were outlined only in a general way; property purchased at inflated prices could be reduced substantially by condemnation procedures that required payment at fair market values. Besides, Jonsson reminded, "if the price of land gets completely out of hand, we could put the airport somewhere else." Nevertheless, one farmer in the area who had had his land appraised just six months earlier at $750 an acre now was told that it was worth $10,000 an acre.

Before the end of 1965 TAMS delivered its more definitive conclusions, carefully presented in a handsomely bound, sixty-five page over-sized document entitled "Site Selection Study." It included a wealth of information not just about the site but also about anticipated requirements that the new airport must face in a rapidly changing industry. The study amounted to a sophisticated exercise in the science of air-traffic forecasting. Central questions it sought to address included these: How many and what kind of new aircraft must a new airport accommodate? How many passengers would be arriving and departing each day in 1975? In 1980? In 1985? There were myriad other questions.

Not only was the aviation industry undergoing rapid change, so were the surrounding communities. Ramifications of these developments also were addressed in the report. TAMS projected by 1985 a doubling in population of the 11-county area from 2 million to 4.2 million. Other topics addressed in the report concerned air traffic forecasts, general aviation, military usage, air cargo, runway requirements, prevailing winds, runway length, aircraft noise (expected to continue to increase with new supersonic aircraft), topography and drainage, economic growth, trends in national and international traffic, and airline industry dynamics.

What TAMS recommended and the board approved was the acquisition of at least 10,700 but as many as 18,220 acres. This site, now defined more precisely, straddled the north-south boundary between Tarrant and Dallas counties and extended into six legal jurisdictions—the two counties and four incorporated cities. It was just north of an east-west axis between the two downtown areas. The chosen area was basically rolling farmland. About 15 percent of it was lightly wooded along several small streams flowing sluggishly southward to nearby junctures with the West Fork of the Trinity. Underlying the "very plastic clayey soil" was the Eagle Ford shale rock formation dating from the Cretaceous Period and laid down millions of years earlier when the area had been covered by a sea. (During a drainage ditch excavation in 1972 the fossil of an 80-million-year-old, twenty-five foot long plesiosaur was discovered.) Several significant man-made structures power transmission lines and radio towers—would have to be relocated. A number of farms, some recent residential developments, a church and even four cemeteries were on the proposed site. Perhaps the most unique part of the property was a 245-acre farm/ranch on which a herd of 500 rare deer—Japanese Sika and Indian Axis—were maintained by a Grapevine man.

TAMS expressed pleasure at the site's possibilities. The region was especially "fortunate" in having such land available. "It will be readily accessible to the greatest number of people. . . . [and it] possesses unusually good topographic features," Prokosch wrote in his introduction. Thirty years later Willard Barr of Fort Worth recalled how excited board members viewed the site as "absolutely ideal."

Of course, already existing was the major—if struggling—airport immediately south, Greater Southwest. Prokosch recommended that it "should be considered as part of the new airport complex."

As to the type of aircraft to be served, it would be "strictly jet" because of the rapid acceptance of jets and the accelerating rate at which they were replacing propeller aircraft. The airport would have to anticipate and meet the needs of the mid-1970s and beyond.

Aside from the all-important consideration of site, TAMS made other recommendations in this initial report to serve as guideposts for the future. Since the configuration of the airport and terminal and runways was yet to be determined, TAMS suggested strongly that the entire area of 18,220 acres be purchased rather than the 10,700 suggested as minimally necessary. With the obvious importance of highway access to the site from several directions, TAMS recommended that the Texas Highway Department be notified as soon as possible. Accordingly, it urged consideration of creating a new rapid transit system linking the airport to Dallas and to Fort Worth. Finally, TAMS strongly recommended the initiation of regional planning studies to assess the impact of what was now certain to be the world's biggest airport.

IN THE FOLLOWING months Prokosch, his TAMS project staff of thirteen other individuals, and several affiliated consultants began working in greater detail on the projected needs of the new "DFW" airport—its overall layout and the terminal design. The FAA and airlines were advised and consulted throughout the planning. The work culminated in the "Airport Layout Plan, presented in July 1966 with FAA and air-carrier approval.

The Airport Layout Plan provided remarkable and futuristic concepts of the dynamics of the commercial aviation industry, and it became clearer than ever that here lay the opportunity to construct an airport of world-wide significance, the first major airport to be built to accommodate the new jet age.

The impact of rapidly changing aircraft technology, especially the conversion from piston equipment to jet, was a major consideration. Indeed, the fact that the airport would be constructed for the new "jet age" was always paramount in the minds of the planners. These days, even short- and medium-range trips, previously handled by smaller prop planes, were being taken over by jet aircraft. And these jets had far greater seating capacities than prop planes. Major new jet aircraft purchases were being announced regularly by the nation's airlines. Clearly, jet and prop jet equipment was replacing piston equipment at a far more rapid rate than had been anticipated. By 1970 it was expected that 85 percent of the U.S. carrier fleet would be jet-powered.

And certainly it became clearer every day that the airport would have to be constructed to accommodate far more traffic than first envisioned. In the most recent nine-month period, U.S. airlines had recorded "unparalleled and previously unforeseeable increases in passenger traffic." TAMS' projections showed that more traffic would be handled at the airport in 1980 than previously had been anticipated for 1985. What this meant in real numbers was that the 2.8 million enplanements at Love Field and Greater Southwest would triple by 1975 to 8.3 million!

In 1960 the average number of passengers stepping into a plane in Dallas and Fort Worth had been 21.2. In 1966, just six years later, the estimated number would be doubled to 42.4 passengers per plane. In addition to this unparalleled increase in passengers per plane, the number of landings and take-offs in Dallas and Fort Worth was expected to skyrocket from 66,200 in 1964 to 113,500 in 1980.

What was happening, as clearly demonstrated by these figures, was a revolution in American travel habits that was ever-quickening in pace. Travel by air was more and more becoming the normal way to take a journey of length. No longer was air transportation the province of wealth and corporations. And as people of modest means took to the airways, travel by bus and passenger train was declining and those industries suffering. On an average weekday in 1980 it was estimated that some 100,000 people would pass through the new airport—60,000 passengers, 14,000 related visitors, 16,200 employees, 3,000 vendors, and 6,000 sightseers.

Despite the relative remoteness of the airport and despite its generous land dimensions, aircraft noise was recognized as a possible problem. Greater volumes of traffic and bigger jet-powered airplanes would require heavier take-off weights and greater noise levels. Future flights to more remote destinations assured this. In 1965 the longest non-stop flight from Dallas or Fort Worth was a 1,500 statute-mile journey to San Francisco.

The plan envisioned four principal north-south runways and two northwest-southeast runways. First Stage construction called for two primary runways, each 11,000 feet long, while the "Ultimate Stage" runways would be 12,000 and 14,000 feet. Even at this ultimate stage, the airport's northern and southern boundaries would be three miles from the ends of the primary runways.

Central to the entire operation and the most representative symbol of the airport would be the terminal itself. Prokosch's plans proposed a single, elongated terminal in the center of the property rather than at a front entrance as was customary, connected by a north-south central thoroughfare spine. The terminal would house all requisite facilities for arrivals and departures, and also for business, charter and air taxi operations. It would contain about 1.5 million square feet—one-third of it designated for airline passenger operations, one-third for cargo operations, and one-third for public areas such as concessions. Carriers with operations at the terminal were, in order of their expected gate requirements for passenger travel: Braniff, 18; American, 17; Delta, 13; Trans-Texas, 12; Central, 10; Continental, 10; Western, 2 1/2; Eastern, 2; and Mexicana, 1/2.

Some 19,000 car-parking spaces were envisioned, a disproportionately large number because of the realization that residents of Dallas and Fort Worth as well as Texas overall were unlikely to give up their reliance on personal automobiles, a contrast with East Coast residents more accustomed to mass transit. Studies soon showed that 92 percent of those arriving at Love Field did so by passenger car as opposed to 42 percent in New York City. While rapid transit was envisioned from Dallas and Fort Worth at some future time, this did not appear to be economically feasible, according to the report, before 1980. (This estimate, of course, turned out to be hopelessly overoptimistic.) It was recommended that new highways leading to the airport should be designed to accommodate adjacent rapid transit facilities.

Preliminary estimates of the construction costs of this new airport were "somewhat over $200,000,000," of which some $25 to $30 million would be eligible for federal participation. One half of this larger sum would be required for airfield construction and the other half for the terminal, parking structures, and related facilities. This money would be raised not through taxes but through jointly issued revenue bonds. After construction was complete and the airport in operation, revenues generated by airport activities would make it self-supporting.

MEANWHILE, WITH these ambitious plans in hand, the time had come to create the permanent legal entity for conducting the airport's business. As a first step, the Texas Legislature passed enabling legislation to permit Dallas and Tarrant counties—not the two cities alone, for this was to be a "regional" airport despite the dominance to this point of the two cities—to create a body to be known as the North Central Texas Regional Airport Authority. It would have power to levy taxes and condemn property. Its creation would require voter approval, and an election was set for that purpose on June 6, 1967.

Leaders throughout the two counties offered enthusiastic support for the new authority. Dallas and Fort Worth's elected officials and board members, having set aside all previous misgivings, strongly encouraged voter approval, and so did elected officials from suburban towns. Numerous chambers of commerce added their support. Only minor insignificant opposition arose, centering their complaints on the need to forestall rising taxes. Approval of the authority seemed certain.

But when the polls closed at 7 p.m. after twelve hours of voting, an unsettling result emerged. Dallas County voters rejected the authority by a vote of 26,385 to 24,125. Tarrant County voters overwhelmingly approved it, 25,160 to 8,747. The only voters in Dallas County to approve the proposition were those living in North Dallas, Richardson, Highland Park and University Park, the areas where so many air travelers lived. Voters within the City of Dallas turned down the proposition, 17,104 to 16,014.

The clouds had darkened. Erik Jonsson was away in Washington, D.C., on the day of the election, a measure itself of the false confidence in the outcome. Contacted by reporters, Jonsson said the board would figure out what to do about the situation when it next met on Saturday, four days away. In fact, there was no requirement that the airport be built by the two counties; that power lay within the cities themselves. The obvious solution now was simply for the cities of Dallas and Fort Worth to act alone—as they had been doing all along—to use their own powers of eminent domain to purchase the needed property.

Already the two cities had received about $4 million toward the new airport from the federal government. Plenty more was expected. FAA Regional Director Henry Newman said failure to create a regional airport authority would have no impact on the federal funds. "How they organize and manage it is entirely up to the cities," he said. "It's strictly an internal matter with the two cities. If they are prepared to go on with the project, the FAA is prepared to work with them." Hobart Turman, a Dallas board member, said it certainly would have been better if residents of both counties had agreed to build the airport, but since they did not he was confident that Dallas and Fort Worth would carry on alone. (Years later, one of the surviving original board members, Bayard Friedman, still believed that the failure of Dallas County voters to approve the project was a great mistake. In his opinion many eventual problems would have been thwarted through bi-county ownership, including especially the seemingly endless dilemma over flights originating from Love Field, which presumably would have been under the authority of the board.)

As to why Dallas County turned down the authority, *Dallas Times Herald* political writer Jim Lehrer said that most voters simply had not been able to see how a new international airport could possibly advance their own "life, liberty or pursuit of happiness." This failure to communicate the message was caused, he figured, by the fact that the political parties, organizations, and personalities who were experienced at getting out the vote had been ignored and not placed on the airport team. Neither the Republican nor Democratic party organizations had been asked to help, nor had organized labor.

One of the serious concerns was competition with Houston for air superiority in the Southwest. Houston's Hobby Airport, which for years had played second-fiddle to Love Field in flights and passengers, was to be replaced with a new international airport to open in 1969 with the capability of handling the new jumbo jets. Undue delay in Dallas and Fort Worth could give Houston a new advantage which might not be overcome.

At the Saturday board meeting Jonsson assured Fort Worth members that despite the negative vote in Dallas County, the City of Dallas was determined to move ahead with the regional airport, and that its creation and joint operation were critical for the economic future of the whole area. Already, he said, he had polled members of the Dallas City Council, and they were in full agreement with him. Jonsson now proposed that the two cities replace the interim board with a joint board of their own to supervise construction and operation of the facility, that the two cities share costs on the basis of their relative populations, and that board membership also be based on relative populations.

Board members readily approved this general view of proportionate representation, but the exact configuration required intense and delicate behind-the-scenes work by the two city managers—W.S. (Scott) McDonald of Dallas and Howard D. McMahan of Fort Worth—and their legal staffs. Finally, a formula was worked out to the satisfaction of all board members and approved by them on April 12, 1968. Dallas, with seven-elevenths of the combined populations of the cities, would provide seven-elevenths of the financing and would have seven of the eleven board seats. Fort Worth would have the remaining four-elevenths financial responsibility and four board seats. Since the new board would not have taxing, land condemnation, or bond-issuing powers of its own, these important functions would remain the province of the two municipalities of Dallas and Fort Worth.

All board members would be elected by their respective city councils for four-year terms. They would serve without compensation. To establish overlapping terms, six of the initial appointments would be for two years and five for four years. Members could serve a maximum of two consecutive four-year terms. The board would elect its own officers each February. The board would set policy, and—taking a note from their mutual council-manager forms of municipal government—would have a full-time executive director as their chief administrative and executive officer. This person they already had found in Thomas M. Sullivan, a 54-year-old Oklahoma-born airport veteran who had been hired from the Port Authority of New York City as the airport's chief administrator.

This new agreement, dependent upon Dallas and Fort Worth city council ratification, met with political resistance in Fort Worth. There, the new mayor, DeWitt McKinley, lamented the agreement as "nefarious, iniquitous and 'unchartertutional.' " Disappointed especially at the numerical superiority of Dallas on the board, McKinley declared that "this turns over control of the airport to Dallas completely and forever." He charged Fort Worth's representatives on the board as having sold out their own city.

But the mayor found little support in his criticism. Fort Worth's City Council ratified the agreement and appointed its first four members to the new board: returning interim members J. Lee Johnson III and former mayor Bayard Friedman, and adding to the board R.M. "Sharky" Stovall, and J.C. Pace Jr.

Dallas council members expressed no qualms, for the plan's basic structure had been engineered by their own mayor, Jonsson. Many years later Jonsson frankly discussed his goals in a candid manner which likely would have offended his Fort Worth colleagues. "I wanted absolute control of that board if we needed it. . . . It was worth a lot of money to have it," he said in a 1993 interview. Jonsson reasoned that even if one of Dallas' board members for some reason sided with Fort Worth on a particular issue, the remaining Dallas members still would retain a 6-5 voting edge. Bayard Friedman insisted in 1998 that Fort Worth board members recognized clearly that Dallas was the bigger partner, and the seven-four board make-up seemed fair and was entirely satisfactory to them.

The Dallas City Council, pleased with the airport progress, gave Jonsson freedom to pick his own fellow Dallas board members. Those he chose, in addition to himself, were Elgin B. Robertson, Morris G. Spencer, Frank H. Hoke, Carl I. Thomsen, George M. Underwood Jr., and A. Earl Cullum Jr.

The time for conflict between the two cities clearly had been over for a long time, and this was no time to resume it. In the months and years during airport construction board members would work harmoniously with an amazing paucity of negative headlines concerning any disagreements. A long-time employee who began working for the new board as soon as it was formed recalled that board members worked "beautifully together" without any discord. "They were determined, dedicated and self sacrificing. All they were interested in was building the airport."

The new board's first assignment was to get organized. This took place on May 1, 1968. Board members picked "Jonsson and Johnson" as their leaders—Erik Jonsson as chairman and J. Lee Johnson III as vice chairman. Additionally, Fort Worth's Bayard H. Friedman was elected secretary. As their executive director, board members voted to retain the man chosen in February 1968 by the interim board as their administrator, Thomas M. Sullivan.

Board members established four sub-committees: by-laws, construction, finance, and operations. Each board member was named to one committee, and this is where much of the basic work was done. Jonsson, as chairman, was ex officio on each committee.

As the board settled into its routine in the months ahead it developed a pleasing pattern of brevity. By the time an agenda item reached the full board for deliberation, the details already had been ironed out by the committee and staff. The actual board meetings, as a result, were often surprisingly brief. Before long, office workers began conducting a pool with the winner being the one who picked the shortest time for the meeting. Occasionally, the official sessions would last no more than ten minutes.

There was a definite understanding at the time, according to Friedman, the secretary, that chairmanship of the board would rotate between the cities. Following a single term by Jonsson, he would be succeeded by a Fort Worth chairman, and the rotation would continue to alternate between the cities. That agreement—if indeed all board members had agreed to such a plan—was forgotten or overlooked in the years ahead as Jonsson continued to serve with great authority and Fort Worth members seemed reluctant to upset the progress being made.

In these first meetings the board, working with Sullivan, established an organizational structure for airport operations centering around six basic components: engineering, finance, property and facilities, planning, operations, and administration. Directors of these departments would report to Deputy Director J.R. Mettler, who in turn reported to Sullivan.

Their job descriptions provided a basic picture of the many aspects of running an airport. Five of the executives had been hired August 1, 1968. Sullivan himself was charged with recommending policies to the board for planning, constructing, maintaining, operating and regulating the airport, and also for implementing those policies adopted by the board. He was responsible for "development and maintenance of the architectural and functional integrity of the Regional Airport as a whole." Sullivan's administrative assistant, G.R. Stanford, not only helped Sullivan as directed, but he also was responsible for administering programs in personnel, budget, and organizational procedures.

Deputy Director Mettler was charged with coordinating the efforts of the six major staff components and also for "developing and maintaining programs to increase public understanding and appreciation of the Regional Airport."

The director of engineering, Ernest E. Dean, was charged with preparation, recommendation, maintenance and implementation of the long-range physical master plan of the airport. (Dean, who later would succeed Sullivan as the airport's executive director, had been hired from TAMS, where since 1965 he had been on-site supervisor of early planning and feasibility studies.) The director of finance, Richard H. Laman Jr., had the task of developing, recommending, and implementing funding patterns for the airport's financial development and operation. Laman, a certified public accountant, had been director of finance and treasurer for the San Diego Unified Post District before joining DFW. The director of planning, Jack D. Downey, would coordinate with major airport users to ensure that their multiple needs were met. Downey had a bachelor of science degree in civil engineering from the University of Missouri. Before joining DFW he was director of advanced program planning for Trans World Airlines. Two years later Downey would become deputy executive director of the airport.

Three staff positions were unfilled because of the early date. The director of operations would be responsible for coordinating all aircraft and passenger support systems, with airport safety the paramount consideration. The director of property and facilities would be charged with use and lease agreements of the facilities and also with economic projections related to the use of the facilities. The director of administration would oversee budget, personnel, and organizational procedures.

In the board's report to the two city councils, an important cautionary word was sounded. All commercial flight activities at both Love Field and GSIA would have to transfer to DFW when it became operational. Otherwise, the airport could never be a self-sustaining, self-supporting project. How to achieve this delicate matter, especially of phasing out Love Field where at the moment twenty-four new passengers gates were being constructed, would be a matter requiring great tact and wisdom on the part of the cities. The board itself could only plan, construct and operate the new regional facility.

Not forgotten either was the requirement to coordinate activities with the surrounding communities that would be impacted so deeply by their gigantic new neighbor. In this regard the board planned a liaison committee for "constant communication" with them, an assignment to be undertaken principally through the North Central Texas Council of Governments.

The board sought to impress upon the city councils the enormous size of the project ahead. "[It] is equivalent to the task of designing and building from scratch and in five years a city of the size and population of Wichita Falls, Texas, all upon the condition that it be self-supporting, that it be modern and up-to-date upon completion, and that it be prepared to accommodate many years of future requirements."

AS THE PLANNING continued into 1967 it was increasingly evident that earlier size estimates were too conservative. The airport would have to grow even in the planning stage, and once built, it would have to continue to expand. This was especially evident in the December 1967 "Airport Master Plan" which combined and updated previous plans into a single document. Requirements had "increased markedly," the document stated. The number of gate positions requested for passenger use by the airlines had jumped from 75 to 106, and rentable space requested had climbed from 329,900 square feet to 446,910.

More activity at the airport, of course, would also impact highways leading there. At an informal shirt-sleeve session in 1967 State Highway Department officials, airport board members, and FAA representatives worked out a long-range plan for adequate highway access. They conceived of major highway interchanges at both the north and south ends of the central thoroughfare spine. The idea was to ensure that traffic entered and departed at both entrances to the airport rather than being dominated by a single entrance. The plan called for most of Dallas' traffic to enter from the north side via an extension of Interstate 635, and most of Fort Worth's traffic from the south via State Highway 183.

One point emphatically made which would continue to be emphasized over the years to come was that if there was a single constant, that constant was change. It was the "first benchmark of airport planning." Ever-changing requirements had to be accommodated by flexible plans. Since the planning itself was being conducted over a period of several years, technical changes in air transport were occurring so rapidly that the earliest plans were becoming outdated. For instance, when TAMS issued its "Site Selection Study" in 1965 it estimated that in 1975 there would be 5.2 million air passenger enplanements. Now, just two years later, that figure was revised upward by nearly 60 percent to 8.35 million. Moreover, changes in the aircraft themselves—especially expanding sizes—were an important factor. What this meant, in TAMS' words, was "enlarging noise envelopes," another way of saying that the airplanes would be "louder." They also needed longer runways. "The concepts of controlled expansion and noise abatement land control are the primary criteria of future airport planning," the report stated.

Certain of the futuristic projections in the "Master Plan," on the other hand, would not materialize in the twentieth century. There was discussion of the need to provide instrumental landing systems for V/STOL aircraft, with the assumption that this "vertical short take-off" aircraft would become just around the corner a fixture in commercial aviation operations. It also was assumed that the Concorde SST and the gigantic, 318-foot long Boeing 2707 SST would be fixtures as early as 1985. Helicopters also were foreseen as playing a significant role in short-haul traffic between the downtown districts and the airport. Large-roof areas of remote passenger parking facilities would be "ideally suited" to accommodate helicopter landing facilities.

The working concept was to have a "restraint-free" airport—that is, an airport that would enable both passengers and aircraft to enter and leave with little or no delay. By now it was understood by all that the new facility, when completed, would be the largest in the world. Sullivan did not expect it to hold the "largest" appellation for long because of the "break-through in concepts and design." It would stand forever, though, as "the pioneer in a new breed of airports to match the new breed of aircraft."

Whereas generally the new airport was envisioned in terms of passenger-carrying capabilities, the air cargo potential was astonishing in itself. With 200 cargo gates ultimately planned, *Engineering News Record* magazine noted that if air cargo aircraft developed to match 747 capacity, the DFW airport could handle more freight than any seaport in the world. A capacity of 90,000 tons in 1975 would become 160,000 tons in 1980 and 410,000 tons in 1985.

In the Master Plan's introductory letter to the mayors of the two cities, Prokosch concluded optimistically: "We believe that the project, as a whole, can become operational in 1972."

THOMAS W. SULLIVAN had developed some serious concerns about TAMS' concept for a single, elongated, and spine-like terminal. Although such a design was customary for airports, Sullivan began asking Ernest E. Dean, sometimes with a caustic edge, questions as to how Prokosch had come to his conclusions about it. Consequently, Sullivan, thinking much further into the future, suggested and the board agreed in July 1968 to hire two architectural firms to re-examine the terminal concept. One firm, Hellmuth, Obata and Kassabum, was located in St. Louis, where it had been founded in 1900. Over the years its architects had designed a number of outstanding, award-winning buildings, among them the Smithsonian Institution's National Air and Space Museum and the Galleria Shopping Center in Houston. The other firm, Brodsky, Hopf and Adler, was in New York City. These two companies, Sullivan said, had broad experience in airports. He had worked with both of them in New York.

Sullivan told the board that he had seen "basic weaknesses" in the plan for an elongated terminal. "You're limited in the roads serving the terminal under this plan," he said. "If you have a bad wreck or a fire and a crowd gathers, you will have activities disrupted throughout your terminal." Fort Worth board member Stovall, alarmed at the change, urged the board to delay hiring the two new firms for at least a week for further consideration. Sullivan said there was no time for delay; the project already was behind schedule and work must begin as soon as possible. The board agreed with Sullivan.

Sitting in the audience during this discussion was Walther Prokosch, who remained silent. Afterwards, he expressed puzzlement. "I'm confused. I'm not certain what our status will be. I want to get a clarification," he said. Then, as one newspaper reported, a wry smile crept across his face: "I guess I should have brought my press clippings."

In an informal meeting with the Fort Worth City Council the next day, Sullivan sought to explain further the decision and to soothe any wounded feelings. What the two new architectural firms would do, he said, would be to merely "audit" the terminal design concept over the next eight weeks. TAMS, Sullivan said, had done an "outstanding job" and would continue with its plans for the runways, aprons, sewage lines, treatment equipment, and other important ingredients of the overall project. "We're not junking anything," he continued. "It's possible some of the concepts presently in the design [of the terminal] won't be there at completion, but some wouldn't have been there no matter who did the architectural work." While TAMS had completed its important assignment in developing a master plan, it would continue to be the general consultant with responsibility of overall management and coordination.

The two men most responsible for the review would be Gyo Obata of the St. Louis firm and Richard Adler of the New York firm. Obata was described as the creative dreamer, and Adler the technical planner. But it was Obata who was actually "the boss," as Sullivan later described their separate roles. "We will work with him completely," he said, describing him as "a little fellow, charming as can be." Obata, a California-born Japanese-American, had won twenty-four design awards in the past dozen years. He had degrees from the University of California at Berkeley, Washington University at St. Louis, and Cranbrook Academy of Arts at Detroit. Adler, a native of New York City, was a graduate of Pratt Institute.

In an August 1, 1968, "airlines technical meeting, Obata elaborated on his overall approach to his assignment. "We honestly feel that a building is not meaningful unless it really functions, and that the whole viewpoint of our study of the TAMS assignment was to really determine how functional, how economical, how flexible, how simple and clear it is for a human being to operate out of this terminal building." Obata told those present that one could not look at the terminal design in terms of previous experience because "we are coming into a new generation of airplanes. . . and all traditional methods no longer apply." The criteria for evaluating TAMS work, he said, had been given them by Sullivan.

Meanwhile, Sullivan was advising Obata of his own concepts. And they were big. Not only would the DFW airport become the air capital of the Southwest, it likely would be the air capital for the Midwest and possibly the air capital of the entire nation. The "principle prerequisite" for an airport terminal, he told him, should be a concept that would accommodate the maximum movement of aircraft, passengers and vehicles and "which also could be expanded in the future with the least inconvenience to the passengers, airlines, and airport operations. Sullivan's administrative assistant, G.R. Stanford, advised Dallas Assistant City Manager George Schrader that the only way Obata's recommended modifications would be accepted would be if they offered "substantial improvements in passenger convenience, efficient operations, and/or economic construction."

At a "Tops and Technical" meeting in July, attended by representatives from the board, engineering firms, and the major airlines (American, Braniff, Continental, Delta, Eastern, Frontier, Ozark and Texas International), Sullivan elaborated privately on the hiring of the two new architectural firms. TAMS had never actually had a contract with the board to do architectural work, he pointed out. What especially concerned him about Prokosch's design was the congestion in the terminal that was anticipated with the monster-sized airplanes of the future. He elaborated:

> I am really worried. . . . If you took one 1,000-passenger airplane and put them [sic] into American Airlines at Kennedy, that terminal building would jam up that terminal, or certainly have it at its peak. Two would jam it up. This is a pretty big terminal. It would do more than that to the United, Delta at Kennedy, because they only have one roadway there. Just bring one into Braniff-Northwestern, and you have had it. This bothers me because in this particular area, we are going to have two of these 1,000 passenger planes and 1/3 will change from one plane to the other. All kinds of automobiles coming in. We are talking about a lot of 727's and 747's and 1011's and DC-10s, and if passenger growth is anything near what is predicted—and we have never guessed right—I said that

what I wanted to do was to design this terminal building to meet the ultimate capacity of the runways.

Sullivan wanted to keep walking distances—so lengthy in major airports—to a minimum, and also to have a terminal building that could be expanded as needed, as well as parking lots, roadway frontage, and aprons.

Sullivan urged the airlines to come up with their own advanced thinking in such areas as ticketing and baggage handling. "I would offer our terminal as a guinea pig," he told their representatives in a planning session. Sullivan expressed his firm belief that within three to five years automated ticketing would be in use. Otherwise, the volume of passengers would be simply too great to handle.

At this July planning session he explained Obata's chore. He was to take a maximum number of movements of airplanes, put them into a composite airplane, bring it to a gate, and arrange for the movement of passengers going everywhere else. If the TAMS concept did not perform satisfactorily, Obata would have to produce an alternate plan. And he had just eight weeks to do it. Sullivan reminded the skeptics that this was not an impossible task. "We came up with the design of Idlewild [now JFK] in three weeks—in three weeks we had a brand new plan."

There was considerable concern among board members and airline executives about the delay inherent in Obata's review. There were two good reasons for concern. First was the felt need to meet deadlines and to open the new airport as close to the projected date of 1972 as possible. A second reason was the rapid growth of traffic at Love Field, which soon would swamp that facility. The FAA estimated that at its present rate of growth, Love Field would have 9.7 million enplanements in 1975 with total passenger movements of approximately 19.4 million. The average number of operations per hour at Love Field between 8 a.m. and 8 p.m. already was seventy-two, a figure projected to rise by 1972 to 159 operations per hour.

In order to make some very advanced and futuristic planning, TAMS and the DFW staff took advantage during 1968 of the FAA's Computer Simulation Facility, National Aviation Facilities

Experimental Center. Here, simulation studies were projected beyond 1985 concerning air space saturation and absolute maximums for enplanements. DFW became the first new airport to use the FAA's modern facility.

IN ARTHUR HAILEY'S best-selling novel, *Airport*, published in this same year, 1968, a reporter asks a prominent authority to identify "the most imaginative" airport executives around the nation, the ones who could look beyond the present and foresee the future. One of the four executives singled out in this blending of fact and fiction was Tom Sullivan.

Indeed, Sullivan envisioned DFW as far more than a mere facility where airplanes and passengers came and went, and he saw aviation not just as a business involved in transportation but as a powerful agent for social change. World-wide flights soon would be accessible to all at reduced costs, he believed, and the airport itself was the mixing pot where all sorts of people came together.

Aviation, he believed, was gradually shrinking the size of the globe, and the best was yet to come. More to the immediate point—and this was why aviation was so particularly important to inland cities such as Dallas and Fort Worth—it had freed cities from their traditional dependence on trade routes dominated by natural geographical features. New forces, controllable by humankind, were at work.

Aviation was creating social mobility on a scale never known before, a mobility that was expanding consciousness and awareness throughout the world. Old prejudices and barriers to understanding, once reinforced by distance and unfamiliarity, were melting away. "We shall open up new avenues to people who do not know the history and the quality of life here in the Southwest," Sullivan said. Especially, of course, was mobility essential to business and industry. "The creative processes of buying and selling depend on face-to-face communication. A salesman must be able to go quickly and to anywhere. . . . Scientists and educators must have frequent and easy contact with their colleagues everywhere knowledge is pushed." And as passenger costs for air travel declined, as Sullivan confidently foresaw happening, people from all economic levels and classes would be able to expand their awareness and understandings of other peoples and cultures. (In the immediate future Sullivan expected the Boeing 747 to expand its passenger capacity in the economy class to 600. He predicted that between 1975 and 1980 transcontinental airfares would be as low as $50 and trans-Atlantic fares as low as $69.) The futurist Marshall McLuhan envisioned a "global village" made possible through instant communications in which one part of the world could know immediately what was happening in another part of the world. Sullivan saw this happening in more practical terms through the first-hand experiences gained through travel.

In the coming years—"by the time our airport will be built, or very, very soon thereafter"—a huge passenger aircraft will be developed, Sullivan believed, that would fly three times the speed of sound at about 2,000 miles per hour and travel from DFW to London in just two and a half hours and to Tokyo in five and a half hours. The new DFW Airport, Sullivan insisted, must be prepared for that day. And by being prepared, he emphasized, "this airport can and will make the Dallas-Fort Worth area the crossroads of the nation."

He foresaw in twenty-five years a rocket ship that would take off from DFW for outer space and reach distant corners of the globe "in times impossible for us to conceive today." He predicted that this rocket aircraft would "shoot up to 100,000 feet, fire a mild booster and eventually reach 7,000 miles per hour." He was convinced that it was imperative to think big and to make sure that sufficient space was reserved at DFW to accommodate such a vehicle when it came to pass.

What Sullivan wanted to avoid at DFW was a situation he had seen in New York City. As chief of aviation planning for the Port Authority of New York he had been greeted with complaints, frustration, and skepticism when, just after the dedication of Idlewild Airport (now JFK), he had urged immediate planning for yet another airport. Because another airport was not built, the result, Sullivan said, was congestion that already was causing passengers in New York to sit at the end of runways for an hour to two hours before takeoff. The same phenomenon, he said, was happening at Chicago's O'Hare and at other busy airports. He believed that these inconveniences ultimately would cause an exodus of industry and commerce from these congested situations to new areas where air transportation was faster and more convenient. The new DFW airport, containing more acreage than JFK, LaGuardia, Los Angeles, and San Francisco airports combined, would offer the desired speed and convenience.

Sullivan pointed out, in what would be an oft-repeated statement, that the DFW airport would hold the equivalent of a good-sized city with a daily population by 1985 of about 140,000 people coming and going. These numbers seemed to dictate the creation of innovations in ticketing. Sullivan speculated that in the future a passenger would insert a credit card into a machine, pull out the ticket that was generated with gate assignment, and proceed promptly to that gate for boarding. At some point the passenger, using the same identification number as on the ticket, would place his luggage in a container that would go directly to the airplane.

Certainly there had to be plenty of space for expansion at the airport. DFW must be "an open-end airport, capable of immediate expansion," Sullivan believed. "That capability, coupled with our awareness of the possibilities, will guard against much of the unpredictable."

Sullivan had come to believe that the elongated TAMS terminal reflected the past and present, but not the future. The news that came in September, then, after this summer of ruminations, should not have been a surprise. Sullivan recommended that the TAMS terminal plan—award-winning or not—specifying a slender, elongated, two-mile terminal be replaced with a new plan worked out under Obata's direction in just eight short and frantic weeks. Instead of a single huge terminal, there would be four (with enough space for nine more) separate, de-centralized half-loop terminals. Multiple terminals would eliminate the congestion inherent in a single terminal, and the half-circles would provide enough perimeter for the airplanes to come right up to each gate. The terminals would permit separate and convenient parking areas for each terminal, speed up completion dates by permitting separate contractors for each terminal, and eliminate congestion of aircraft. All this gained, and yet it would cost about $30 million less than the Prokosch terminal.

Each terminal would have three levels for separate functions— the ground level for a service road, airline operations, and a transit system; the second level for passenger lounge areas and concessions; and the third top level for departures. All gates would be adequate to handle jumbo-jet aircraft like the Boeing 747. The 252 gates ultimately planned for DFW would equal the capacity of all three New York airports combined.

An obvious concern was how to transport passengers making connections from one terminal to another. The solution was to install a yet-to-be defined "horizontal" elevator or rail system linking all terminals. This was a matter of some importance, for linkage of the separate terminals by a fast, efficient, and safe system was obviously essential. It was envisioned as a computer-controlled system of ultra-modern, streamlined, capsule-type cars running on tracks and carrying from six to ten passengers each. Such systems already were successfully in operation in large steel plants and coal mines.

The airport now carried a projected cost of $285 million, or $350 million with interest. Target date for completion was fall 1972.

The airport board, having been concerned already about delay but now excited about the new concept, quickly approved the new plans on September 28, 1968, after a briefing attended by city councils from both Dallas and Fort Worth. The concept's flexibility, economies, and convenience gained special praise. At opening the airport would offer 105 passenger loading gates, more than triple the number at Love Field. This number could be expanded ultimately to 205 gates. Erik Jonsson quickly summed up the new terminals' advantages: "This will be quicker to construct, cheaper, more flexible, more pleasant for the air traveler. We'll be getting more for less." Sullivan assured the board that if grading started in November the airport would be ready by late 1972.

As a newspaper writer described the genesis for the idea, it was Obata's "high regard for efficiency, bolstered by his customer-level familiarity with airports the world over, [that] culminated in a revolutionary new airport concept." Given the massive amount of land space to be taken up by the airport, Obata said, he had decided that efficiency would best be served by decentralization. "What we decided on is almost like going back to the old airports in small towns where there's a single hangar and terminal for a single plane at a time," Obata said the smaller sizes of the buildings would represent "human" scale rather than monumental scale. This quality was reflected in another way, too. Walking distance for those arriving by car would be only 300 feet as contrasted by an airport such as O'Hare where passengers might have to walk for distances as great as a mile.

How such "human" qualities could exist in the *biggest* airport in the world was, in many ways, a puzzle. Especially puzzling was figuring out just how big the airport would be. A feature article in the *Dallas Times Herald*, accompanied by a unique map, helped make the point. Familiar Dallas locations were superimposed on a map of airport property, and it could be seen that the airport's boundaries would hold—with abundant space left over—Love Field, the State Fair grounds, Texas Stadium, Addison Airport, Red Bird Airport, Greater Southwest International Airport, the Dallas Central Downtown Business District, the Southern Methodist University campus, White Rock Lake and its surrounding green belts, Kiest Park, and Laurel Land Memorial Park.

SIX

Building the World's Biggest Airport

✈

There was enough concrete [in the runways] to pave a four-lane highway between the airport and Oklahoma City....enough to cover the entire principality of Monaco with a layer three feet thick!

The revised master plan required quick approval by both city councils if the airport's 1972 completion date was to be realized. And before work could begin, revenue bonds—$35 million worth—had to be sold. Bid specifications had to be drawn up, advertised and processed.

Fort Worth approved the new plan immediately. Dallas, however, balked, citing the unresolved matter of Fort Worth's Greater Southwest International Airport as the problem. Would GSIA now be incorporated as a part of the new airport? Would it be dismantled? Would its acreage be purchased from Fort Worth? If so, for how much?

Dallas City Councilman William E. Cothrum pressed these questions with Mayor Jonsson at the Dallas council meeting. Councilwoman Sibyl Hamilton wondered if the airport would have "undisputed air rights over GSIA." Jonsson couldn't say for certain. In light of this, the council instructed City Attorney Alex Bickley to pose three questions to Fort Worth: (1) Would GSIA be available to the DFW airport at a price to be negotiated? (2) If the board did not need GSIA outright, could air rights be obtained? (3) Would suitable right-of-way approaches to the regional airport be made available through GSIA property?

Fort Worth was not pleased at the delay. Dallas was "dragging her feet," complained Mayor DeWitt McKinley. "Fort Worth approved an airport authority; Dallas County defeated it. We sold bonds and Dallas waited for a more favorable market. We have shown our good faith. I don't know what Dallas wants. Does she want a free ride? Does she want an unreasonably low price for her land?" Fort Worth Councilman Frank Dunham questioned whether Dallas was acting in good faith. "Will they give us a schedule for the phasing out of Love Field? . . . . It's time for Dallas to show her hand or throw in," he said. The *Fort Worth Press* editorialized that Dallas' attitude seemed to indicate that its citizens believed they were "about to be victimized by some sly, clever Fort Worth plot."

Fort Worth's City Council held an emergency session to respond to Dallas' questions. R.M. Stovall, member of both Fort Worth's City Council and the airport board, signed a letter of response that stated in part: "As we understand it, GSIA is not needed, but if GSIA is needed within the next 12 months to complete the new regional airport, it will be available at a fair price based upon its value at the time it is acquired."

Still, the Dallas City Council was not satisfied. To some, Fort Worth's response seemed ambiguous. Before the week ended, though—pressured surely because of the unsettling negative comments from Fort Worth—the council sent a letter to Fort Worth, agreeing to pay 7/11 of the costs for buying GSIA if it were determined within the next twelve months that the property was needed.

This seemed to settle the matter, and Dallas approved the master plan, clearing the way for the board to issue $35 million in bonds to fund initial costs. Much of this would cover costs for preparation of the site—in other words, grading and drainage. Bonds for this purpose were sold on December 2, 1968. Meanwhile, specifications for bids to commence work already had been solicited. The winner among nine bidders was a Michigan firm, Holloway Construction Co., which offered to do the work for $17.9 million, $2 million less than the engineers' original cost estimate.

This done, an official groundbreaking ceremony was announced for Wednesday, December 11, 1968, a date which happened to be the birthday of the late Amon G. Carter and the fiftieth anniversary of the first flight that Erik Jonsson had taken when he was a youth in New Jersey. Invitations went out to several hundred officials.

News of the groundbreaking ceremony inevitably led to renewal of a perennial question—would the airport actually be ready to open in 1972? "That's the $64 question right now," said architect Richard M. Adler. Sullivan was not nearly so uncertain, and he quickly pointed out that Adler's remarks *must* have been misconstrued. The airport, he said with what turned out to be false optimism, would definitely be open for business in late 1972. The airlines themselves also were privately skeptical that the job could be completed by late 1972 or even by early 1973. But Sullivan insisted that it would be ready—so long as the airlines themselves did not delay their input on the terminal structures.

The site selected for groundbreaking was a field of four-foot tall weeds at the juncture of the Dallas and Tarrant County lines on County Line Road, just at the point where the city limits of Grapevine, Irving, and Euless came together. Approximately 300 invited guests attended the ceremony. They were taken to the remote site by bus from the Inn of the Six Flags, in the process frightening a small herd of cattle into a minor stampede. After most of the guests had been assembled for entertainment by a Texas Christian University band, the first air passengers ever to land at the future airport arrived by helicopter. The passengers included the men who would operate four bulldozers as groundbreaking tools: U.S. Secretary of Transportation Alan S. Boyd, Dallas Mayor and Airport Board Chairman Erik Jonsson, Vice Chairman J. Lee Johnson of Fort Worth, and Executive Director Thomas M. Sullivan. Three blasts from a 105-mm. howitzer, manned by U.S. Marines, startled the crowd. Four bright, helium-filled balloons carrying a bag of dirt from the groundbreaking were released to head immediately north, apparently en route to Oklahoma. (The winds soon shifted to the east, the balloons landed almost a hundred miles away in Como, and the man who found them claimed a $100 U.S. Savings bond as his reward.)

At a luncheon immediately afterward at the Inn of the Six Flags, the master of ceremonies, George Haddaway, veteran editor of Dallas-based *Flight* magazine, reminded that this day was Amon G. Carter Sr.'s birthday. "He was one of the great and early supporters of aviation, not only in this area but nationally, as well," Haddaway said. "We shall always remember him for his foresight and vision." Then, keeping things on an even keel between the two cities, Haddaway observed that this day also marked the fiftieth anniversary of Erik Jonsson's first airplane ride.

Transportation Secretary Boyd, who had commented briefly at the groundbreaking, now made more formal comments. Boyd said the airport was destined to be one of the six major hubs of the world, joining London, Paris, Tokyo, Los Angeles and New York. As an aviation facility it would be "far ahead of anything else in the world." Boyd called attention to one of its unique features— the six-lane thoroughfare that would pierce the very center of the facility. "Such an idea would—only a few years ago—have qualified a man for residence in an asylum." But Boyd also had a word of caution, saying that an important planning task ahead must not be forgotten: the development of nearby "reliever" airports for corporate and private aviation. "I urge you to look into this arrangement now. The non-airline planes more and more everyday are furnishing valuable transportation services," he said.

Among the approximately 350 local and national political, government and civic leaders present for the luncheon was the CAB's Ross Newmann, who labeled the groundbreaking a "splendid step in the right direction." But, said the man who had refereed the dispute between the two cities, "I have to say that it was very, very difficult to take the first step."

After the exuberant luncheon, Dallas' J. Erik Jonsson walked up to Fort Worth's J. Lee Johnson III. "You can kiss me now," Jonsson said playfully. "Erik," Johnson replied, "there are some things I just won't do for Fort Worth."

Inspiring though the groundbreaking and luncheon were, they must have been particularly arduous for Sullivan. He went home afterwards "with the flu and just a touch of pneumonia" and stayed in bed for three weeks afterwards.

At this point only a little more than half of the 18,335 acres had been purchased by the two cities. (Since the board itself lacked the power of eminent domain, purchases were made by the cities of Fort Worth and Dallas.) Land costs, now estimated to be $35 million instead of $21 million, earned menacing headlines: "Airport Costs Spiral." Overall airport costs now mentioned in news stories—unofficially—were something more than $500 million instead of $285 million. *Dallas Times Herald* writer Dick Hitt cited a much higher figure in his popular daily column. "If the recently disclosed mark of $500 million stuns you, how does a billion hit you? That's the figure mentioned as a ceiling possibility by a high-ranking city official at a recent cocktail conversation."

Fort Worth's Mayor McKinley, still skeptical, said he had lacked confidence in the airport cost estimates "from the very beginning." McKinley complained that the board was withholding information and conducting much of its business in closed sessions. Vice Chairman J. Lee Johnson III of Fort Worth, expressed a contrary point of view. The only thing that concerned him was "whether we are building this thing big enough." The final cost of the airport, whether $500 million or a billion dollars, would not cost taxpayers anything but the purchase of the land, he said.

McKinley's complaints would spur a break with the Fort Worth city councilman and airport board member Stovall. In the spring of 1969 Stovall made the airport an issue in his decision to run for mayor against incumbent McKinley. Describing the airport as "the single most important thing being undertaken today in the Fort Worth-Dallas area," he said McKinley several times voted contrary to the interests of the airport. "I don't think he is 100 percent for the airport," Stovall contended. McKinley denied the charge, but the issue of McKinley's support for the airport became a major aspect of debate between the two men in their joint appearances. Stovall was emphasizing an issue that resounded favorably with the voters—they ousted McKinley and made Stovall their new mayor.

TO THE UNTRAINED eye, it was difficult nearly two months after the groundbreaking to discern much progress toward building what would be the world's biggest airport. There were twenty-seven earthscrapers, eighteen bulldozers, and nearly a hundred workers at the area, but not a single building had been started. The workers were involved in site preparation, an undramatic but essential part of construction. They were clearing trees from the land and they were moving dirt—about 200,000 yards of it already. They were also building a water transmission line from Fort Worth to bring water necessary for construction. (Ultimately, with completion of the airport, Dallas would supply two-thirds of the water needed and Fort Worth one-third. Four separate above-ground tanks connected by miles of underground pipelines would hold more than twelve million gallons of water.) Among the many workers were TAMS architects and engineers who were carefully inspecting the quality of the fill material that would underlie the runways and provide a cushion for the great weight of concrete runways and the pounding of huge airliners. A year later in March 1970 an aerial photograph showed a huge, flat landscape with miles and miles of ten-foot drainage pipes (big enough to drive a pick-up truck through) lined up, ready for installation. At this point only about half of the grading and thirty-six miles of the drainage work had been completed. Even so, the job was on schedule!

The issue of rising costs, a subject of growing speculation, was addressed at a board meeting in early February when Sullivan sought to explain the matter. As he outlined to the board's satisfaction, the basic cost for the facility had climbed only from $285 million to $299 million, and this was being attributed to the addition of a medical center, two crash-rescue buildings, and a maintenance complex. Other new costs, however—interest accrued during construction, legal and financing fees, development expense, and contingencies—added $112 million. Still other new expenses included service facilities to be built by airlines, other commercial costs, and federal government expenditures, bringing "total airport investment" of $601 million. Jonsson, totally non-plussed and appearing to confirm columnist Hitt's recent speculation, said the airport's costs might reach a billion dollars. "We are talking about a vast project," he said. Costs for the suburban cities would be "a flat zero," and the only added expenditures for Dallas and Fort Worth would be for land, he emphasized.

Original estimates of land costs of between $21 and $25 million, it turned out, were far too low. By summer the two cities already had spent $22 million, with just 10,238 of the 18,335 acres acquired. Final costs for land were expected to almost double the original estimate, now anticipated at nearly $50 million. Recent land purchases had been the most expensive. By April 1969 it had become evident that Dallas especially would need more money for its land purchases. Fort Worth officials were quoted in the press as believing that Dallas had wasted taxpayers' money by paying too much for its land purchases, citing an average of $3,057 per acre for 4,376 acres. Fort Worth had paid an average of just $1,415 for 6,000 acres. The result was that in June 1969 both city councils agreed separately to issue additional warrants to complete the purchases—$16 million for Dallas and $7 million for Fort Worth. More financial help came in April 1970 when an additional $50 million in revenue bonds were sold. At the end of 1970 Dallas City Council once more had to issue additional warrants, this time in the amount of $9.5 million, to cover its share of the cost of land acquisition, $40 million. With Dallas paying 7/11 of these costs, the total cost for airport land ultimately reached $62 million, three times the minimal amount of $21 million that had been predicted.

A MAJOR ASPECT of the airport remained unresolved—an efficient system for moving passengers with connecting flights from one terminal to another. By 1975 as many as 1,600 persons an hour, or five million a year, would be using the system, most of them carrying considerable luggage and most of them having little more than an hour to connect with their flights. By 1985 the system would carry more than 36 million passengers a year. Many airports simply used buses for this purpose, and the board hired a transportation consultant to study the efficacy of buses as opposed to their own preference, an automated system. As the airport's deputy executive director, James R. Mettler, described it: "The transit system we envision for this airport incorporates the idea of small units moving four to six people within the terminal complex." DFW's goal was a compelling one: "To develop the most sophisticated automated requirements of any rapid transit system anywhere." It conceivably would transport not just passengers, but baggage, freight, supplies, mail, and trash.

A one-million dollar grant to the airport from the Department of Transportation's Urban Mass Transit Authority sought not only to assist DFW in finding the best solution for the airport but also a possible solution to transportation problems in urban environments around the nation. Part of this grant would be used to analyze separate systems being developed for the airport by Varo Inc. of Garland, Texas, and Dashaveyor of Venice, California.

First of the two systems to be unveiled in prototype was Varo's "Monocab," billed as a "horizontal elevator," an electrically powered vehicle suspended from an overhead track above ground-level congestion. The Monocab, introduced in March 1970, was about the size of an automobile with a seating capacity of six, although a twenty-four seat model also was being developed. Under this concept a passenger could summon a specific "cab" by pushing a button for a particular airline or parking lot. Dashaveyor's proposal for the "people mover," unveiled in January 1971, featured electrically powered cars running on rails and capable of carrying as many as thirty passengers. The cars would travel at speeds of about 35 miles per hour. The system, according to Dashaveyor officials, could be extended to downtown Dallas and Fort Worth, with cars running at speeds of 80 to 90 miles per hour.

Bids from these two competitors were opened in February 1971, and by then the two competitors had added others to their team. Varo had been joined by LTV Aerospace Corp. of Dallas, and Dashaveyor had arranged for two partners, Morrison-Knudsen Co. of Boise, Idaho, and Fischback & Moore of New York City. Both bidders had enlarged their proposals so that the system they designed would be capable of serving far more than the DFW Airport. Bids opened at airport offices revealed that Dashaveyor was low bidder, with two separate offers of $27.3 million and $36 million. Varo's bid was for $48.5 million.

A month later the board rejected both bids as too expensive and too complex. Both bidders unsuccessfully urged the board to reconsider its decision. New specifications would call for a simpler, less sophisticated system, one that probably would not necessarily carry freight and garbage. Passengers and their baggage now would be the focus of what had been labeled the AIRTRANS system.

Sullivan urged Varo and Dashaveyor to submit new bids in the competition. Would the airport's opening now be delayed? No, assured Ernest Dean.

The important matter of who would build the "people mover" or AIRTRANS system finally was settled in June 1971 when the board awarded the contract to Vought Aeronautics of LTV Corporation, choosing that firm's bid of $20,979,822 even though it was $3 million higher than Westinghouse Air Brake's bid. LTV's plan, as board member and construction committee chairman George Underwood explained, provided "better engineering, a shorter construction time, [and] a better guideway system." Also, it was believed that LTV, as a local company, could provide better service to the system than Westinghouse, located on the East Coast. LTV's plan envisioned automated cars running on rubber tires at ground level via computer programming on a U-shaped guideway. Airline passengers would have to wait an average of ten minutes for a car. The system would cover a twelve-mile route, delivering not only passengers but luggage, mail, supplies, trash and employees between the four terminals and other points. The bid had been based on a "contrived" plan, and the actual award to LTV was $30,980,872. This was hailed as good news for the local economy, for it meant 1,750 new local jobs.

For LTV, which had as its original and primary business the building of military aircraft but which now was seeking diversification, winning the contract was its second major coup in two weeks in the area of ground transportation. The firm had won a Department of Transportation contract on July 1 for $1.2 million to design a mock-up of a 150-mile per hour, 60-passenger tracked air cushion vehicle for rapid transit systems. Now LTV officials envisioned "people-mover" contracts for rapid transit systems everywhere.

Initial routing of the AIRTRANS system would be between stations at the four half-loop terminals that now had been determined to represent the "First Phase." And construction of the loops was ready to begin in July 1971. While the airport would open with four loops only, by the year 2000 as many as thirteen loops were expected to be operational.

The fact that awarding the AIRTRANS contract had been delayed actually meant a delay in the airport's opening, despite earlier assurances. Instead of April 1973, the airport would not be ready until July 1973.

TO THE GENERAL public, the scope of DFW continued to be difficult to comprehend despite the vast amount of publicity. A poll conducted by the *Times Herald* led the newspaper to conclude that the airport and its projected impact were "incomprehensible to the average citizen." Only a few of the respondents knew that DFW would be the world's biggest airport, or that it was to be one of six major air centers in the world, or that it was expected to exert a major stimulus on economic growth and development in the area, or that its costs largely would be covered by fees charged to commercial air carriers and other users. Most people vaguely compared it in size and traffic to New York's Kennedy Airport, although in reality DFW would be more than three times the size of Kennedy with a planned flight traffic that would equal the combined volume of Kennedy, LaGuardia, and Newark. "Tell me, just how big is 18,000 acres?" asked one person. The newspaper reporter had an answer: nine miles from north to south and 8.5 wide.

There was another way to gauge its size. After the board in 1971 hired a chief of security, Leonard (Len) Limmer, he erected a chain-link fence around the airport property perimeter to define the property. The fence was thirty-five miles long. In early meetings the engineering staff, Limmer later recalled, wanted a fence with security gates at all entrances around the airport, even those not going directly to the terminals. Those entering airport property would have to identify themselves, and a special tag would be given them for their windshields. Limmer preferred and won acceptance for an "open" airport with easy access.

Sullivan had found Limmer in the Dallas suburban town of Mesquite, where Limmer had become at the age of 27 the youngest police chief in the state. He had been recommended for the DFW position by Dallas City Manager George Schrader, who had promoted Limmer to police chief when he had been city manager in Mesquite. In Mesquite Limmer had suggested to Schrader the possibility of uniting in a limited way the fire department with police functions. The idea had not materialized, but when Schrader told Sullivan about Limmer's idea, he was intrigued. As director of the Port Authority of New York Sullivan had worked on the same concept. Limmer was hired to head the airport's security force and given Sullivan's approval to hire security personnel who would be cross-trained in police, structural fire, aircraft fire rescue, and emergency medical services.

By the time the airport would open in January 1974 Limmer had hired and trained through various academies nearly 300 officers who were uniquely qualified. Integration of these activities was more logical, productive, and economical than more traditional methods, and it also meant higher salaries for the highly trained officers, although an overall savings had been achieved by combining the functions.

References to the new DFW Airport described it as a "regional" airport, a misleading term. Even at this date plans were well under way for direct international flights. In February 1969 Sullivan began writing letters to the major large international carriers such as Lufthansa, Trans World, Pan American, and Alitalia asking their plans for using DFW both at the opening and also for the years 1980 to 1985. The new airport, now being designed by "two nationally renowned architectural firms, a principal engineering firm, and others," not only would be the "world's largest airport," but it was the board's "real desire to build the finest airport facility in existence," Sullivan told the carriers: "If international carriers are to directly serve this large

Southwest United States travel market, we must incorporate facilities in the plans we are now preparing." To that end, Sullivan desired their needs as to "terminal gate requirements, terminal building passenger areas, and inspection space requirements."

Sullivan also privately sent layout plans for the airport to international airport planners in Paris, London, Tokyo, and New York asking for their candid comments, good and bad, on the design. "I do not ask for an exhaustive review, but simply your impressions and any points of softness," he told the president of the Japan Airport Terminal Company in Tokyo.

The goal to offer non-stop international flights appeared to be a certainty in September 1971 when Japan Air Lines announced its hopes of flying directly into DFW. The announcement was made in conjunction with the formation of a new Japan-Texas Association by twenty-eight leading Japanese business executives and a number of Texas business leaders. (Japan Air Lines also had requested the right to land at Chicago's O'Hare, but space there was so limited that permission was doubtful.) Sullivan was "delighted" at the news, pointing out that if the route was approved it would be the first foreign-based airline to come to DFW. Within six months the new North Texas Commission, an organization formed to "market" the area, announced plans to place in Tokyo its own trade ambassador, former State Department official John F. Shaw. His goal was to promote trade between Japan and the Dallas-Fort Worth area. The Commission chose Tokyo for its first international office rather than London or Paris or Frankfurt because of Japan's greater promise as a partner for the area.

The North Texas Commission membership consisted of a number of blue-ribbon business and civic leaders who launched a $1.5 million annual advertising and sales promotion for the area. In its efforts to promote the new airport, the Commission, struggling for a simple way to describe the greater Dallas-Fort Worth area, came up with a new term, "Southwest Metroplex." This soon became shortened to the "Metroplex," a word which soon became the standard descriptive term for the area.

A few days later the newest CAB member, Robert D. Timm, visiting DFW and saying he had not been able to "conceive of anything so vast and visionary," predicted that by 1980 it would be the nation's leading air hub. As to Japan Air Line's pending request for CAB approval to land at DFW, he could not say when or if it would be granted. But there seemed to be little doubt that it would be. DFW's "sheer size, location and scope of facilities will attract international airlines," he said.

Euphoria seemed to have set in, for within the week the nation's new Secretary of Transportation, John Volpe, described DFW as a "facility that by any stretch of the imagination will be a pacesetter for the rest of the nation." He said he expected DFW to be "an international airport of real significance." But in November 1971 the chairman of the Civil Aeronautics Board, Secor D. Brown, said that new international flights must await an economic recovery by American airlines before approval.

Among the myriad concerns anticipated with the airport's ultimate opening was the reaction of nearby residents to the noise generated by overhead flights, a common problem with so many airports and one which board members hoped to be alleviated because of the airport's massive spaces. G.R. Stanford, one of Sullivan's top aides, had an idea in April 1969 that he privately proposed to Sullivan. An excellent opportunity exists, he said, to start developing an "experience pattern" for those who work and live near the airport. Begin letting these residents experience "over-flights" on a limited basis to inure them on a gradual basis to the noise levels, he argued. This, he said, could be done by altering the flight patterns of the training aircraft now operating out of GSIA. Such flights on a limited basis would permit the area's residents and workers to "start becoming accustomed" to the noise. "If such an experiencing period does not occur, we may be besieged with numerous complaints shortly after the start of operations," he said. Whether or not Stanford's recommendations were followed is not known.

Work on the facility had been remarkably free of accidents and injuries until the spring of 1971. On Monday, May 10, 1971, the side of a forty-foot ditch being dug for a utilities distribution tunnel collapsed without warning. Many of the workers managed to scramble free, but three who were laying concrete at the tunnel's deepest part could not escape. Millions of tons of shale entombed the men. Their bodies, encased in shale and concrete, could be freed only with jackhammers. An investigation revealed that the cave-in occurred as an "unseen shale plug" had slipped out, causing the collapse. There was no negligence on anyone's part, a TAMS report showed.

GROUNDBREAKING for the $2.5 million air traffic control tower, a 196-foot structure which was the responsibility of the FAA, took place on July 15, 1971. It would be the first of a new futuristic type to be used as a standard by the FAA. The control tower's "cab," eleven-sided with 620 square feet of floor space, would rest atop four pre-cast concrete shafts.

FAA administrator John H. Shaffer, who spoke at the groundbreaking, urged airport officials to make DFW the best in the world. Being "biggest," he avowed, was "not all that essential." In an interesting aside, Shaffer also observed that in his opinion airlines were "missing the mother lode" in their emphasis on gaining more and more passengers. Air freight ultimately would offer more revenue, he predicted.

Building runways sufficiently strong to withstand the pounding of the new generation of huge aircraft was an important aspect of the construction process. The matter was raised with some urgency in Dallas in July 1971 at an air safety forum sponsored by the Air Line Pilots Association. In opening comments, Captain I.L. Moor charged that runway pavements "all over the country" were literally coming apart. Without citing specifics, Moor said that runways being built at new airports were being constructed "to outmoded standards." Concrete for DFW's runways was yet to be poured, and Ernest E. Dean responded. Dean said DFW's new runways would easily handle the biggest and heaviest aircraft.

Before concrete could be poured, though, underlying soil at DFW had to be stabilized with massive doses of lime. The mammoth runways, requiring some 600 million pounds of cement, would require a year and a half to be completed. During this period some 60,000 loads of concrete—twenty-five tons per load—would be hauled.

Board member and Fort Worth Mayor R.M. Stovall predicted that these enormous demands would create a shortage of cement and an increase in its price. His comments received wide coverage and prompted a mini-controversy. A spokesperson for area cement companies quickly denied Stovall's predictions. Supplies on hand were ample, he said, and production capacity was more than adequate to handle all demands for cement, including the massive amount scheduled for DFW.

In November 1971 bids were solicited for paving, one of the largest jobs of its kind in the world. The amount to be spent was expected to exceed $50 million, which would pay for 3 million square yards of concrete for runways that would be from 13 to 17 inches thick. This was enough concrete to pave a four-lane highway between the airport and Oklahoma City. It was also enough to cover the entire principality of Monaco with a layer three feet thick! When bids were opened just before Thanksgiving, 1971, the low bid, submitted by H.B. Zachary Co. of San Antonio and South Prairie Co. of Wichita, Kansas, was just over $57 million. The job was awarded to them in December 1971.

Although its runways certainly would be strong enough and lengthy enough to accommodate the Concorde, whether or not DFW would host regular flights of the new airplane was not certain. Environmentalists' concerns had arisen about the sonic boom accompanying the supersonic airplane. By August 1971 five Texas senators had introduced legislation to prohibit supersonic flights over Texas. An Associated Press news story stated with exaggeration that passage of this legislation "would wreck the future of the new airport because its whole concept is built around the SST and other aircraft of the future." State Senator A.R. Schwartz of Galveston, one of the sponsors of the anti-SST legislation, said simply, 'We can do without the SST and its sonic boom."

But negotiations to bring the Concorde to DFW for the opening continued. Clearance was obtained from the FAA and the State Department. Monsieur Henri Ziegler, chairman and chief executive of the Societe Nationale Ineastrielle Aerospatiale, which with British Aircraft Corporation was building the Concorde, even visited DFW to review the situation first-hand. Ziegler expressed great admiration for the nearly-finished airport, and he continued to favor the visit, although he wanted assurance that the presence of Governor John Connally as commissioner general of the dedication ceremonies would not be political in nature. Ziegler also expressed great concern that because of alleged noise problems all U.S. carriers except Braniff had canceled their options to purchase the Concorde.

The early rush to buy land in the area of the airport still had not diminished. Two years in advance of the opening, what was described as the "largest land development boom in Dallas, Fort Worth and Mid-Cities history" was occurring. A newspaper article ticked off thirty-one major multi-million dollar developments planned, the bulk of them in Irving, Grapevine, Grand Prairie, Coppell, Hurst, Bedford, Euless and Arlington. They ranged from commercial parks to housing developments.

When a corporate relocation specialist wrote in 1967 to Sullivan—apparently an old friend—concerning a large but unnamed corporation's interest in moving its headquarters to the Dallas-Fort Worth area, Sullivan wrote back enthusiastically. "I am not a member of the Chamber of Commerce for this area, Bozo, but believe you me, in the year and a half that I have been here, my associations with the civic leaders and the progressive planning on their part and on the parts of the two city councils, the wholesome attitude of the people in the community, and the ideal weather conditions lead me to the conclusion that it is one of the finest areas in the United States. The completion of the Airport will make it the finest."

In August 1971 the board executed an agreement with AMFAC Inc. of Honolulu to build a 450-room, $10 million hotel at DFW. AMFAC agreed to pay the board a percentage of its gross sales, a sum anticipated to bring DFW about $255,000 annually. The chairman of a regional safety committee for the Air Line Pilots Association questioned the advisability of placing the hotel at such a central location adjacent to the control tower. In the draft of his reply, presumably sent, Jonsson advised that the hotel's location had been studied carefully and that the FAA had concurred that its location was proper and not hazardous.

LOVE FIELD continued to deal with a rapidly growing volume of traffic even though its days as the major airport for the area clearly were limited. It was predicted that by 1973, just before DFW would open, Love Field would be the tenth busiest airport in the world. A study for the North Central Texas Council of Governments determined that by 1975 Love Field would be confronted with a chaotic traffic jam, having outgrown by nearly four million passengers its maximum capacity of eight million. American Airlines and Braniff were its dominant carriers. American had seen passenger departures at Love Field nearly double in five years to more than 27,000 in 1968. With no new airport in sight until at least late 1972, American was obliged to undergo a $10.3 million two-year expansion program at Love Field. Its $8 million passenger concourse opened on December 3, 1968. Aside from the practical relief it gave, the new facility contained what the airline described as "a major addition to the art treasures of Dallas"—a 35-foot long, motorized Alexander Calder sculpture suspended in the main lobby. Two days after American's new concourse was unveiled, Braniff opened its own new terminal at Love Field, a $9 million facility which doubled its available space. Neither of these major projects appeared to lessen the two carriers' enthusiasm for moving to the new airport when completed. They were additions that simply had to be done to accommodate their customers at Love Field.

While commercial flights had ended at GSIA, Fort Worth's second municipally owned airport, Meacham, still was active and also in need of greater space. A new runway, control tower, and administration building costing a total of $1 million were announced in October 1968. And the growing amount of business was causing a shortage of hangar space.

A question of increasing importance was just what would happen to Love Field after the new DFW Airport opened? The executive director of the North Dallas Chamber of Commerce, Gordon Rose, pointed out in October 1971 that the end of Love Field as one of the nation's busiest commercial airports would "undoubtedly have the greatest effect on North Dallas of any development in this entire decade." The organization's president, Tom James, named a Love Field task force to address the issue of its future. "When the $200 million payroll of Love Field and its allied businesses is at stake, we must be concerned," he said. "We will be affected." James said at the organization's annual meeting that his part of town would suffer unless Love Field continued intrastate and short-range feeder flights after the opening of "Grapevine International." Passengers would find it most inconvenient to "fight through 17 miles of clogged traffic to board a plane to a destination only 250 miles away," he said.

Those closest to Love Field, though, knew that while its future would be different, it would be promising. The man who had been aviation director for the City of Dallas for twenty years and now was vice president of Southwest Airmotive, George Coker, pointed out that the present volume of business and corporate flying alone was sufficient to cover the costs of maintenance and management operations. And corporate flying was expanding rapidly.   Jonsson himself also foresaw Love Field as a facility for corporate and private "pleasure" aircraft. And, he thought, once DFW became saturated, it could be used as a "backup."

W.C. "Dub" Miller, former city councilman and long-time Dallas Chamber of Commerce aviation committee member who headed up its Love Field task force, foresaw a busy future for shorter commuter flights within 500 miles of the airport. "Once air traffic passengers discover they are going to have to drive from 20 to 24 miles to the new airport terminals for a short flight to Houston, Austin or San Antonio, they will ask for commuter flights at Love Field."

In fact, one upstart new "commuter" airline operating out of Love Field already was doing that. Southwest Airlines, owner of three Boeing 737-200s, in the summer of 1971 began a schedule of six round-trip flights between Dallas and San Antonio and twelve between Dallas and Houston's new Intercontinental. Southwest had won permission to inaugurate these flights only after a lengthy legal battle against Braniff and Texas International, both of whom had argued that there was no need for new service to those cities. In the fall of 1971, with its Houston leg failing miserably, Southwest gambled and shifted its primary Houston operations away from the new but distant airport to the older but nearer Hobby Airport. Because of Hobby's convenience to downtown

Houston, business people began flocking to Southwest's flights there. Realizing at once the promise of this new opportunity, Southwest quickly moved all its Houston flights to Hobby and achieved spectacular success there. The new airline's economical, no-frills service (no meals on these short flights, only peanuts and soft drinks), elimination of reserved seating in favor of a first-come, first-served policy, and bold and imaginative advertising programs were very appealing.

Southwest's new success in Houston seemed ominous for its chances at the new DFW Airport. Would Southwest resist a move there in order to retain its far more convenient location at Love Field?

Bond ordinances both in Fort Worth and Dallas had decreed and the major airlines had signed agreements in December 1969 to move all their operations to the new airport when it opened. These agreements had been signed with the airlines at a brief but impressive public ceremony with top executives from the major airlines—Braniff, American, Delta, Eastern, Frontier, Ozark, and Texas International. (This was prior to Southwest's entry into the market.) Jonsson, as chairman, and Friedman, as secretary, signed the documents on behalf of the board. An important caveat was left unspoken at this public moment. Four of the airlines placed a condition on their agreement—they would consider the agreement null and void unless all other carriers signed the letter. Continental Airlines complained that the agreement was too open-ended. In a note to his files, Sullivan recorded that Ross Newmann had assured him that the CAB would not permit any carrier to have a competitive advantage by staying at Love Field once the new regional airport was operational.

Complicating the problem was the fact that the leases of major airlines at Love Field extended to as late as 1979, and of course the fact that more than $27 million had been spent in recent years to remodel the airport's facilities. "Unfortunately, we don't know what we're going to use these facilities for," confessed a Delta Air Lines official.

As anticipated, though, it was Southwest that uttered the first protest against the move to DFW. Southwest had not signed the December 1969 agreement because it had not been in existence at the time. "There's no object in us being out there," said its president, M. Lamar Muse in November 1971. "Our sole purpose is to serve the local commuter." Muse said it would be suicidal for his airline if it were forced to operate solely out of DFW. Thus, he said, he would ask the DFW board for a waiver to continue operations out of Love Field. This he did in March 1972.

This news was distressing. A source "close to the regional airport" predicted to news reporters that "this could lead to dire results for our project." The concern, of course, was that one deviation by a single airline could set a precedent that would permit others to follow. Before the end of the year Braniff International stoked up the fires when its chief executive officer, Harding Lawrence, announced that his airline, the largest operating in the area, would retain its own flights from Love Field if any other airline did. Braniff competed directly with Southwest with flights to Houston and San Antonio, as did another airline, Texas International.

In June 1972 the airport board filed suit in federal court against Southwest to require it to move to the new facility. Three weeks later Southwest responded with a counter-claim, and its president, Lamar Muse, said his airline might be forced to move to Addison Airport in North Dallas if it lost its battle in court.

Meanwhile, the battle in the marketplace between Southwest and Braniff was also heating up. Boasting of its efficient, no-frills service, Southwest had made a drastic price reduction to $13 on its Dallas/San Antonio flights. Braniff responded with its own $13 fare between Dallas and Houston's Hobby, where in view of Southwest's success Braniff now had transferred some of its flights. Southwest, still in the red as a new airline with heavy start-up costs, could hardly afford to match this reduction on its popular Houston flights. "They're trying to destroy us just like they've tried to do since we were applying for certification," declared Southwest's Muse. Braniff's Edward Acker responded: "I'd hardly call it a war. We think of it as another competitive experience."

In an imaginative counter-play, Southwest decided to offer the same $13 fare for any Dallas-Houston customer who asked for it. But those who would agree to fly at the standard $26 rate would be given in appreciation a bottle of fine whisky or an ice chest. It didn't take long for those passengers traveling at company expense to choose the $26 price and to take home the whisky or ice chest. The third airline with flights between Houston and Dallas, Texas International, felt obliged to enter the fray before losing all its passengers, and it also began offering a $13 fare between the two cities.

Lurking behind this intensive, high-profile battle was the question of whether Southwest would be permitted to stay at Love Field after DFW opened. If forced to go to DFW, Southwest's future would be imperiled. And if it could remain at Love Field, so convenient for "commuter" passengers, Braniff and Texas International likely would demand the same privilege. If these airlines remained at Love Field, DFW's fees from airline activity would be significantly reduced. The issue loomed larger and larger as a major concern for DFW's welfare.

In March 1973 the issue was heard in a non-jury trial before U.S. District Judge William M. Taylor Jr. The cities of Dallas and Fort Worth and the airport board asked for a "speedy" declaratory judgment that they had the authority to require all carrier services, both intrastate and interstate, to move to the new airport. Southwest argued that its "commuter" flights to San Antonio and Houston could best be done from Love Field because of its more convenient location, and that there was no authority to order their transfer to DFW.

FAA Regional Director Henry Newman testified in behalf of DFW, stating that continuation of Southwest's Love Field operations would be a violation of the principle that created the new airport. An airport planning consultant testified that permitting Southwest to stay at Love Field would cause others to do so too, and the result could bankrupt DFW. "We believe if Love Field is designated an intrastate airport for Southwest, you're really talking about a 23 percent diversion of passengers," said R. Dixon Speas.

The struggle, in the minds of many, pitted a tiny, three-airplane airline against not only Braniff but against both city councils and the DFW airport board. Muse, testifying before Judge Taylor, said he believed Braniff was trying to bankrupt

Southwest, and that Braniff was seeking to do what it had been unable to achieve in Houston—that is, keep Southwest out of Hobby.

The president of Frontier Airlines, Al Feldman, stated that if any of the eight interstate carriers who had agreed to the sole use of DFW failed to honor any part of their bargain, his airline would consider its contract null and void. This did not include Southwest, he said, because it had not been founded at the time of the signing. It did, however, include Braniff and Texas International, both of whom had announced that they would return to Love Field if Southwest were permitted to stay.

After the month-long hearing Judge Taylor issued his opinion. Southwest could continue to fly out of Love Field. Love Field was a public airport, Judge Taylor said, and while the City of Dallas was not obliged to provide Love Field as an airport for Southwest, as long as the airport remained operational it was "not legally permissible" to exclude Southwest.

"It was a victory for the commuter," proclaimed Lamar Muse. Fort Worth's city attorney, S.G. Johndroe Jr., said the decision would cost DFW Airport $3.65 million a year.

Several weeks later Southwest entered its third year of existence, having piled up as a start-up airline a $5.5 million deficit. But projections showed the next quarter to be profitable for the first time. The airline, boasting of a brash advertising campaign and flight attendants clad in bright, sexy hot pants, seemed to have accomplished the impossible. (In February 1975, the U.S. government indicted Braniff and Texas International for conspiring to put Southwest out of business. Both airlines pleaded "no contest," and paid $100,000 in fines.)

THE FACT that appointment to the DFW board was valued and prestigious became clear in January 1972 when a young and independent candidate in Dallas, Wes Wise, bucked the establishment to become mayor of the city. Jonsson, having served four terms on the board, had chosen not to run for re-election, but he maintained his keen interest in the airport and wanted to retain his seat on the board. His term, along with those of Frank A. Hoke and George Underwood Jr. (all of whom had been on the board since its formation), would expire on January 31, 1972. Wise made it known that as mayor he should have one of those seats. The question was, whose seat? Wise said that he did not necessarily want to replace Jonsson, but he believed that the office of mayor should be represented on the airport board and that he would consider it a "personal affront to the office of mayor" if he were bypassed.

Dallas City Council members, somewhat tormented over the issue, finally agreed to appoint their new mayor to the board and also to re-appoint Jonsson. The third appointee was Henry Stuart, a former City Council member and now president of Addison Airport. Hoke and Underwood, even though they had coveted re-appointment, were disappointed.

An interesting bit of byplay had occurred beforehand. The council had forced Wise, before agreeing to appoint him, to assure them that he would not support Fort Worth Mayor R.M. Stovall as the next chairman of the airport board. Wise earlier had told the council that he believed the chairmanship should be passed along to Fort Worth. As it turned out, on February 1 the new airport board unanimously re-elected Jonsson to be their chairman. J. Lee Johnson III and Bayard Friedman were re-elected as vice-chairman and secretary. Jonsson thus began his fifth term as chairman of the board.

One of the questions Wise raised at his first board meeting was the status of a planned extension of Loop 635 from Stemmons Freeway in northwest Dallas to the north end of the airport. The extension would give easy access to the north end of the airport for residents of affluent North Dallas. The project had been included in a ten-point program of priorities drafted in 1968, but it had not yet been funded by the Texas Highway Department. There also was discussion of a new Interstate 30 between Dallas and Fort Worth with a link to DFW, but there were no funds available.

In February 1972 Wise and Stovall returned from a visit to Washington, D.C., and reported that the Department of Transportation had promised to pay two-thirds of the cost of developing a rapid transit system to connect their two cities to the airport. The system, known as Tracked Air Cushion Vehicle

(TACV), would be supported by a thin cushion of air and would run at speeds of up to 150 miles per hour along a concrete guideway. Total cost for developing the system was anticipated to be $15 million, with the two cities jointly being responsible for $5 million. This was the system which LTV Aerospace Corporation had selected six months earlier with plans to build a full-scale mock-up.

THE NUMBER of workers at DFW had climbed to 2,000 by February 1972, and in the summer that number doubled. The heightened activity was accompanied by an ever-increasing rise in the value of property in nearby communities. "The land boom at a Texas airport," was the headline in *Business Week* in the spring. The article pointed out that in 1967 land in Coppell had been selling for about $1,000 an acre; now the going price was $10,000 an acre. At year's end, a tract of land in Euless purchased by International Airport Center, Inc., for $3.6 million represented more than $55,000 an acre. All this was accompanied by a building frenzy that now was at the $1 billion mark in the area with more construction on the drawing boards. Kenneth M. Good, whose company owned 4,000 acres, called the airport "probably the most significant project in the U.S. in the last 20 years in terms of its impact on real estate values." It was predicted that the town of Grapevine would skyrocket in population within three decades from 7,000 to 50,000 population, and that tiny Coppell would jump from being a sleepy farming community of less than 2,000 to a city as large as Waco.

Trying to bring some order into the rapidly changing area was the North Central Texas Council of Governments (COG), the organization with headquarters in Arlington containing some 137 governmental jurisdictions as its membership. One of COG's achievements had been persuading nearby communities to pass ordinances setting up a Joint Airport Zoning Board with authority to see that no hazards to air traffic were created around the airport among the various municipalities.

Even with the rather frenetic pace toward urbanization in a huge area surrounding the airport, there was an anomaly that would continue for some time into the future. A farmer whose family had operated a 120-acre farm in the area since the turn of the century and who had sold that property to the airport, now turned around and leased back from the airport an even larger area, some 2,000 acres, within airport boundaries. On this acreage he was raising wheat and milo. This practice of leasing unused airport land for agricultural purposes would continue for many years.

In April 1972 a major milestone was reached with the completion of the new administration building. The staff of approximately fifty workers moved their operations from their former offices in the Great Southwest Industrial District to the new facility. The buff-colored, two-story structure with basements was located on the east side of the airport on Valley View Road and East Airfield Drive. The modernistic structure had been built at a cost of $1.48 million. Executive offices in the north end of the structure were divided from reception areas by floor-to-ceiling glass walls. Sullivan's office was in a suite on the northwest corner of the second floor, as were those of Jack Downey, second in command, and Ernest Dean, deputy executive director.

As to the rest of the airport, Sullivan said in July 1972—a year ahead of the new opening date—that the work was "on schedule, which, incidentally, is incredible." The reasons, he said, were "good contractors, good prices, good weather, and good staff." Almost 40 percent of the entire airport now was complete. The eight airlines that had signed the agreement to move from Love Field to DFW upon its opening would have ninety days in which to do so after the airport was certified as complete by the board and the FAA. But the problems of moving piecemeal to the new facility meant that the move likely would be done at one time. The last project to be finished would be a critical element—the AIRTRANS people mover.

As the year 1972 drew near an end, excitement about the possibility of direct international flights increased. Negotiations were on-going, although Sullivan predicted direct overseas routes could not become a reality until 1975. Officials from many foreign air carriers had visited the airport, and three airlines—Braniff, Delta and Pan-American—already had petitioned the CAB to link DFW to Europe with new flights.

Could there possibly be enough passengers to accommodate regular international flights? The key to this, explained John Thompson III, director of transportation for the North Texas Commission, lay in a system of "feeding" passengers to the airport from surrounding areas and states such as West Texas, Louisiana, New Mexico and Oklahoma. The NTC pointed to a new survey which showed that already there were more "feeder" flights arriving daily in Dallas' Love Field than in New York City. "We can show we're already a gateway; give us the international flights," Thompson said. Some of the foreign carriers earlier had viewed Houston as a more appealing outlet for new foreign service. But studies indicated that Dallas and Fort Worth already supported more than twice as many flights as Houston, and the average income of Dallas and Fort Worth residents was higher.

Early in 1973 the board began thinking seriously about the dedication ceremony, authorizing $450,000 to cover costs of the event. Foreseen were a gigantic air show, an open house, a gala benefit ball, and the hosting of national and international dignitaries—perhaps even a visit from President Richard M. Nixon. Texas Governor John M. Connally would be commissioner general.

A special invitation was extended to the new British-French Concorde supersonic jet. The 1,300-mile-per hour aircraft had never visited the United States even though a reproduction model by the joint British-French builders already had toured Africa, Australia, and the Middle East. Concorde officials expressed pleasure at the invitation, but whether or not it could fly across the United States continent or begin scheduled service at American airports still was uncertain. If the same noise levels were required for the Concorde as for the DC-10 and Lockheed 1011, it would be impossible for the Concorde to land at major American airports.

By early 1973 the airport was sufficiently advanced in construction to permit tours by special parties—editors from the Texas Press Association, groups from the American Association for Retired Persons, and others. What they saw was a mammoth facility that was about 75 percent complete. It would have four half-loop terminals and sixty-six gates with plans to have more than 250 gates in thirteen terminals by the year 2001. National attention more and more was focusing on the airport. As a writer for Copley News Service wrote after his tour in February 1973: "They've done it again in Texas. . . . Building the biggest and best—the No. 1. . . . An eye-popping, mind-boggling spectacle." Big enough, the writer added, to hold New York's JFK, Chicago's O'Hare, and Los Angeles international airports combined.

Another news story declared that DFW Airport had attracted wide attention from the news because "it is the only major airport ever constructed anywhere in the world which is being completed on its original time schedule." The claim, of course, was exaggerated since the original goal had been to complete the airport in 1972. It was and had been apparent that DFW would easily surpass Houston's new airport, Houston Intercontinental. Even the *Houston Post* complained that the airport was not living up to its name since it had daily direct service only to Mexico. Houston's 9,000-foot runway was far short of the distance recommended for the 747; DFW would easily exceed that requirement.

On Thursday, May 17, 1973, five months prior to the projected completion of DFW, U.S. Secretary of Transportation Claude S. Brinegar had the privilege of being the first person to step from a fixed-wing aircraft to the tarmac at DFW. Brinegar flew to DFW in a U.S. Coast Guard executive jet which needed only a bit more than half of the 9,000-foot runway for landing. The official came to DFW for a three-hour review on the status of the project, which now was reported to be 88 percent complete. Erik Jonsson briefed Brinegar, U.S. Representative Jim Collins and Dallas County Commissioner Roy Orr on the airport.

In July 1973 a group of twenty board members and area civic leaders journeyed in the opposite direction, going to Washington, D.C., on a four-day trip to familiarize federal officials there with the new airport. Of special concern was the push to acquire direct international flights. One day, said C.A. Tatum, president of the North Texas Commission, the new airport would mean to the area what the deep-water port meant to New York City and the railroad to Chicago's development. J.C. Pace Jr., president of the Fort Worth Chamber of Commerce and a DFW board member, reminded representatives of the Civil Aeronautics Board that CAB prodding had helped crystallize plans for a regional airport, and that now the CAB should be responsive to the "need for services which will help the airport fulfill its purpose." While it was apparent that no international flights could be in operation by the time of the October opening, future possibilities looked good.

Sullivan's determination to have the airport completed by October 1973 seemed by the spring to be a sure bet. Ernest Dean reported to board members in May that the Braniff terminal was 96 percent complete; the joint Texas International/Ozark/Frontier terminal 85 percent complete; the American Airlines terminal 82 percent complete; and that he was "quite pleased" with the progress of the Delta-Continental terminal.

In fact, contracts required that all construction be completed and ready for an "acceptance inspection" by July 15. Afterward, contractors would be given sixty days to correct any deficiencies and to make last-minute changes. A possible snag was AIRTRANS, which was experiencing difficulties. "We're working very hard," said Dean amid reports that the problem lay in the quality of the ride. Some sixty of the sixty-eight cars had been completed and tested by June. The system was to provide service not just between the terminals, but also with the hotel, two remote parking facilities, mail facilities, and a maintenance area. Despite the problem, Dean told the board that the October 1 opening date still was on target.

SEVEN

Dedicating a Dream

✈

*Midway betwen Dallas and Fort Worth, a shotgun marriage
between two ancient civic rivals has produced
a colossus of a jetport that is more than
twice the size of any ever built.*
New York Times

In fact, the airport was ready for its dedication even before
October 1, although by now disappointed board members had
agreed to a request by the airlines and delayed the actual opening
for flights until October 28. But there was no need to postpone the
dedication, and on Thursday, September 20, 1973, DFW Regional
Airport hung out the "welcome" sign for the first of a four-day,
Texas-size festival. It was an event of national and international
significance that rarely if ever had been matched in aviation
history. Airport officials, city and business leaders, dignitaries
from throughout the world and local citizens celebrated a facility
that very soon would become one of the nation's most important
transportation hubs and that already was acknowledged to be the
world's biggest airport. The airport was basically completed,
although the Marina Hotel was unfinished and AIRTRANS was
not ready for service.

To organize a party of such magnitude the dedication
committee had toiled for many months. John M. Connally, the
former governor of Texas and the former secretary of the U.S.

Treasury, served as the very visible "commissioner general." Official hosts were the DFW Regional Airport Board, the North Texas Commission, the Federal Aviation Administration, and the Junior Leagues of both Dallas and Fort Worth. Working with Read-Poland Public Relations, the committee issued invitations to 140 heads of state and as many ambassadors, along with 40,000 invitations to other guests. President Richard Nixon, who was extended a special invitation to come and serve as the keynote speaker, headed the guest list. White House officials gave some early indications that the President would attend, and the Secret Service requested clearances for the large press corps that accompanied him. Nixon didn't make it after all, though. Newspaper headlines suggested a preoccupation with two important concerns—the growing controversy concerning Vice President Spiro Agnew and alleged kickbacks and continuing inquiries by a U.S. Senate committee into the Watergate affair. Nixon sent White House counselor Anne Armstrong, a Texan, in his place.

"Massive," "huge," "big Daddy," "Texas-size," "mammoth," "gigantic" and other such adjectives could be heard throughout the weekend. One Kilgore resident said that the new airport was so big birds at the north end would fly to the south end for the winter. Outside observers also were fascinated with DFW's size. The *Washington Post* noted that the airport would just barely fit into the entire District of Columbia. In the frequent references to other U.S. airports, DFW was cited as "three times as big as New York's Kennedy," "twice the size of Chicago's O'Hare," and six times as big as Los Angeles International." The *New York Times* reported: "Midway between Dallas and Fort Worth, a shotgun marriage between two ancient civic rivals has produced a colossus of a jetport that is more than twice the size of any ever built— and likely to provide lessons to the world on how pleasant a jetport can be."

The lessons were not easy ones. It had been a long and busy decade since the mayors of these two fiercely competitive cities had agreed to set aside past animosities and explore the possibilities of creating a new regional airport. Their shared vision for creating one of the world's great airports—combined with the strong nudge of the federal government—had provided the impetus to join forces and create perhaps the greatest achievement in the history of either city. FAA Administrator John Shaffer, speaking some months earlier at the groundbreaking ceremony of the DFW Control Tower, had summed up well the role of transportation in building all the world's great cities—Rome and its roads, London and the sailing ship, New York City and its deep-water steamship port, and Chicago and its railroads. "No city has yet reached its greatness by aviation," he said. But now he predicted that the facility being built by Dallas and Fort Worth would "fulfill this destiny."

THURSDAY, THE FIRST day of the $450,000 extravaganza, was designated as International Press Day. In attendance was the largest contingent of news representatives ever to assemble in the metroplex—more than 450—far surpassing even the number of journalists who had descended upon Dallas to cover the Kennedy assassination. (The numbers of visitors at the airport actually was far greater than anticipated, for the journalists' numbers were swelled by the unexpected presence of some 500 non-journalists who complicated the day's events.) After breakfast, the news people went into the skies aboard a Braniff Boeing 747 for a forty-five minute aerial tour of the area. From this aerial vantage point Fort Worth Mayor Stovall and Dallas Mayor Wise identified landmarks and discussed with the reporters and editors the way in which the airport was destined to impact the entire region.

Following a briefing on what would happen during the next days of the dedication, the journalists explored the terminal complexes and operational facilities, took rides on AIRTRANS and visited the airport press center. In a rare opportunity, the FAA opened the DFW Airport control tower, the tallest in the world, to the news media. FAA guides explained how controllers would be monitoring landings, takeoffs and movement on taxiways and aprons.

A highlight of that first day was the arrival of the British-French Concorde SST in its first landing ever on U.S. soil. Earlier, in announcing the Concorde's visit, Tom Sullivan had said, "Next September 20th at 11:00 sharp, the Concorde will land at this airport. I just can't tell you how thrilled we are to have that great big beautiful bird land at our airport as a first." The sleek-winged aircraft, built jointly at a cost of $340 million by the British and French as a harbinger of the future, arrived at Braniff Gate 10, carrying with it additional aviation writers from throughout the world. They had traveled to DFW via Caracas, Venezuela, making the 2,559-mile flight in two hours and 22 minutes. With an average cruising speed of 1400 miles per hour, the Concorde traveled at twice the speed of sound. However, since U.S. regulations didn't permit commercial supersonic flights because of the sonic boom, it had slowed down over the Gulf of Mexico before entering U.S. territory. As one newspaper reported, the Concorde could have shaved about ten minutes off its flight time if it had been allowed to fly at supersonic speeds over the U.S.

To give spectators a good view of the already famous airplane, it had been expected to conduct three passes over DFW before landing, but a small mishap spoiled those plans. Just prior to the first flyover the pilot had to gain altitude quickly when a small aircraft was spotted in the area. Concorde Chief Pilot Jean Franchi pulled the plane into a climb from 1,000 to 3,500 feet, quickly reaching a speed of about 350 miles an hour. The plane subsequently made two more passes, but the third was canceled because of limited visibility and increasing air traffic in the area.

In this historic moment, DFW Regional Airport's promise of direct access to the world seemed fulfilled. The *Concorde Bulletin* had predicted that the Concorde's arrival at DFW would bring together two innovative concepts in air travel—"an airport which should still be modern in the 21st Century and a supersonic transport whose entry into passenger service will herald a 12-hour world, in which no major population center will be more than half a day's flying from any other." Erik Jonsson noted the significance of the Concorde's arrival this way: "It is fitting that the first landing of this plane in the U.S. is here at DFW Airport— the airport of tomorrow."

The Concorde's arrival also symbolized prospects for new commercial trade in the United States. In addition to its media passengers, the airplane was carrying representatives from France and Britain with hopes of promoting Concorde sales in the U.S.

Their message was that the aircraft was not the noisy, pollution-causing vehicle many feared in an emerging age of environmental concern. In fact, this opportunity to influence public opinion was one of the primary reasons for the Concorde's visit to DFW. In a letter to Monsieur Henri Ziegler, chairman and chief executive, Societe Nationale Industrielle Aerospatiale, the vice chairman of the airport board, J. Lee Johnson III, had written that the dedication of the airport, "the world's largest and most revolutionary air transportation facility," would serve as a prime opportunity to "display the environmental compatibility of this aircraft, particularly in areas of sound and emission control, and thereby allay some of the unfounded fears of the environmentalists throughout the world as well as in the U.S." The opportunity for firsthand, personal observation would seem to be the most reasonable and expeditious manner in which the merits of the Concorde could be recognized by the general public, Johnson had said.

(Though DFW officials would later propose a "Texas Connection" to bring the Concorde to the airport on a regular basis, the "plane of the future" was viewed as very costly, and by the beginning of 1973 most American airlines already had dropped their options to purchase Concordes. Following this visit for the dedication, only Braniff Airways continued to express interest in the possibility of leasing one or two Concordes from British Airways.)

This first dedicatory day ended with a press preview party at the Inn of the Six Flags, which had been designated as the off-site headquarters for the world press, a place where media representatives were provided access to special facilities equipped with typewriters, telephones, telegraph, teletype, photo and television transmission equipment. From this location the journalists filed their reports to publications and broadcasting stations around the world. Tom Sullivan, earlier that day, had reminded them in a press conference that they were sharing in "the greatest thing which has happened in the world of aviation."

Press reactions to the new airport varied in tone. Airport officials had worked so hard to ensure positive public perceptions of the new facility, but some journalists focused on difficulties experienced during the day rather than on the airport itself. Their most common complaint, "poor organization of press activities," had been caused by the presence of those 500 or so unexpected non-journalists who showed up that day and made it less manageable. Media representatives had found themselves vying with non-journalists for information packets and opportunities to tour the facilities. Because of the size of the crowd, activities often had been behind schedule. Even press conferences sometimes were jammed with the curious, noted *The Dallas Morning News*, "leaving the press at the back of the room or standing in doorways."

All in all, however, Press Day was a success and media coverage was positive. Many commented on the revolutionary design of the terminal. A representative of the Paris architectural magazine *L'Architecture d'Aujourhui* noted that "the planning is incredible. It is especially good because the people don't have to walk far from their cars to the planes." Several writers commented on the lessons to be learned from such an undertaking. A producer for Japan Broadcasting Corp. in Tokyo said his station was there to learn about the techniques used to reduce noise and air pollution. "We have a lot to learn from this airport," he said. Unsurprisingly, many journalists noted the size of the facility, often quoting Concorde Pilot Franchi, who, when asked about his impressions of the new airport, said, "It's big. Concrete must be cheap around here." Others perceived challenges for motorists arriving at the airport. *Business Week* transportation editor Brenton Welling Jr. noted the need for additional signage. "I think a lot of people are going to get very lost for a long time," he said. Perhaps Fort Worth writer Martha Hand best summarized the impact of the tour on the visiting reporters: "Big as a Texas brag, bold as a Texas sunset, the port is mind-boggling in its magnificence and its functional simplicity."

WITH PRESS DAY completed, dignitaries began arriving for Friday morning's festivities in a spectacular caravan of cars, each bearing the flag of the visitor's native land. The first event was a VIP reception at the Texas International/Frontier terminal, followed by a tour of the airport. Fifty-one nations were represented by diplomats and United Nations officials who had arrived, somewhat ironically, at Love Field via commercial airlines and met there by members of the DFW Regional Airport Board. Representatives from the Chief of Protocol's Office in the U.S. State Department were on hand to help the sponsors of this gala, the Dallas and Fort Worth Junior Leagues, with logistics and languages. Those in attendance were truly distinguished, and the number of them was most impressive. They reportedly constituted the largest delegation of ambassadors ever assembled for a single event in the nation outside of Washington and New York.

That evening the VIPs were guests of honor at the International Charity Gala, the most extensive hospitality effort ever organized in North Texas. The party for an estimated 5,000 guests, held in the Delta Terminal, spread out for more than a half mile. In keeping with the international travel theme, "passports" (tickets for the gala) were mailed to invitees from Airport Commissioner General and Mrs. John Connally. As guests arrived at the Delta-Continental terminal, "customs officials" checked all passports before allowing entry.

The see-and-be-seen $50-per-person affair, chaired by Dallas Junior League member Carla Francis, featured international fare prepared by European chefs. As guests strolled through the terminal, they encountered fourteen smaller parties, each offering foods and entertainment unique to a particular region of the world. Performers ranged from Peter Nero to Doc Severinson to Willie Nelson to Paulette to the Jason-Wilson trio. Both the magnitude and the panache of the event were captured by writer Claire Eyrich:

"Architects and decorators had created a playland of separate entertainment areas, framed in stage sets and mobiles. . . and hung with rich-hued 10-foot banners, all with the single theme of 'Celebration'. . . A wonderland, created in the midst of the world's largest airport, with thousands of tropical trees, tens of thousands of branches of ti leaves and jade-tree foliage, together with hundreds of potted jade and lemon trees, was the background for masses of colorful coleus and blooming yellow chrysanthemums. . . Folding screens and giant cube-shaped decorative partiches in classic themes borrowed from a dozen nations divided these entertainment areas into convenient 'ballrooms' in the heart of the big airport. . . The effect was at once overwhelming in its immensity and informally 'with it' in the midst of formal splendor." Writers knowledgeable on social affairs would later bill the event as the "jettiest, jazziest ball of them all this season, bar none."

Such a mammoth party could not escape some mishaps, however. Once again, a flood of unexpected guests, about 2,000 more than the 5,500 that had been expected, decided to attend the event. Parking became a nightmare. Traffic jams were so bad that DFW Commissioner General Connally and DFW Board Chairman Jonsson were late for their own party. Once inside the airport gates, some guests waited for more than an hour to reach parking attendants. It took up to thirty minutes to reach a buffet table, and lines outside the restrooms required about a forty-minute wait at the peak of the evening. When the party ended, the situation got even worse. Some guests reported two-hour waits to retrieve vehicles from valet parking. Others just gave up and took a bus home.

SATURDAY, the day of the formal dedication, dawned hot, humid and windy. The ceremony began at 10:30 a.m. at Dedication Plaza, adjacent to the on-site press center in the American Airlines terminal. Flags from the fifty-one nations represented flapped in the brisk south wind behind the platform, especially built for the ceremony and seating 1,069 guests. More than twenty school marching bands from the area added to the day's festive nature.

This was the day Tom Sullivan and the two cities had anticipated for almost ten years. In fact, the excitement surrounding the event seemed almost too much for the 60-year-old Sullivan. As he prepared to leave his office that morning for the ceremony, he felt familiar pains reminding him of three earlier heart attacks. These attacks had not kept him from accepting his post with the new airport, however, and they weren't going to keep him from sharing in this celebration. He continued on to the Plaza and joined other airport executives for the official dedication of the new airport.

Commissioner General Connally, master of ceremonies, shared the podium with Texas Governor Dolph Briscoe, White House official Anne Armstrong, and Mayors R.M. Stovall of Fort Worth and Wes Wise of Dallas. They greeted a crowd of about 45,000 people, including foreign dignitaries, local business and civic leaders, and local citizens. A six-person congressional delegation led by U.S. Representative Jim Wright from Fort Worth were special guests, as was U.S. Senator Lloyd Bentsen. And so was another federal official with a very special interest in the proceedings: Ross Newmann, the Civil Aeronautics Board hearing examiner who had decided a decade before that Dallas and Fort Worth needed a new regional airport.

Erik Jonsson kicked off the celebration. "Dedication of the new DFW Airport brings to reality a dream which has been around for a long time—so elusive it had become known as the 'impossible dream.' " In chronicling the events leading to the development of the new airport, Jonsson suggested that the drama involved in the ten years prior to the dedication might never truly be captured: "Looking back over the long trail that brought us here, it is literally impossible to recount all of the elements that were part of the project or the other minor and major perils we encountered along the way. When you consider all the many diverse interests that were brought together, the reshaping of long-time antagonistic attitudes of the communities, I guess we have seen something of a miracle."

Newmann cited DFW as a model airport for years to come. It was, he said, "a real pleasure to come back here ten years after the beginning of this airport controversy and to see this great new airport dedicated today based on the cooperation, trust, faith and good will of the cities of Dallas and Fort Worth." Following Connally's official dedication of the airport to "the young faces of the future, here and around the world," Governor Briscoe called the dedication "one of the most significant events in the history of the State of Texas." This new facility, he said, represented "one of the greatest technological achievements in the history of transportation." Looking to the future, Briscoe noted that this new airport would serve as Texas' gateway to the world, providing the potential for international air transportation. It would be "a tremendous factor in the years ahead."

Transportation Secretary Claude S. Brinegar—who on May 17 had enjoyed the honor of being the principal passenger on the first plane to make an official landing at DFW—addressed the national significance of the event. "America occasionally needs to be reminded of its greatness. Your remarkable airport is such a reminder you can justly be proud of it," he said. "Your airport's very name— Dallas Fort Worth— suggests strength. Here are two great cities that have put aside natural rivalries in recognition of a regional need that could only be met by joint action. . . Never before has our nation seen such a dedicated and thorough approach to airport and community planning."

Anne Armstrong offered official greetings and praise from President Nixon. "This port on the prairie is proof positive that the pioneer spirit of Texas will continue to create greatness," she said. "When Texans put their minds to a project, the sky is the limit." Congressman Jim Wright said that the "real miracle of this facility is the one of human cooperation." It stands as a monument, he said, to the proposition that "there is nothing which free men, working together in harmony and with unity of purpose, cannot achieve."

Following the official dedication, a spectacular two and a-half hour air show entertained the afternoon crowd. Aircraft passing in front of the spectators ranged from a 1929 Ford tri-motor to 1930-vintage bi-planes to a DC-3 of the 1940s to the sleek and supersonic Concorde. It also featured the British Vulcan, a 13-year-old delta-wing bomber, and the U.S. Army's Silver Eagles, a precision-flying helicopter team whose antics of dives and controlled spins were accompanied by plumes of multi-colored smoke. The U.S. Army's Golden Knights parachute team created moments of silence when it dropped one of its members from a mile above the terminals. The crowd favorite, however, was the British-built Hawker Harrier VTOC (vertical takeoff and landing) jet fighter flown by a U.S. Marine who zoomed in low and then climbed 10,000 feet in seconds at a speed close to 700 miles per hour. Local celebrity and world champion acrobatic helicopter flyer Charlie Hillard from Fort Worth led the "flying Red Devils as they climbed, dove and stalled through smoke trails in the show's finale."

An "Honored Guests Luncheon" celebrated both visiting dignitaries and their wives at two separate sites, a separation by sex that brought some controversy. While the male VIPs enjoyed an invitation-only affair at the site of the dedication, their wives were transported to the Dallas Cowboys' Texas Stadium for a fashion show and luncheon where twenty-five Texas designers had created special designs for the occasion.

These separate affairs proved to be troublesome for event organizers. The Fort Worth chapter of the National Organization for Women (NOW) was disturbed at this separation, and they had shown up at the women's luncheon at Texas Stadium. In a flyer they distributed to the wives as they stepped off buses the protesters charged that since the airport was designed for the 21st Century, it was now time to "put 20th Century ideas behind us." Since the airport had been paid for by the taxes of both male and female citizens, there should have been no discrimination based on sex, they contended. "Sending all the women to a fashion show and all the men to a political luncheon assumes that only women are interested in the fashion industry and only men are interested in the political process. . . The DFW Airport insults the intelligence of both men and women by segregating the luncheon and failing to offer the same opportunities to both men and women."

THE FINAL DAY of celebration, Sunday, brought more crowds to the airport to share in the festivities. While official ceremonies were over, the public open house continued and so did the aircraft display and the afternoon air show. The formal ceremony concluded with a flyover of F8 jets coordinated by volunteer airline pilots who also set up and manned a communications command post throughout the dedication weekend.

The day had been a cacophony of sights and sounds. Besides the dedication ceremony, a day-long public open house allowed local residents and visitors to see the new facility. Besides the airport itself, visitors viewed the world's largest static display of commercial and military aircraft ever assembled on one airport. The Concorde SST remained on display throughout the weekend, as did the world's largest aircraft, an Air Force C5A. Other attractions included a Boeing 747 jumbo jet, a Lockheed L-1011, a Lufthansa transport model with a swing-away nose, a 1928 Ford Tri-Motor, and a variety of antique and military transports.

On this final day many contemplated the achievement. Dallas Mayor Wes Wise said it well: "Clearly we have demonstrated once and for all, a cooperative and friendly spirit between the cities of Fort Worth and Dallas, which will herald in a new era of prosperity and improvement in quality of life."

Wise's Fort Worth counterpart, Mayor R. M. Stovall, echoed his thoughts: "The people of Dallas and Fort Worth had a dream: a dream of providing in the Southwest metropolitan region the world's first and largest regional air transportation facility. As we embark upon the next few weeks in the history of this great area, many of the visions of that dream are becoming a reality with the formal dedication and the pending operation of the first phase of the DFW Regional Airport. . . . All this points to the advent of a new era of prosperity for the Southwest Metroplex. A prosperity born of the visions and hard work of dedicated citizens of this great region."

On this last day of the four-day ceremony, the *Dallas Times Herald* published a special airport edition, the biggest in its history, which contained a special article written by Sullivan. Building the airport, he said, was "the kind of opportunity that comes once in a lifetime." It represented a rare chance "to start from scratch in creating a magnificent new airport armed with all that knowledge of past mistakes, and blessed with a very precious commodity, thousands of acres of open space." The fact that it had taken the two cities so long to come together might have been a blessing, he wrote. "Not only does D-FW benefit from all the bitter lessons of other airports, but it comes at a point in time when those other facilities have reached points of strangulation, both in air space and land space. Thus, the airport here is not simply another airport, but rather is the ultimate airport whose very stark contrast to outdated facilities will dramatize its uniqueness and accelerate its recognition as a world aviation center."

THAT NEW ERA meant a new role for the airport that had served the region's aviation needs for more than half a century. Dallas' Love Field would cease to be the city's major air-carrier airport, but it would become the nation's largest general aviation facility. To commemorate the transition, Love Field officials held a dedication of their own just a week before the dedication of the new DFW airport. In a private ceremony beginning at 11:00 a.m. on Friday, September 14, about 100 invited guests celebrated Love's Field's "re-dedication" as a general aviation airport. The event reflected the joint efforts of community leaders, the Dallas Chamber of Commerce and civic groups.

The purpose of the gathering was to call to the attention of decision-makers and area residents the continuing importance of Love Field in the region's economy. "In changing its role, a *Dallas Morning News* editorial noted, "Love Field is ideally designed and located to serve the growing needs of corporate and general aircraft. After another half century, Dallas will still proudly recognize it as one of the great aviation centers of the country." A report prepared by Arthur D. Little, Inc. in anticipation of the opening of DFW Regional Airport summarized the role Love Field could play in the continued economic growth of the area:

> The role of Love Field should be considered in its broad importance to Dallas. It has been said that Dallas is a port, but rather than having a sea, Dallas is surrounded by an ocean of air and its airports are the key link to increased commerce. In *Goals for Dallas* the importance of the Dallas/Fort Worth Regional Airport in making Dallas a world air center has been noted. In addition, the need for more private aircraft and short-hop commercial facilities has also been recognized. Exceptional aviation facilities have made it possible for Dallas to become the largest city in the United States without water transportation. As part of the aviation system, which contributes so much to the growth of Dallas, Love field has a long and valuable life ahead of it for short-haul (non-scheduled) aviation and for the growing business of executive and private aircraft. . . Love Field as a

general aviation airport will play a vital though specialized role in stimulating the continued economic growth of Dallas.

With the dedication of the new airport and the re-dedication of Love Field accomplished, attention now turned to a pressing matter—the ending of passenger service at Love Field and the beginning of service at DFW. This transfer was rife with the possibility of complications and problems. In the midst of all the hoopla surrounding the dedication activities, airport and airline officials had continued to huddle privately to negotiate the airlines' moves from Love Field to DFW.

In early August, members of the airport board had approved a request from the carrier airlines to postpone the airport's operational opening to 12:01 a.m. October 28. The minutes of the board's monthly meeting explained that most of the United States would revert to Standard Time on October 28, and that historically was the occasion for major alterations in airline schedules. Schedule changes result in expenses to the carriers, they explained, and delaying the switch to that date would lessen the uncertainties confronting passengers as they became acclimated to the new airport. Additionally, the extra time would be beneficial to the airlines in teaching their employees about the operation of their new facilities. Not only would much of the equipment and facilities be new, but in many cases, passenger and baggage handling concepts would be different from those in use at Love Field. "Service to the public will be considerably enhanced by the additional training and familiarization time afforded by an October 28 starting date," the board concluded in approving the request.

However, board members were adamant about not wanting any more delays. For a while, it appeared that no more would occur. As late as September 9, airport officials continued to assure the board that the facility would be ready for business on the target date. "October 28 means a fully operational airport," Erik Jonsson told board members at their regularly scheduled monthly meeting.

As the date of the dedication drew near, however, it had become increasingly evident that the operational opening would, in fact, again be delayed. Six of the eight tenant airlines—American, Braniff, Continental, Delta, Eastern and Texas International— had become increasingly nervous that the airport would not be completed in time for them to make a smooth transition to the new facility before the busy holiday season. At a news conference on September 20, Sullivan said that although the project was "on time and within budget," some airlines had discussed yet another delay to be sure their personnel could cope with the complexities of the new facility and equipment.

Delays in opening, of course, meant a delay in receiving revenues from airport operations. Thus, a few days after the dedication the board on September 27 asked Dallas and Fort Worth city councils to approve a "contingency" request to sell $18,150,000 in revenue bonds to cover expenses involved in delaying the operational opening. Should further delay occur, the board emphasized, the airlines—not the taxpayers—would be responsible for paying off these bonds since the facility would be ready for occupancy on the target date.

Both cities approved the sale of bonds, and on October 1, a reluctant board again approved the airlines' request for a delay—this time until January 13. The amount also included debt service on the existing construction bonds and lost landing fees and concessions income. Tom Sullivan expressed the disappointment of board members. "I must say that I make this recommendation with bitter reluctance, but they (the airlines) have good reasons for their request."

DURING THE NEXT two months, as the airlines prepared for the move west, legal issues threatened to delay the move even further. Of great concern was the continuing controversy over Southwest Airlines' desire to remain at Love Field. Although U.S. District Judge William M. Taylor, Jr., had ruled in April that the cities could not force Southwest to move to DFW, airport officials and the two cities appealed the ruling, and on November 1, 1973, DFW officials traveled to Washington, D.C., to lobby the Civil Aeronautics Board to require all airlines serving Love Field to move their flights to DFW on January 13. The CAB's response was that, for the same reasons cited in the District Court decision, the

CAB had no authority over Southwest flights. So, as DFW airport officials prepared for the operational opening of the new airport, Southwest Airlines continued to offer intrastate commercial air transportation services from Love Field without any intention of joining the other airlines in moving to DFW.

Another legal dispute which threatened the opening of the airport arose over a dispute about whether unauthorized taxicabs could pick up passengers from the airport. It stemmed from the exclusive rights given a ground transportation service authorized by the board and approved by the state to a new entity, SURTRAN. This new agency, created exclusively for airport service, operated under the umbrella of the municipally-owned Dallas Transit System. It would hold a monopoly on bus, limousine, and all in-bound taxi service from the airport to the two cities. SURTRAN's buses, almost fifty of them, would operate from three terminals in Dallas and one downtown Fort Worth terminal. About a hundred distinctive SURTRAN taxi-cabs bearing distinctive orange and gold colors would carry passengers to and from the airport. To provide this taxi-cab service SURTRAN made an arrangement with a joint venture of Yellow Cab Company of Dallas and Fort Worth Cab and Baggage Company of Fort Worth. While any taxi driver hired outside the airport could deliver passengers to the terminals or inside the property, only SURTRAN taxi-cabs could pick up passengers at the airport. Other cab drivers would have to "deadhead" back with no passengers and no return fares. This situation infuriated the independent cab drivers, who alleged that an unfair monopoly had been created and who, along with other transportation services, went to court in protest.

An Austin court agreed and issued on January 3 an order denying SURTRAN a monopoly on public transport to DFW. The fate of SURTRAN suddenly became uncertain. The order, issued by the 200th District Court in Austin, was made at the request of a number of excluded carriers—Continental Trailways Bus System, American Bus Lines, Airport Coach Service and National Terminal Services, Inc. As the suit was pending, Judge Dee Brown Walker of the 162nd District Court in Dallas issued another restraining order prior to the airport's opening, stopping

SURTRAN's temporary bus service between Dallas Love Field and Fort Worth. At the cities' request, however, District Judge Charles D. Mathews dissolved this restraining order on January 8, permitting SURTRAN to furnish temporary taxi services until the date of the airport's opening. Another hearing set for early in the year would determine the cities' right to grant an exclusive franchise to SURTRAN.

In addition to these legal issues, an impending fuel crisis threatened the potential profitability of the new airport. This followed an announcement by the federal government that airlines could expect only 85 percent of the fuel allocations they had received in 1972. It was feared that significant cutbacks in flights would have to occur. In spite of a later statement by the federal government that U.S. airlines could expect 95 percent of their 1972 fuel quotas, many airlines still announced cutbacks. *Fort Worth Star-Telegram* writer Jim Street captured the mood of the time in his weekly column. "As with the cliché about the weather, so it was with the energy crisis: If you don't like your allocation, just wait a day or so. It— the energy crisis—has been changing so rapidly that one is never sure that what he writes one day still will apply when published the next."

As the new year approached, it appeared finally that the cuts in fuel would not significantly affect the operations transferring from Love Field to DFW, but certainly most of the major airlines would reduce the number of flights. Only Braniff anticipated an increase in flights when the new airport opened with a total of 147 departures and arrivals from both airports representing an increase of ninety-five at DFW; Continental would reduce its flights from fifteen to fourteen, Delta would go from fifty to forty-five; Eastern would eliminate two weekend flights, leaving five daily flights; and Frontier, Ozark and Texas International would remain unchanged, with fifteen, seven and fifty-eight operations, respectively.

While not as significant as earlier feared, these cutbacks in flight schedules created an unexpected decrease in landing fees anticipated by DFW Airport officials. Moreover, in addition to this reduction in flights, some of the airlines would be using smaller, lighter aircraft, such as 727s and 737s. From these estimates, officials anticipated a drop of about 14 percent in landing fees.

DESPITE THESE legal complications and energy crisis concerns, excitement mounted as the official move date drew closer. The board's January 7 meeting was particularly important as members were asked to approve the documents necessary for the airport's operational opening. The fifty-two item agenda that day included a "use agreement" making the eight airlines official tenants of the airport on opening day. The board also accepted four facilities as being ready for occupancy.

On January 10, the new FAA control tower was dedicated in a 10:30 a.m. ceremony. Actually, the 196-foot tower had been operating on a test basis for months with special FAA aircraft in place of jets. The new $2.5 million "space age tower" with eleven windows on an 11-sided, 620 square-foot cab housed two complete control centers. One set of controllers worked air traffic on the east side of the airport and another worked the west. The semi-automated system controlled traffic within a 30-mile radius of the airport, allowing controllers more time to focus on safe and efficient landings and takeoffs and ground movement. FAA spokesperson Alexander P. Butterfield recognized the significance of the tower's completion as he addressed the small crowd gathered for the dedication. "We are observing the last major milestone in the development of the world's largest, and in so many ways, the world's most fantastic airport. So it's a very special occasion." Indeed, all the critical services necessary for the operation of the new airport were now in place.

During the final few days before the opening, the airlines finalized training of on-site personnel, completed equipment checking and conducted last-minute tests on new operating procedures. Most of the airlines had begun to move non-essential equipment there early in the week to help with a smooth transition. American and Braniff alone moved more than 10,000 pieces of equipment, including 1,000 major ramp components. While most of the items could be moved by van, the large equipment—such as the 155,000-pound tugs used to move widebody jets—had to be transported by flat bed trucks.

One of the particular problems in preparing for the opening was in obtaining appropriate training in a timely manner for the security personnel. "Sullivan didn't want 250 people sitting around from September to January with nothing to do but draw salaries," Public Safety Director Limmer recalled. Not only did this require finding and hiring a large security force almost simultaneously, but it meant that the proper training academies had to be found to train them at the right time. This was accomplished by using just about every government entity in the area that had police, fire, or emergency medical technician academies. The new security officers were certified all three ways—as police officers, firefighters, and emergency medical technicians.

Crunch time, of course, was Saturday, January 13, as flight service prepared to actually switch from Love Field to DFW immediately after midnight. All was ready except for a portion of AIRTRANS. Early in the day the airport board had met in an emergency session and concluded that because of unresolved problems AIRTRANS service would be offered only for the section that carried passengers from terminal to terminal. Though the move to DFW was scheduled to coincide with the airlines' lightest period of flight schedules, it was still a bit tricky. Some of the heavy equipment required at Love Field until almost the last moment had to be moved to DFW in time for the beginning of service there. The transfer, called the "largest mass move of an entire industry in the Southwest" and costing more than half a million dollars, required the services of all the professional movers in the area. It was reported that "there was as much activity on Stemmons and John Carpenter Freeways as there was in the air during the Christmas holidays."

But the move was completed, and at one minute past midnight on Sunday, January 14, 1973, incoming flights to Dallas were diverted to the new DFW Regional Airport. The "impossible dream" was realized when an American Airlines Boeing 727 flown by Captain Vern Peterson of Cooke County touched down at 12:07 a.m., exactly on schedule. The flight had originated in New York City with stops at Memphis and Little Rock. Captain Peterson pulled the Boeing-built aircraft into Gate 6 at the

American terminal to an awaiting crowd of more than 1,000 people, many of them bearing welcoming signs, and including the mayors of Dallas and Fort Worth, airport board members, airline officials, and members of the press. A band was playing a musical tribute for the occasion as the first passengers, Dr. J.W. Parker and his wife Patricia of Fort Worth, stepped off and received a silver medallion as a memento of the occasion. Each of the other passengers, who included American's president, George A. Warde, got a bronze medallion. American Airlines presented a yellow rose to each traveler along with a first-flight certificate. By noon Sunday some 110 flights had arrived and nearly 120 flights had departed, with the first outgoing flight an American Airlines non-stop flight to Los Angeles.

As for Love Field, aside from Southwest's continuing operations, the last major airline activity occurred there nearly an hour past the midnight hour on January 14. At 12:45 a.m. a Braniff flight, which had had connections with several other late-evening flights and could not conveniently be transferred to DFW, departed for Kansas City and Chicago.

In little more than minutes, Love Field had yielded its title as the world's tenth busiest airport to DFW Regional Airport.

EIGHT

Preparing for Takeoff

✈

Covering DFW Airport will be like
trying to cover an entire city.
Bill Case, *Dallas Times Herald*

Within the first year of operation, more than 14 million passengers would be served by DFW through more than 900 scheduled air carrier operations each day, making the airport one of the busiest in the world. Commuter, charter, general aviation, and military movements added some 150 more operations daily. Though the airport been designed to serve "strictly jet" aircraft, general aviation services were provided at Gate One of Terminal 2E. There, operators could deliver or pick-up passengers, refuel, and access catering and sky cap services. A comfortable waiting area in the terminal and hourly weather reports (with a direct line to the Flight Service Station) quickly earned the praise of pilots and brought more general aviation craft than anticipated into the new facility. The services were provided by Ozark Air Lines under an arrangement that provided the airline about $6,000 per month to handle fuel arrangements and light maintenance; render passenger assistance; collect landing and parking fees; provide communications; and disseminate flight information.

That first year, the airport included two parallel, north-south principal runways augmented by a crosswind runway accommodating up to 1,000 aircraft movements daily or up to 125 aircraft movements per peak hour. Three terminals were operational, with sixty-six passenger gates. Nine major commercial airlines and eight commuter airlines offered more than 800 flights a day. The nine majors included American Airlines, Braniff Airways, Delta Air Lines, Continental Airlines, Frontier Airlines, Eastern Airlines, Texas International Airlines, Ozark Air Lines and Mexicana Airlines, the only foreign flag carrier.

Braniff, the largest of the air carriers, was the sole occupant of its own "half-loop" terminal, the only airline with that much space. The terminal faced eastward from the west side of the main airport spine road looking toward Dallas. The Braniff terminal had eighteen arrival and departure gates, all with enclosed passenger loading bridges. The company's $52 million investment in five facilities included the 426,000-square-foot passenger terminal, a 68,862-square-foot automated cargo facility, a 136,000-square-foot maintenance hangar, a 48,500-square-foot flight kitchen and a 15,400 square-foot ground support equipment maintenance building. The passenger terminal, more than twice the size of the company's Love Field space, offered automated baggage handling and ticketing machines. Frankfurt-Short-Emery-McKinley was the architectural firm chosen to construct the maintenance facility; George L. Dahl, Inc. was the architect and engineer of the other three structures.

At the time of the airport's opening, Braniff employed more than 5,000 people in the Dallas-Fort Worth Metroplex and already was contributing more than $115 million annually to the local economy. When Braniff started in 1928 it had three employees and one Stinson-Detroiter airplane. It offered one daily round trip from Oklahoma City to Tulsa. Since then Braniff had grown to an all-jet airline with more than 10,000 employees worldwide. Dallas continued to be the airline's "home town" and the hub of its domestic route system, as it had been since 1942.

Already having 270 flight arrivals and departures daily from its Love Field location, Braniff now looked forward to significant global expansion from "the world's largest airport." Chairman

Harding Lawrence cited the opening of DFW as an opportunity for the Dallas Fort Worth region to become an international gateway for world trade and tourism. "With the new Dallas Fort Worth Airport as the cornerstone," he said, "air transportation can be both the catalyst and the vehicle to stimulate and achieve a new era of growth, development and prosperity for the Metroplex."

Braniff recognized the growing importance of air cargo in its new terminal, which had the capability of handling 150 million pounds of freight a year. In fact, the two "cargo cities" located at either end of the airport had the potential to accommodate 200 of the largest cargo planes then in existence and to ship as much freight as that handled by the world's largest seaport. American Transportation Association data showed that within the next few years, U.S. airlines were expected to spend $900 million for 133 additional freighter aircraft. DFW was designed so that it could become a central hub of international air freight activity in the years ahead.

With the exception of Mexicana, the other signatory airlines were located on the east side of the airport. American Airline's facilities were in the middle of the giant building complex, opposite the Federal Aviation Administration control tower. Eastern Airlines shared the central-most passenger terminal with American, while Delta Air Lines occupied space in the most southern of the four terminals. Continental, Frontier and Texas International shared space in the northern corridor.

Mexicana Airlines, located in the Braniff Terminal, was the only non-U.S.-based airline, offering one daily flight to Guadalajara. Both Braniff and Texas International also provided international service, flying direct from DFW to several Mexico cities. American, Braniff and Delta afforded additional access to other countries through connecting flights between North Texas and the South Pacific, Caribbean, South America and Europe. At DFW's opening, more than forty-five major route applications were pending before the U.S. Civil Aeronautics Board, with more than half representing international destinations. The fact that all of the applications had been submitted by U.S.-based carriers, however, illustrated the need to attract more foreign flag carriers.

ON THE LOCAL LEVEL, figuring out how to move people to and about the new airport had been a significant issue throughout planning and construction. For those traveling to the airport from either side of the Metroplex region, the solution had been the creation of the SURTRAN system which offered 24-hour bus and taxi service to and from the two cities and surrounding areas. A week after the airport opened, the city of Arlington became the first suburban city to provide SURTRAN bus service for Arlington residents to the airport. Residents could either have someone drive them to catch a bus or leave their car at the SURTRAN terminal. Riding SURTRAN cost $2.50, or $5.00 round-trip. Storing a car at the terminal cost $1.50 a day for passengers. Simply to drive their own cars to DFW and place their vehicles in the remote parking area at the airport also cost $1.50 a day. Private helicopters and airplanes offered alternate transportation to the new airport. Commuters from Love Field to DFW could actually take a ten-to-fifteen minute jaunt on Metroflight Airlines for $12.00—a bargain considering that taxi service cost $17.00 to $20.00!

At DFW's opening, only State Highway 114 and State Highway 183 provided access to the airport. In Dallas a 9.1 mile extension of Interstate 635 beyond I-35 (called Spur 635 since it was not federally funded) was eagerly anticipated by the growing number of travelers using airport services. The completion of the western spur of Loop 820, which would improve traffic flow around the airport, was high on the Texas Highway Department's list of priorities. Other projects included the completion of Highway 121 to connect the northern part of the airport property with the extension of Highway 635 from Dallas. Ultimately, a section of the new I-20 would connect with Highway 360, providing greater access to the airport.

The ready cooperation of the Texas Highway Department was critical to the success of the airport, as planners had recognized early on. Just two weeks after the airport's opening, Sullivan presented a resolution adopted by the airport board commending the Texas Highway Department for its role in developing the huge airport complex. At a luncheon meeting during which State Highway Commissioner Charles E. Simons was recognized,

Sullivan said, "There is no question but that highways are a key link to the success of any public transportation system. . . If it had not been for the Texas Highway Department's wholehearted support and professional approach to building the vital network of highways, the Dallas/Fort Worth Airport could not have been brought to reality."

Once travelers arrived at the airport, they were expected to use the new $33 million people-mover AIRTRANS, which transported passengers and employees between terminals and gates. The system, custom built for DFW by LTV Corporation, was hailed as the most advanced and largest completely automatic ground transit system in the world. The forty-passenger, rubber-tired cars were propelled by electric motors through a concrete U-shaped guideway. The average ride time from one point in the airport to another was ten minutes and cost passengers 25 cents. Ultimately, fifty-three AIRTRANS stations would link the terminals with each other and with remote parking areas, the Airmail Facility, the airport hotel, and the FAA control tower. Passengers would board one of the fifty-one vehicles designated for "people-moving," while baggage, mail and refuse were moved on an additional seventeen utility vehicles. System capacity was 9,000 passengers, 6,000 bags and 70,000 pounds of mail per hour.

At the time of opening, though, AIRTRANS was not completely up to specifications. At the January 8, 1974, airport board meeting, LTV had assumed responsibility for the delay and assured members that the total system would be completely operational by July 1974. In the meantime, the SURTRAN ground transportation system was pressed into service to provide back-up support.

AIRPORT POPULATION, estimated at 23,000-25,000 upon opening, was expected to increase to 100,000 daily by 1980, when it would have 60,000 passengers, 14,000 related visitors, 16,200 employees, 3,000 vendors, and 6,000 sightseers. The size and significance of the airport to the region was reflected in the opening of the *Dallas Times Herald* DFW Airport News Bureau. Veteran aviation reporter Bill Case, who headed the new office, explained that "covering DFW Airport will be like trying to cover an entire city." The total facilities of the DFW Airport equaled those required by a city the size of Wichita Falls."

The airport's size and status also was recognized in another unique way—by the awarding of its own special U.S. Postal Service zip code (75261) for individuals and institutions located on airport grounds. A major regional airmail and distribution facility was operated by the U.S. Postal Service. The 130,000-square-foot facility, employing 275 Postal Service workers, served the North Texas region and also as the exchange point for most of the airmail sent from the U.S. to Mexico and Canada. To celebrate the first day of postal service for DFW Airport, the airport board authorized the production of a special envelope with regular airmail postage. The full color design by E.A. "Ted" Schuman showed an aerial view of the airport and included a summary of airport facts.

DFW reportedly was the first airport in the world to have its own telephone exchange. In fact, the facility had two exchanges— one for internal use and another for external calls. The $20 million system, built by General Telephone Company, became operational on May 20, 1973, when Airport Board Chairman Erik Jonsson placed a call to Transportation Secretary Claude S. Brinegar in Washington, D.C. The enormous system used 22,708 circuit miles of cable and operated from a 54,000 square foot headquarters building. Public telephone calls—which were only a dime in other parts of the Metroplex—cost 25 cents.

Other "city" services reflected the size and stature of the facility. Banking services were provided by an affiliate of Main Street National Bank of Dallas and Town North National Bank, Farmers Branch. A medical center, which was the nucleus of the airport's medical emergency control system, served the routine medical requirements of airport users and personnel. Emergency service was available 24 hours a day.

The Airport Marina Hotel greeted its first guests on Wednesday, January 9, when the first 200 rooms in the 12-story Fred Harvey hotel were ready for occupancy. Billed as "the only hotel in Dallas-Fort Worth with its own international airport," the hotel was located almost in the center of the airport complex.

With three entrances from the AIRTRANS system, visitors had easy access to the hotel, which would offer 600 guest rooms, an 800-person capacity ballroom, penthouse restaurant and club, coffee house and pub. Guests could also enjoy a health spa, game room, year-round swimming pool, shopping arcade and barber/beauty salon.

Seeking to live up to its characterization as "the friendliest" airport, DFW offered special accommodations for the handicapped and others with special needs. Entrance ramps, reserved parking spaces, Braille markings on elevators, restroom accommodations, and graphic signage all aided handicapped visitors. The all-volunteer Dallas Fort Worth Regional Committee for Foreign Visitors also provided information, counseling and other services for airport users. Formed by Mrs. Clyde Emery of Southern Methodist University, the committee assisted foreign travelers with language problems and in becoming familiar with the DFW area. The group also aided city officials by greeting visitors of state and other VIPs.

Vendors played a major role in conducting airport business. Parking was handled by Airport Parking Company of America. Dobbs House offered thirty-six food and beverage concessions, five gift shops and two duty-free stores. Airport Shops Inc. of Atlanta operated four additional gift shops. Airplex Stands Inc., a division of Zale Corporation, had fifteen news stands throughout the airport. Gibson Enterprises operated three barbershops with four chairs each.

What the airport did not have was a chapel. Despite a three-year effort on the part of the Greater Dallas Council of Churches and clergy from Fort Worth and Dallas, the go-ahead for a chapel had not been received. In fact, it would be several years later before a chapel would finally be built to serve the airport community. Today there is a chapel in every terminal.

THE EXECUTIVE in charge of daily operations at the new airport was 27-year-old Fred Ford, the youngest man in the industry to hold the position of operations director at a major airport and the youngest man ever to achieve the Accredited Airport Executive rating. Interestingly, it was not his credentials but a bout of mononucleosis that brought Ford to DFW. Seven years earlier (at the age of 20) he had been forced to bed for several months in his home, which just happened to be located at the foot of the runway at Boston's Logan Airport.

While recuperating, Ford avidly followed news reports of a local controversy between Logan Airport officials and nearby residents who were unhappy about the fact that 747s would soon be introduced to their area and—they thought—create a significant increase in noise pollution. Curious about the situation, Ford wrote to the aircraft manufacturers asking them about the noise factor. After learning that the 747s, in fact, "wouldn't make as much noise as some of the old piston jobs," Ford wrote the local newspaper to share this information. The newspaper published his letter, and the head of the Massachusetts Port Authority saw and was impressed by it. The rest, as they say, is history.

Ford became the first executive trainee of the Massachusetts Port Authority, completed a two-year course, and in December 1969, was named director of aviation for the city of Springfield, Missouri. Just about two years later, he joined DFW Regional Airport, first spending one year in Washington, D.C., to serve on the President's Aviation Advisory Commission before returning to the Metroplex to accept the operations post at the new DFW Regional Airport. Officially titled deputy executive director, Ford was responsible for operating what quickly came to be known as "the airport of the future."

DFW Airport drew both praise and criticism from early users of the facility. Reactions ranged from confusion over the location of certain services to delight from passengers who were able to park so close to their departure gates. The worst kinks in the system seemed to involve lost or damaged luggage and a lack of information and signage for intra-airport and ground transportation. Though the complaints were few, media coverage of the incidents that did occur was rather widespread, drawing the ire of airport and city officials. They charged that media representatives seemed to be looking for things that went wrong rather than recognizing the significance of the achievement represented by the new facility. In a statement to the Dallas City

Council, Dallas Mayor Pro Tem George Allen said, "What should be the crowning glory of this entire region for years to come has been marred by nit-picking criticism. The Dallas-Fort Worth Airport is magnificent, far ahead of anything else in the world. Yet people have been griping about the smallest things imaginable." As it would turn out, however, negative coverage of these "smallest things" would be forgotten in the years to come as the airport's overall significance to the North Texas area would be recognized and appreciated.

One complaint common to most airport operators but noticeably absent at DFW was noise. As *Dallas Times Herald* aviation reporter Bill Case reported, this was in glaring contrast to Love Field, "which over the years, produced thousands of complaints and dozens of lawsuits charging property damage and value depreciation." At DFW, only fourteen noise complaints were received during the first ten days of operation. Even so, airport officials quickly made adjustments to address the grievances, requiring pilots to fly a mile farther north and to make their turns over Lake Grapevine rather than over the city of Grapevine as originally allowed.

Of course, the sheer size of the airport significantly reduced noise pollution. Four-and-one-half mile buffer zones without any buildings extended beyond each end of the runways, followed by another mile where private housing was banned. At a time when public opposition to jet noise and pollution was growing, DFW's large land mass helped it avoid the environmental protests that had blocked or stalled the development of airports in other cities.

While land mass alone took care of most of the ground noise, the reduction of flyover noise required more sophisticated measures. In planning, airport designers and engineers had to calculate the potential noise generated by air traffic at DFW and determine how to best minimize noise levels. The project involved the calculation of a "Noise Exposure forecast," which is a combination of the frequency of flyovers, timing—day or night—noise levels and the annoyance factor to the person on the ground. Engineers simulated the noisiest airplane landing and taking off on a hot Texas day—the kind of day when noise is generally considered most objectionable. When an acceptable level was to alleviate the concerns of local residents as well as how best to route air traffic.

DFW REGIONAL AIRPORT'S Department of Public Safety, composed of 205 staff members, had a big job serving a "community" of 25,000 airport employees and about 100,000 daily visitors. The initial class of thirty-two DPS officers had begun their training in March 1973. The first DFW police force included twenty-two women. Because of the special needs of an airport community, the officers were cross-trained in police work, firefighting, crash rescue, communications and other safety skills. An on-site jail facilitated the work of police officers, whose duties included traffic control, anti-air piracy and terminal security.

Safety in the sky, of course, was also a priority for airport planners and, according to those responsible for air traffic in and out of DFW, the new airport was a great success. Both air traffic controllers and airline pilots hailed DFW Regional Airport as the safest in the nation. Noting that DFW had "many of the safety features airline pilots have been clamoring for so many years," Captain Bill Alford, chairman of the Airline Pilots Association of America, called DFW "the most nearly perfect airport in the country."

Alford's successor, J.J. O'Donnell, identified the specific features applauded by the Association's pilots as including "grooved runways long and wide enough to handle today's needs with ample growth potential for the next twenty-five years; obstruction free approach and departure routes with zoning protection against construction of hazards to air navigation; high speed turnoffs which improve operational safety and runway utilization; fringe area zoning by surrounding communities to reduce noise and air pollution conflicts; concrete runways to accommodate aircraft over one million pounds; safety criteria in the design of cross-over bridges and blast fence protection for motorists; passenger loading and unloading facilities which provide a convenient and safe system; and runway signs and marking system which provide night visibility to flight crews superior to other airports in the nation."

Citing the collaboration of the Airline Pilot's Association and the airport board in designing the facility, O'Donnell said, "We are pleased that airport management accepted 75 percent to 80 percent of ALPA's Airport Committee recommendations, which resulted in achieving standards over and above minimums required by FAA regulations for airport design and construction."

The air traffic control system was put to the test—and received high marks—during the airport's first three days of operations in the midst of one of the worst fog "storms" ever experienced in North Texas. The airport started with five instrument landing systems—the most ever commissioned by the FAA in conjunction with the opening of a new airport. In July, the terminal radar approach control systems were relocated from the Greater Southwest Airport, combining all control operations in the DFW Tower. (The systems had remained at Southwest until DFW completed the installation of the state-of-the-art automated radar terminal service.) The move was timed to coincide with the operation of two new advanced air traffic control systems that made the DFW system the most sophisticated in the world. The new systems, designed to assure the safety and efficiency of aircraft movement in the DFW area, offered state-of-the-art computerized control and communications equipment. The Automated Radar Terminal System (ARTS III) provided controllers with computer-generated data tags on the radar scopes showing the aircraft's identity, ground speed and altitude. The Terminal Communications Switching System (TESS) offered flexibility of communications for the overall air traffic monitoring and control of air traffic within a 50-mile radius of the airport. The system carried thousands of messages simultaneously, each on its own frequency, over a single coaxial cable laid around the airport. Cost of the new tower and radar equipment was estimated to be about $15 million. The center was operated by some 121 air traffic control specialists and supporting personnel.

AS THE AIRPORT became operational, the issue of who would head the board in succeeding years surfaced. There was some discussion of the alleged agreement between Dallas and Fort Worth that the position would rotate between the cities. While

Fort Worth's Mayor Stovall and later Bayard Friedman recalled that the idea was generally agreed upon, once ensconced in the chairmanship, Jonsson had declined to quit his post. He reported that he had "no plans" to step down. By this time the airport was functioning so smoothly and relations between Dallas and Fort Worth were so positive that any disappointment on the part of Fort Worth members was quietly swallowed.

At the February 7 airport board meeting, the past officers—including Jonsson as chairman and Johnson as vice chairman—were unanimously re-elected. In responding to why a change in the chair had not been made, Johnson said that "the time was not right." The board also welcomed two new Dallas representatives, W.H. (Bill) Roberts from the Dallas City Council and Irving Baker, a Southern Methodist University administrator and the first black appointed to the board.

Interestingly, the issue that received the most attention by board members at that meeting—the first since the opening of the airport—was not the election of new officers. Rather, it was the fees charged for various services at the new airport. Visitors had expressed keen displeasure about having to pay 10 cents to go to the bathroom, 25 cents to make a phone call, 25 cents to drive through the airport property, three dollars to park their cars, and—the most abhorred, it seemed—receiving only 95 cents back when a dollar was inserted into a changer. Dallas Mayor Wes Wise voiced considerable dismay about the number of complaints he had received from local residents upset with the fee structure, and particularly the dollar bill changers. Referring to the money changers as a "psychological horror" that had already created some public relations problems, Wise asked for—and Board members agreed to—a review of service fees to be conducted by the operations committee. (Two months later, at the April meeting, the board would approve the recommendation of the operations committee that no change be made with respect to the money-changers. The fee was necessary, they reported, to maintain the privately owned machines.)

THE NEW AIRPORT meant drastic changes and economic progress for the communities surrounding the facility. Even prior to its opening, its impact on the North Texas economy was estimated to reach $637 million annually by 1975. That was more than ten times Dallas and Fort Worth's investment in the land on which the airport was built.

The opening of the airport was a great day for area home builders too, for suddenly the housing market was booming with an even greater than anticipated demand for new homes. Construction added hundreds of millions of dollars to the regional economy through job creation and purchases of goods and services. The airport's annual payroll was approximately $100 million, which was estimated by economists to yield a multiplier effect economically of from two to three times the direct value, meaning that the total economic impact of the airport was between $200 and $300 million.

Grapevine, the city which held 8,000 acres of the airport northern property including the terminal buildings, was expected to receive $1 million in tax revenues annually from the airport. Not surprisingly, Grapevine Mayor W.D. Tate called the airport "the largest and most exciting industry in the region." The mayor of Arlington, located in the area just south of DFW, viewed the airport as "the most important event of this decade for this region." These words rang true as the airport quickly became the economic engine that fueled the growth of the neighboring areas.

In February 1974 DFW received a Headliner Award at the annual Newsmakers Ball in Fort Worth for having generated the most national publicity for Fort Worth and Tarrant County. The airport brought more than just publicity to Fort Worth, of course. For the first time in many years, downtown Fort Worth began feeling a resurgence of energy and renewed optimism for future economic development. Employment was good in 1973 and expected to be better in 1974. In his state-of-the-city address, Fort Worth Mayor Stovall noted economic predictions that the airport would bring a sharp increase in the population of North Central Texas by attracting businesses and industries.

In fact, a number of corporations with one million dollars or more in total net worth already had moved their corporate headquarters to the DFW area in 1973, and more were on their way. Other companies established operating facilities or subsidiary offices. A major factor cited in their decisions to relocate and/or expand was the opening of DFW Airport. Airport officials observed that their efforts to gain additional international air routes were strengthened by the increased interest in the area and the involvement of Metroplex companies in international trade. At the same time, however, their hopes for global expansion were somewhat diminished by a new CAB policy designed to reduce the nation's route structure in order to bolster airline profitability. (At the time of the airport's dedication, the CAB had not granted any new routes in more than two years, explaining that airlines' profit margins or rate of return on invested capital had dropped below the established 12 percent level of "healthfulness.")

Concerns that the CAB would thwart international expansion caused a group of Dallas and Fort Worth business and civic leaders to go to Washington in September to bid for direct international air service into DFW. Dallas Mayor Wes Wise and Fort Worth Mayor R.M. Stovall were among the travelers who met with representatives of the U.S. State Department and the Civil Aeronautics Board to seek support for international (as well as domestic) expansion of flights at DFW. The primary objective of the visit was to convince government officials that international service was both needed and economically feasible. Mayor Stovall observed that many foreign airline executives seemed to have the wrong impression that the airport already had international service to Europe and also that the area it served was smaller than it actually was.

This conversation with government officials continued, and in February 1974, Charles F. Butler, director of the Civil Aeronautics Board's Bureau of International Affairs, traveled to DFW at the invitation of the North Texas Commission. While there, Butler explained that the factors to be considered in deciding for or against European routes for DFW were whether the new routes would be economically advantageous (given the sharp increases in fuel prices) and whether the new routes would lure foreign visitors to the U.S. as well as provide access for Americans to travel abroad. Noting that the major obstacle to new trans-Atlantic routes was the energy crisis, Butler said that the first European first European route from DFW likely to be authorized would be one to London, which was considered most lucrative.

THE COMPLICATED LEGAL proceedings that were being played out in two federal courts continued. The central question still was whether Southwest and Braniff (which had kept some flights at Love Field) should be allowed to continue operating out of Love Field. The conflict escalated in February 1974 when Braniff reported an expansion of commuter flights out of Love Field, and Texas International Airlines (TI) announced that it planned to place commuter flights at Love Field in order to remain competitive with Southwest and Braniff. Arguing that such a move on TI's part would be a clear violation of the contract between the airlines and the cities of Dallas and Fort Worth, city officials threatened to take legal action to thwart the plan.

The clash worsened when American Airlines refused to pay the full amount of a bill for landing fees at DFW during the initial weeks of operation. The company argued that Braniff would be paying a greater share of the costs at DFW if it did not operate any of its flights from Love Field. Thus, American contended, it was being forced unjustly to subsidize Braniff operations. According to a letter from American to airport officials, the difference in the amount billed and the amount paid "represents that portion attributable to Braniff International's refusal to transfer all scheduled flights to DFW." Since landing fees were a major source of revenue for construction and operating costs at the new airport, this was no small matter.

The options available to the cities in attempting to resolve the issue were to file suit against Braniff and TI to force them to keep all flights at DFW or to wait for a ruling on a petition filed earlier with the Civil Aeronautics Board. The petition asked that the agency force all federally regulated airlines to operate from the new facility. It was also suggested that as a last resort, Dallas could close Love Field.

While Dallas officials felt strongly that their city had a "moral and contractual obligation" to Fort Worth to see that all flights operated out of the new airport, they also believed that Love Field should not be closed. The airport, they thought, would continue to play a strong role in the local economy and in meeting the general aviation needs of the area. At the same time, with Dallas operating two airports and Fort Worth only one, Fort Worth taxpayers were, in effect, subsidizing Love Field by supporting DFW. The situation was particularly delicate given the 1968 Concurrent Bond Ordinance agreement between the two cities, which required the cities of Dallas and Fort Worth "through every legal and reasonable means. . . [to] promote the optimum development [of the airport] to assure the receipt of gross revenues to the maximum extent possible."

In furtherance of that mandate, on February 23 the cities of Dallas and Fort Worth filed suit in federal court in Fort Worth to prevent Braniff and TI from operating commuter flights out of Love Field and to require American to pay landing fees at DFW. Dallas City Attorney Alex Bickley said at the time that while he would prefer a ruling from the CAB to prevent a lengthy legal battle, CAB officials had said a hearing on the matter could delay the ruling a year. This was particularly upsetting to Dallas Mayor Wise, who blamed the federal government for being negligent for the CAB's failure to amend the certificates of the airlines to require their exclusive operation from DFW. "I think the federal government has been remiss in this whole affair. . . I think for them to come into Dallas-Fort Worth and say you must have a regional airport against the wishes of many Dallasites and then not come to our rescue in a crucial situation such as this is certainly bad."

In the next legal maneuver, TI filed suit against the City of Dallas to obtain terminal space at Love Field. Arguing that it was entitled to the same consideration as its two competitors who already had space there, TI requested access to a facility that would allow it to service flights from Austin. The city's refusal to grant space was both arbitrary and discriminatory, the company argued.

The issue broadened in early March 1974 when Delta jumped into the debate with a request to intervene in the lawsuit on behalf of the cities. Delta's plan was to force Braniff and Texas International to use only the regional airport for its commuter flights. If the situation were not resolved, Delta attorneys argued, the airlines footing the bill at DFW might eventually be unable to underwrite the full cost of operating the airport and retiring its debt. That would mean that taxpayers would be forced to share the financial burden—something Airport Executive Director Thomas Sullivan had promised would never happen. The U.S. District Court granted Delta the right to intervene in the suit, which was heard in Fort Worth federal court on March 13. District Court Judge Joe Burnett issued a temporary injunction permitting TI to begin commuter service to Austin the next month.

In late March, Braniff asked the federal court to dismiss or postpone proceedings initiated against it by Dallas and Fort Worth, pending a ruling by the CAB and a ruling of the U.S. Court of Appeals in New Orleans on the controversial Southwest Airlines decision. At the same time, American sought a court order to block the cities from increasing the fees at DFW if other airlines used Dallas Love Field for commuter flights. Citing the original use agreement between the airlines and the airport, American argued that "such continued breaches of contract could bring about progressive intolerable financial pressure" on the other airlines that had been operating in good faith from the facility. The airline also asked that Braniff Airways be required to move all operations to DFW, that TI be forced to remain at DFW, and that the cities of Dallas and Fort Worth require that the affected airlines use DFW exclusively.

In a surprise move influenced by questions about whether the original suit had been filed in the appropriate court, the cities asked U.S. District Judge Eldon Mahon to drop their civil suit against the three airlines (Braniff and TI to stop service at Love Field and American to pay landing fees bill). On March 27, the judge agreed to dismiss the suit without prejudice. Within minutes, American and Delta filed suit in a Fort Worth federal court in a similar attempt to stop Braniff International from using Love Field for commuter flights and claiming that the cities had allowed Braniff to breach the agreement to cease operations at Love Field and move them to DFW. This suit was intended to remove any concerns regarding federal court jurisdiction in the case.

The Dallas and Fort Worth city councils considered more drastic actions in late March, with each considering ordinances that would close the "city" airports to commercial traffic. The Dallas ordinance was designed to solve the problem of competing commuter flights at Love Field and DFW. The Fort Worth ordinance would ban commercial flights at Meacham Field as a preventive measure, given that no commercial flights were then operating there. The Dallas City Council tabled the ordinance temporarily after a heated debate between city officials and Southwest Airlines representatives. The key spokesperson for the airline was attorney Herbert D. Kelleher, who argued that it was "total nonsense" that the financial structure of DFW would be impaired if Love Field remained open. In questioning Dallas' "moral" obligation to Fort Worth, he said, "I ask whether you are representatives of Dallas or a guardian angel for Fort Worth." The legality of a city taking such action was also questioned.

Despite these concerns, the Fort Worth council shut down Meacham Field to all commercial airline traffic on April 15. Council members voted to approve an ordinance to provide $200 fines for any commercial flight operating out of the airport. About two hours later, the Dallas City Council took similar action closing Love Field and Red Bird Airport in Dallas to commercial traffic. The ordinances would take effect on May 1.

These dramatic actions were certain to lead to further legal action, so there was no surprise when Southwest Airlines sought a permanent injunction against the City of Dallas on the matter. On April 17, U.S. District Court Judge William M. Taylor Jr. issued a temporary restraining order prohibiting the City of Dallas from enforcing the ordinance. Taylor called the city's action an "open defiance" of his earlier court ruling that allowed Southwest to continue operating from the municipal airport.

Early in April, the DFW-exclusive airlines tried a new tack. Delta, Continental and American threatened that they would be forced to also offer flights in and out of Love Field unless all scheduled carriers were forced to suspend operations at the Dallas airport and operate exclusively out of DFW, thereby sharing in the costs. Two days later, Southwest proposed a compromise that involved the airline paying any landing fee at

Love and Meacham Fields that the two cities and board determined to be fair and not to exceed $1 per thousand pounds of maximum certificated gross landing weight. In exchange, Southwest would be granted a waiver permitting it to provide air service to any Texas points through Love and Meacham on a permanent basis and the cities would dismiss the appeal pending before the U.S. 5th Circuit Court of Appeals and any other attempts to force the airline out of Love Field.

The proposal was viewed as discriminatory and illegal by Fort Worth Mayor Stovall, who said it likely could not even be considered without the approval of the eight airlines under contract to use the new airport. Dallas Mayor Wise agreed that the proposal was a bad idea, citing still other problems including the negative impact on DFW Airport's chance to gain international air routes. He said that the foreign carriers wouldn't be interested in scheduling stops at DFW unless they were convinced that DFW was the airport of the region.

The potential erosion of flights from DFW back to Love Field reminded some of an earlier time when just such a situation had resulted in the demise of Greater Southwest International Airport, which had been proclaimed upon opening as "the nearest thing to perfection in planning, in design and in functional layout of any airport in its class anywhere." Among those who expressed concern was retired Civil Aeronautics Administration (now FAA) Aviation Director William G. "Bill" Fuller, who had helped to create both Meacham Field and GSIA. DFW might be destined for the same fate if airlines continued to move flights back to Love Field, Fuller feared.

Such concerns were not abated when both Southwest and Braniff received court approval in mid-April to continue their Love Field flights temporarily. At the same time, two new airlines—Apollo and Tricon—appeared in federal court, requesting permission to intervene in the Southwest suit and to begin services at Love Field. These airlines added a twist to the controversy because they were not under the control of either the Civil Aeronautics Board or the Texas Aeronautics Commission. The size of their aircraft provided a special exemption from CAB jurisdiction and the fact that their flights would be interstate placed them beyond the control of the TAC. Thus, one more government agency—the Interstate Commerce Commission—could be pulled into the debate.

In an effort to stop the bleeding, U.S. District Judge Taylor called on the Civil Aeronautics Board to get involved and help devise a solution. Citing the "urgent national importance" of the matter, Taylor said, "It is apparent to me that this is not purely a local matter but one that affects the interest of the traveling public nationally and internationally." Even so, the CAB declined to participate, saying it was up to the Texas Aeronautics Commission to solve the problem. In a letter to Judge Taylor, CAB General Counsel Richard Littell acknowledged that the CAB had anticipated that—upon the completion of the new airport—air services to the DFW area would be provided through a single regional airport.

"However," he continued, "the operations now being conducted by Southwest Airlines Company under authority by the certificate issued to it by the Texas Aeronautics Commission, and the possibility that other interstate carriers might be licensed by the Commission, are factors which were not before the board at the time of its earlier actions looking toward service to the Dallas Fort Worth area through a single airport." Even if the CAB were to amend the certificates of all CAB-certificated airlines to require service exclusively at the new airport, he said, it "would not of itself provide a solution which would be satisfactory to all of the various interests concerned." The Texas Aeronautics Commission, on the other hand, had the authority to resolve the issues by requiring Southwest to restrict services to the new airport or by "holding that the municipal authorities can exclude scheduled operations from Love Field." So, it seemed, the problem would have to be resolved without the CAB's help.

A particularly troubling aspect of the dispute was that it seemed to be re-kindling tensions between Dallas and Fort Worth. Media reports suggested a brewing spat between the two cities' representatives on the airport board. Perhaps in an effort to quell negative publicity that could hurt the new airport's ability to attract new business, Fort Worth Mayor Stovall contended that all was peaceful, telling *The Dallas Morning News* that all members of the board were working together in the best interest of the airport. "There is definitely no feud between the Dallas and Fort Worth members of the airport board. We are all pulling together in the same direction."

This was the same theme that the DFW "traveling team" of business leaders carried to the West Coast and other points in the U.S. during the succeeding months on business development trips sponsored by the North Texas Commission. NTC President C.A. Tatum said at the time that if the subject of the status of Love Field came up, "we're going to tell them Love Field will be closed to commercial air travel and the DFW Airport, the greatest in the world, is the airport of the Southwest Metroplex."

Before year-end, of course, a different tale would be told—one involving a victory for Southwest Airlines and the continuing operation of commercial air service out of Love Field. The story would play itself out in the highest court in the land with the two cities and DFW Airport officials appealing the lower court's ruling (granting Southwest the right to remain at Love Field) all the way to the U.S. Supreme Court. By refusing to hear the case, the Supreme Court effectively upheld the lower court's ruling that municipalities lack the authority to exclude state-certificated and authorized air carriers of intrastate passengers from a city-owned public airport.

SHORTLY AFTER the operational opening of the airport, the board had begun to consider a successor to Executive Director Thomas M. Sullivan. While Sullivan had said he had "no immediate plan" to retire, he was expected to announce his retirement when the new airport was running smoothly. That time came on April 8 when Sullivan asked the airport board during a Monday afternoon news conference to grant him early retirement. Citing health problems that precluded his continuing service as executive director, he said that he had been proud to see "the great dream of the two cities come true."

Sullivan's role in that dream already had been widely recognized, and his stepping down would signal a new phase in DFW's history. Upon the completion of the facility, Jonsson had said that DFW Airport would not have been built without

Sullivan's "unique capability" to understand the complex interrelationships on such a project. "He is probably the only guy in the country who understands designers, engineers, contractors, airline people, bankers, lawyers and political leaders and can relate successfully to all of them to make it happen."

Sullivan was succeeded by Ernest E. Dean, DFW Airport's deputy executive director and the former resident manager for the international engineering firm of Tippetts-Abbett-McCarthy-Stratton. Dean had been involved in the DFW project from the beginning. In fact, he conducted the original site selection process in preparation for the construction of the airport. When the airport opened, Dean first served as chief engineer. He was later promoted to deputy executive director, engineering. Recognized as a leader in aviation, Dean was the natural choice for the top job at DFW. Under his leadership, the new airport began its flight toward becoming one of the finest in the world.

NINE

A Decade of Growth

✈

*I don't know if I'll go to heaven or hell, but I do know
that I'll probably have to go to Dallas
for a stopover first.*
Disgruntled Houston resident

During its first year, DFW Airport was operating at only about 10 percent of the potential of its ultimate design. Already, though, it was one of the busiest airports in the world. This new transportation center quickly confirmed what airport planners had anticipated—the need for tremendous expansion to meet the demands of an increasingly mobile public. Airport-related employment reached 13,452 in the initial year with airlines, other tenants and the airport board allocating about $187.5 million in salaries alone. Payroll for the 4,565 additional support personnel at locations off airport property brought the total payroll to $254 million. The direct economic impact of DFW (including payrolls, airline and concessionaire expenditures and the purchase of goods and services) reached $350 million by year end. Executive Director Ernest Dean was pleased to report that the new airport was both viable and successful: "I believe it is a fair assessment to say that the years of planning and building that went into this project have resulted in an airport which, measured by the breadth and depth of services available to all those who make use of it, is unmatched in the world today."

The airport grew quickly, with aircraft operations topping the 1,000 average daily mark within three years. Air freight also increased with more than 65 million pounds of mail and 150 million pounds of freight and express shipments of air cargo moving through the airport on an annual basis. By 1977, DFW had become the fourth busiest airport in the United States and the fifth busiest in the world. Based on air carrier operations, the Texas airport was third in both the nation and the world and was the third largest U.S. connector of interline and intraline transferring passengers. DFW quickly exceeded traffic loads at other major airports, and by the end of its first decade was loading twice as many passengers as Houston Intercontinental and a third more than New York's LaGuardia. It was probably about this time that a familiar story comparing the number of flights in and out of DFW to Houston began to be told. The tale quoted a disgruntled Houston resident who complained, "I don't know if I'll go to heaven or hell, but I do know that I'll probably have to go to Dallas for a stopover first."

Two new signatory airlines—Air Canada and Flying Tiger Line—joined the DFW family in 1978, signing agreements to back and retire the revenue bonds that financed the airport and guarantee adequate revenues to operate and maintain the facility. Piedmont became a signatory carrier the following year, offering daily nonstop service to several cities in the Carolinas. Domestic services expanded almost exponentially with most of the airlines serving DFW quickly adding new destinations and expanding service to existing locations. A long list of new carriers also began service at DFW, offering transportation to all parts of the nation.

The new airport ranked among the five safest airports in the world, according to the Aviation Safety Institute, which cited DFW for its "excellent runway design" and finely organized air traffic control system. In fact, Institute officials noted that if Love Field were not in the corner of its airspace, DFW probably would have been first in safety.

INTERNATIONAL EXPANSION continued to top airport officials' wish list. They were particularly eager to obtain the first intercontinental air route from DFW, and, subsequently, to attain official "gateway" status (as the connecting site or destination of foreign flights). Though the Civil Aeronautics Board initially was slow to approve international route requests, it finally granted DFW transatlantic "gateway" status on January 15, 1975, providing for DFW carriers to fly nonstop flights to Europe. By year end 1978, more than 800,000 international passengers had passed through U.S. Immigrations and Naturalization Service at DFW. A total of 385,000 passengers departed DFW for foreign destinations, with 418,000 more arriving directly from foreign countries.

The largest international market was Mexico, followed by Great Britain. Nonstop service to London—finally inaugurated in 1978—carried more than 90,000 passengers across the Atlantic during the first six months of operations. Getting this service off the ground had not been easy. Braniff was the first of the DFW carriers to request non-stop routes between DFW and Europe, filing route requests as early as 1973 in anticipation of the airport's opening. In October 1977, amidst considerable controversy over which airline should be awarded the lucrative DFW-London route, the CAB finally ruled on Braniff's application, denying its request and awarding the route to Pan American instead. Fortunately for Braniff, that decision was overturned later in the year by U.S. President Jimmy Carter, who awarded Braniff the authority to provide nonstop service between DFW and London. His decision, the President said, was based on his interest in adding strong regional domestic carriers on international routes, increasing international competition and promoting "price innovation."

As could be expected, Pan American's reaction was swift and harsh. The reversal was a result of "backstage lobbying" by Texas politicians, the company contended. "Pan Am is outraged," said Pan Am Board Chairman William T. Seawell. "We do not believe that the President's decision was governed by considerations of foreign policy. Rather, it appears to have been dictated by [politics]."

Nevertheless, the President had the ultimate authority in these matters, and Braniff set the inauguration date for its new service on March 1, 1978. Flight time was delayed, however, by the very "pricing innovations" President Carter had hoped to promote. A bitter airfare dispute broke out between the U.S. and British governments when Britain refused to approve Braniff's "cut-rate" fares (ranging down to $349 for a round-trip on standby), arguing that the airline's "discriminatory pricing" gave DFW an advantage over other U.S. cities. Britain soon conceded, however, and the first scheduled nonstop 747 flight from DFW to Gatwick Airport departed the Braniff Terminal at 7:00 p.m. on March 18. According to Airport Board Chairman Henry Stuart, this flight was the most significant event at the airport since its opening. "That was a turning point," he later would recall. "Braniff's ability to fill that flight focused the Civil Aeronautics Board's attention on Dallas-Fort Worth as an international center, and it caused other international airlines to focus their attention on Dallas-Fort Worth."

The European market was tapped, and about two months later, the CAB gave tentative approval on an interchange application submitted by Braniff to participate in flying the Concorde between DFW, Washington, D.C., London and Paris. Scheduled to begin in October, it would be the first time that a supersonic transport would arrive on a regular basis at an interior U.S. airport. DFW Airport officials viewed the event as a milestone: "The Concorde will bring worldwide publicity to the airport and show that we can handle it without any problems."

The supersonic Concorde actually went into regularly scheduled service on January 12, 1979, when two Concordes flown by Braniff pilots touched down simultaneously on parallel runways at DFW. These flights commemorated a first-of-its-kind agreement involving a U.S. carrier and foreign airlines. Under the agreement, Braniff pilots would fly the 100-passenger Concordes subsonically between DFW and Washington, D.C. (to meet U.S. noise restrictions over U.S. soil), with pilots for British Airways and Air France handling the D.C. to London and Paris segments, respectively, at twice the speed of sound.

GETTING THE CONCORDE TO DFW—actually getting authority for the supersonic transport to use U.S. airports at all— had been a long road. Soon after DFW opened, a debate began on whether the plane should operate out of Kennedy (in New York) and Dulles (northern Virginia) airports. The issues were primarily environmental. The Concorde simply could not meet the noise limitations set for takeoffs and landings in the U.S. Also, it was argued, the operation of the Concorde could have adverse effects on the ozone layer that protects life on earth from excessive ultraviolet radiation from the sun. U.S. Transportation Secretary William T. Coleman ultimately made the decision that determined the Concorde's fate in the U.S., but not before considerable public debate on the issue.

Diplomatic concerns also clouded the issue. The makers of the plane—and Great Britain—were longtime allies of the U.S. and had already invested a small fortune (at least $2 billion) in its development. If they were denied access to the American market, the future of the aircraft would be at great risk. The mayors of Dallas and Fort Worth supported the proposition of bringing the Concorde to DFW. So did Texas Governor Dolph Briscoe. The Environmental Protection Agency opposed it. The EPA Administrator argued: "At a time of not just environmental concerns and economic concerns but energy concerns, to continue to push a wasteful technology as the Concorde really makes no sense to me whatsoever." The EPA was particularly concerned about potential increases in skin cancer caused by a reduction of the ozone layer and the possibility that a fleet of supersonic transports could create a layer of atmospheric gases that would have disastrous consequences.

The official response from Britain and France focused on the opportunities presented by supersonic flight. "History shows that each advance in transportation was questioned. At issue were the need for the innovation as well as its possible effects on man's environment. In each case, society found the benefits of the innovation to outweigh the environmental effects. We believe this to be true for the Concorde as well."

Hopeful that the U.S. would ultimately acquiesce, Britain and France launched supersonic travel in the European market with two flights on January 21, 1976. A British Airways flight from London flew into Bahrain in the Persian Gulf in only 3 hours and 38 minutes—more than three hours faster than a subsonic jet could make the trip. The Concorde from France arrived in Rio de Janeiro via Dakar, Senegal, five hours and forty-five minutes later. An article in the *London Daily Mail* expressed the views of the Concorde's makers about inaugurating these flights outside the U.S. "The Americans are the friendliest of allies but the most ruthless of competitors. . . The greatest European civil aviation project in history is compelled to make its commercial debut down a side street."

On February 4, 1976, Transportation Secretary Coleman announced his decision on whether the Concorde should fly in the U.S. Unsurprisingly, it was a "political" one designed to address the concerns of both opponents and advocates of supersonic transportation in the U.S. Coleman said he would allow the SSTs to land at two U.S. airports for a 16-month trial period, limiting the activity to two flights daily into New York's Kennedy International Airport and one flight into Dulles International outside Washington, D.C. The decision could be revoked at any time with four months notice or immediately if the supersonic flights were deemed harmful to the health, welfare or safety of the American people. The environmental and economic effects would be closely monitored during the trial period.

The debate was far from over, however, and later in the month the New York State Legislature made the first move to ban the Concorde from Kennedy Airport. The lawmakers passed a bill limiting noise levels at the airport and sent the legislation on to New York Governor Hugh L. Carey, who earlier had expressed opposition to the landings of supersonic transports at Kennedy. Even if Carey signed the bill, however, the jet could not be barred unless the New Jersey legislature passed an identical bill since Kennedy was run by the New York-New Jersey Port Authority, which had the authority to regulate airport operations. In contrast, Dulles Airport outside Washington, D.C., had no choice but to accept Coleman's ruling because that airport was run by the federal government. But that didn't stop local residents from taking legal action in an effort to bar the Concorde because of noise and air pollution.

In the meantime, the co-manufacturers of the French-British aircraft continued to lobby for entry into the U.S. market. At an aviation industry meeting in Dallas, the venture's general counsel noted that many of their critics were "making a damn sight more noise than the Concorde... Would we dare to release an airplane into service which we even suspected might become a hazard?" At least one U.S. group thought so, as reflected in a lawsuit filed by the Environment Defense Fund seeking to overturn Coleman's decision. At the same time, the New York-New Jersey Port Authority reached a decision to ban the flights for at least six months.

British Airways and Air France were not deterred, however, and the partners filed suit seeking to invalidate the decision of the Port Authority of New York and New Jersey, charging that the action was unconstitutional and in violation of U.S. treaty obligations. The U.S. House of Representatives and Senate also became involved, ultimately rejecting an amendment that would have banned the Concorde from all U.S. airports. The lawsuits continued, and in May 1976, a federal appeals court refused the request of officials in Fairfax County, Virginia, to set aside Coleman's ruling and upheld the government's decision to allow the supersonic jet to land regularly at two U.S. airports. The ruling cleared the way for Concorde service to begin at Dulles International Airport on May 23, marking the arrival of the first supersonic Concorde to fly commercially to the U.S. Less than three years later the Concorde began flying to DFW from Dulles.

IN ADDITION TO EUROPEAN destinations, the international offerings at DFW Airport included new single plane service from DFW to Panama City, Bogota, Guayaquil, Lima and Manias. In anticipation of increased demand for international flights, air carriers also made applications to fly into twenty-three new destinations in the Far East, Middle East, Caribbean and Europe. Both Braniff and Pan American World Airways already had designated DFW as a co-terminal for service to Central and South America, which allowed them to provide service to twenty-five cities in Latin America directly from DFW without having to stop at another "gateway" point.

In recognition of DFW's entry into the international market, the U.S. Department of Customs elevated DFW from a Port of Entry to an official Customs District in 1979. This was a significant event for DFW because it meant that statistics on imports and exports could be reported directly for DFW (as opposed to being included in the totals for all cities in the district), letting the international business community know that DFW had become an international player, generating significant amounts of international cargo and freight on its own. At a brief ceremony celebrating the opening of the facility, North Texas Commission Chairman of the Board Ray Hunt applauded the ten-year effort that was being recognized. "This has always been an international community with first-class facilities. This latest addition, an autonomous customs office, makes Dallas-Fort Worth equal or superior to any major port of entry in the world."

Another indicator of DFW's "international" status was the creation of a new 250-acre Foreign Trade Zone accessible by air, rail and truck. The zone, it was hoped, would further enhance international business at DFW by enabling businesses to manufacture, assemble or warehouse within the area, thereby deferring payment of customs duties until products were placed in the domestic market. (Products going to foreign markets were not subject to U.S. duties.)

The increased international activity at DFW did not go unnoticed by the U.S. Travel Service, a division of the U.S. Department of Commerce. In 1979, the Travel Service accepted the Metroplex for U.S.T.S. "gateway status," making DFW eligible to receive promotion in foreign countries by the U.S. government. The Travel Service also established a Gateway Receptionist Program at the airport to aid foreign visitors to the area. Through the program, U.S. students fluent in foreign languages greeted passengers from incoming international flights to assist them in managing their stay in this "foreign" environment.

Airport officials viewed these developments as important steps toward establishing DFW as a center for international commerce. Indeed, by year-end 1979, DFW had emerged as the seventh largest international gateway in the U.S. The following year proved to be even more exciting, with four new foreign-flag carriers beginning service at DFW. On April 1, Thai International Airways' inaugural flight into DFW touched down with some 250 Thai dignitaries aboard to celebrate the beginning of direct service to Tokyo and Bangkok (with actual service beginning the following year). This would make DFW that only inland city with single-plane service to Japan, from which connections could be made throughout Asia. A few weeks later, Lufthansa initiated twice-weekly freighter service between DFW and Frankfurt, with regular passenger service beginning on May 1.

Air Jamaica arrived at DFW for the first time on June 21, providing nonstop service between DFW and Kingston and Montego Bay. A few months later, British Caledonian—originally scheduled to start operations at DFW the following year—decided to move up the start date for service between DFW and London's Gatwick Airport to October. New markets were also established with single-plane service to Aruba, Caracas, Bangkok, Grand Turk, Montego Bay, Puerto Plata, and Rock Sound. To top off an already great year, Mexicana agreed to become signatory, making it the second foreign-flag carrier in this category and bringing the total number of signatory carriers to twelve.

Airport Board Chairman Jack Evans expressed board members' pleasure with the airport's expansion into the international arena: "The year just ended [1980] has been by far the most exciting for the Airport with the addition of four new foreign-flag carriers. It has been our goal to become one of the world's truly great international air harbors and it appears we have almost attained that greatness."

Much of the credit for DFW's emergence as an international air center was given to the North Texas Commission, whose principal goals were to promote the Metroplex as a center for international trade and commerce, to encourage corporate relocations to the area, to create a positive image for the Metroplex, and—most important to DFW Airport's success—to secure new air routes for the airport. The priorities of the NTC were set once a year based on what domestic and international flight deficiencies existed. The needs were prioritized on the basis of expected traffic, likelihood of achievement, the time involved and economic impact. As M. Keith Graham, who served as vice president for aviation development, noted, "New air routes are not obtained, implemented and exercised by happenstance. They come about through dedicated effort. They are planned and sought after."

As an example of how the NTC worked, Graham explained how Piedmont had come to DFW. "As a result of the air-route analysis we do constantly, we noted that there was no single-plane service from DFW to cities like Charlotte or Greensboro/High Point, N.C., and that there's been a growing air-travel relationship between the furniture industry in the Carolinas and elsewhere in the Southeast and the Dallas Home Furnishings Mart. People at the Dallas Market Center long had complained that their customers were tired of having to make a connection in Atlanta to get back to their manufacturing plants.

"So we spent about five years trying to convince the incumbent carriers to offer non-stop or single-plane service to those Southeastern points, but they were using Atlanta as a hub and wanted everything fed from DFW through Atlanta. From there you could connect on one of their planes to the Southeastern cities. Then it occurred to us there was an airline out there named Piedmont. So we called on them with figures showing the traffic between Piedmont's Southeastern cities and Dallas-Fort Worth, along with some suggestions about how an expansion to here would help them with traffic flow farther west. Voila! A year later Piedmont announced it was coming to DFW, and now its routes from here to Charlotte and other points are some of the most successful in its system and Piedmont is now the third largest operator at DFW, behind American and Delta."

It was somewhat ironic that at the same time international service at DFW was really taking off, air traffic industry-wide had dropped sharply because of a sluggish American economy and rising aviation fuel costs. Airline debt loads had soared to dangerous levels. Thousands of workers were laid off, and employee wages were cut back or frozen. Of course, DFW did not escape unscathed and, in fact, total passenger traffic dropped 4 percent from 1979 to 1980, the first decrease since the airport's opening.

One of the greatest casualties at DFW resulting from the fuel crisis was the loss of Concorde service. In the fifteen months the Concorde had flown in and out of Texas, the cost of jet fuel had climbed 120 percent. Given that the price of a ticket on the Concorde already cost 20 percent more than a regular first class ticket, the company feared that a hike in ticket prices to offset the loss might turn passengers away. In fact, this was not really a viable option since most flights between Dallas and Washington were averaging less than a third of the 100 needed to fill the plane. The airline announced that Concorde service at DFW would be discontinued on June 1, 1980.

IF "UNDER CONSTRUCTION" signs were signals of progress, then there should have been no doubt that DFW Airport was thriving. Not long after the operational opening, the airport had already begun work on new parking and terminal facilities, taxiway expansion and a new warehouse maintenance building. These projects would be only the first of significant new developments at DFW, including the construction of world headquarters for two of its signatory airlines. Within ten years, an expansion program that equaled the original investment of $700 million was completed! While the aerial view of the loop-shaped terminal buildings remained similar, significant changes were evident on closer inspection. For example, instead of two parallel runways with one on each side of the terminals, there were four runways (two on each side), with companion taxiways and aprons. Additional crossover taxiways on the north and south ends of the airport provided for two-way traffic flow that eased delays during heavy traffic periods.

Inside the airport, changes also occurred. The air cargo area was doubled to meet existing demand. A new office building was constructed in the center of the airport to accommodate aviation-oriented firms and agencies. Delta had begun construction of a new terminal at 4E, increasing aircraft parking from sixteen to twenty-one gates (with an ultimate expansion to thirty-eight gates planned). The airline also began a major expansion of its maintenance hangar, which would make it the largest such facility at DFW. Ultimately, Delta would establish a secondary hub at the airport, including two satellite terminals with underground passageways to the main terminal. By 1984, American and Delta would become the number one and two carriers at DFW, accounting for 80 percent of total passenger traffic.

Two of the most significant construction projects at the airport belonged to two of the signatory carriers. Braniff broke ground on "Braniff Place," the company's new world headquarters, on September 16, 1976. The new $25 million complex of four interrelated low-rise buildings occupied 340,000 square feet of space in a wooded area on the west side of the airport and included centers for administration/finance, training, computers and recreation. The company took advantage of new "special facility revenue bonds" made possible by a 1972 tax reform act that allowed issuance of bonds by cities for corporations when it related to airports or air carriers serving an airport. The special bonds were tax-exempt and usually obtained at a rate lower than taxable corporate bonds. Braniff asked the cities of Dallas and Fort Worth to issue $35 million in revenue bonds for the construction of the new facility, agreeing to pay off the 30-year bonds at a rate of approximately $3 million a year, in addition to $142,000 in ground rent.

The new Braniff headquarters was completed and fully occupied in 1979—just a few months after American Airlines announced it would relocate its world headquarters from New York City to DFW. The Metroplex business community had courted American for years, attempting to lure the company to move its headquarters to DFW where its Learning Center (the training facility for flight attendants) and Flight Academy, which trained new pilots and "refreshed" experienced pilots on new equipment and technology, were already located. In the spring of 1978, American's Chairman Al Casey was finally ready to listen to proposals that his company should move its headquarters to the Dallas-Fort Worth area. As Casey later explained, there were several reasons "starting with deregulation" that a move seemed inevitable. "Like survival," he said. "As we entered 1978 we were out of money. We were out of the means to raise cash. We were out of everything. I and the whole management team knew we had to do something drastic. Deregulation would create a whole new world in aviation, and everybody, including American, was cash short for the heavy expenditures we knew lay ahead."

Casey met with DFW Airport Board Chair Henry Stuart and Executive Director Ernest Dean to discuss the matter. Together, they hammered out an agreement in principle that American would move if the airport would build it a new headquarters and reservations center financed with tax-free bonds, then lease the facilities back to the airline at a rate sufficient to pay off the bonds. Within a month of this meeting, Dean received the approval of the city councils of Dallas and Fort Worth to proceed. He delivered to Casey a concrete proposal that included $147 million in tax-free bond financing to pay for the new headquarters facility. Casey accepted the proposal and presented the plan to American's management team at one of their regularly scheduled Monday meetings in June. The group agreed that it was in the company's best interest to make the move.

In November, after intense speculation in the press, American made the official announcement that it would move to DFW. But not without a fight. The company encountered tremendous political pressure from state and city officials to stay in New York. The situation became more tense when a delegation of influential New Yorkers lobbied to get the U.S. Treasury Department to disqualify the proposed bond financing package for tax-free status. In response, Casey called on Texas representatives Majority Leader Jim Wright and Senators John Tower and Lloyd Bentsen who, according to Casey, "lobbied incessantly against the IRS ruling." Though their efforts ultimately failed—with the IRS ruling that non-operational facilities, including airline company headquarters, could *not* be financed by tax-free bonds—they were able to prevent the ruling from applying retroactively. So by the time it was made, American's bonds had already been issued and sold, making the new facility the last building of its kind to be financed by tax-free bonds.

American had purchased 325 acres south of the airport to construct facilities that would house the world headquarters, reservations center, training facilities and utility plant. It was a homecoming of sorts since the company had been formed in 1930 in Fort Worth as American Airways through a merger of four small airlines, including Texas-based Southern Air Transport, which itself had been formed from two small Fort Worth-based carriers. American's first chairman, C.R. Smith, was a Waco native who began his career with Southern. Following the merger, he served as president and chief executive officer from 1934 to 1968, when he became U.S. Secretary of Commerce. In the first flight with flight attendants, American inaugurated the first "red eye" flight between Dallas and Fort Worth and Los Angeles in 1934 with a 12-passenger Curtiss Condor. The company's famous DC-3 flagship began service in Fort Worth at Meacham Field in 1936. American also initiated Texas' first commercial jet service at Love Field in 1959. The company's Stewardess College—now called the Learning Center—opened in 1957. The pilot training facility followed in 1970.

Construction on American's new headquarters began in August 1980 and was completed in early 1983. In addition to the new headquarters facilities which were in the city limits of Fort Worth, construction in Terminal 2E to the north of the American terminal provided seven new aircraft boarding gates and offices for the Federal Inspection Services used by American and the carriers American handled. The new inspection facility established a "one-stop" clearance procedure where passengers could be screened by a single federal inspector handling preliminary processing for both Immigration Services and the U.S. Customs Service. An 800-foot connector building linked the new space with existing activities at Terminal 3E.

A new station in American's new terminal offered weatherproof vestibules and escalator entrances to the terminal concourses. The opening of the new station signaled a new stage for the people-moving system, which had experienced considerable down time and, consequently, customer complaints, during its early years of operation. In fact, the AIRTRANS system had been shut down in September of 1975 because of unresolved disputes between airport officials and LTV Aerospace Corporation, the designer and builder of the system. In January of the following year, the airport board assumed complete responsibility for the operation and maintenance of the system under a contract settlement with LTV. After a four-month shutdown for improvements, the AIRTRANS system began transporting passengers again in January 1976. Although it took a while to work out all the bugs, AIRTRANS was fully operational at almost 100 percent reliability in 1980, carrying more than 7 million passengers and employees on an annual basis.

The East Tower of the Marina Hotel—a mirror image of the West Tower—opened early in 1981, offering 853 additional rooms. Coupled with the 600-room West Hotel, the complex was the largest hotel located on any airport property in the world. The hotel system changed its name to Amfac Hotel & Resorts in 1980, with the DFW complex renamed Amfac Hotel, East Tower and West Tower. The Amfac recreational area, which included the Bear Creek Golf and Racquet Center, opened in the spring of 1980, offering an 18-hole golf course and tennis and racquetball facilities. Another 18 holes was added the following year. Marina officials cited the significance of the development to the region: "With Bear Creek, 1,450 guest rooms, more than 130,000 square-feet of exhibit space and enough night life to satisfy the most socially active guest, we think the Airport Marina can play a major role in bringing major meetings, conventions and trade shows to the Dallas-Fort Worth area and that will be good for everyone's business." In 1983, the DFW Hilton & Executive Conference Center was completed. The Center was located two-and-a-half miles from the north entrance of the airport on a 28-acre site, which included conference facilities, and 416 guest rooms in two nine-story towers.

THE AREA SURROUNDING the airport also was experiencing a building boom. As anticipated, the airport served as an economic magnet, attracting new industries and corporations to the area. Within ten years of the airport's opening, the region had attracted new and/or relocating businesses to the area at a rate of about 225 per year. The Metroplex ranked third nationally (behind New York and Chicago) as a corporate headquarters city. In just five years, the number of single family dwelling permits issued annually in the city of Grapevine increased from about 50 in 1973 to almost 400 in 1978. The "Irving land boom" as it was called created almost unimaginable windfalls for land owners who, less than twenty years ago, had purchased airport land for $30 to $40 an acre, and were now title holders to property going for up to $250,000 an acre.

In every direction, new construction spurred by the airport's success was visible. One of the largest new projects was the 12,000-acre Las Colinas development located in nearby Irving and including an urban center larger than downtown Dallas. Office towers, hotels (including the Mandalay Four Seasons luxury resort), apartments, service centers and residential neighborhoods were either under construction or planned for this new community. Another 500-acre industrial-office park was built in Irving adjacent to the DFW Airport Foreign Trade Zone. DFW Freeport, as it was called, was a multi-use development with twenty-five acres of restaurants, shops, hotels, a jogging trail and tennis courts—all surrounding three man-made lakes in the center of the development. The area would draw an estimated population of 2,500 people upon completion.

Five years after the airport opened, DFW officials held a press conference to announce the findings of a year-long study that found the airport to be a major contributor of more than $3 billion worth of economic impact on the community each year. An Air Transport Association official noted that in twenty-five to thirty other studies his organization had conducted at various airports, they had not seen the level of growth occurring at DFW in any other area of the country. Airport officials were proud of the airport's role in such progress: "Clearly none of this would be taking place if it were not for the airport. Thus the value of the airport to the community cannot be measured simply in the dollars it costs to operate it for the year."

In 1983, construction began on one of the largest housing developments in the Dallas-Fort Worth area. Valley Ranch, located in north Irving, would offer a large base of affordable housing near the Las Colinas business park. Around the same time, construction got underway on a 1,280-acre industrial port at the south end of the airport on the site of the old Greater Southwest International Airport. The Centreport development included a more than 200,000 square-foot office and industrial building and two smaller office and warehouse structures.

Additional high-rise office and hotel buildings along Airport Freeway and Highway 360 would soon follow.

While DFW generally received support for its role in the economic development of the area, the activity on airport property was beginning to strain the relationship between DFW and the surrounding communities. Mid-cities officials were concerned that perhaps the airport had not lived up to its promise to encourage industrial development in their respective cities. Under the 1971 agreement, DFW officials had agreed to encourage businesses unrelated to airport operations to locate outside the airport. Ten years later, however, some of these businesses had moved onto airport property or into the Foreign Trade Zone, which was free of local taxation.

In response, although the land bordering the airport was designated for industrial use only, the City of Irving changed the zoning requirements to allow the development of residential units, including apartments and condominiums in a three-square-mile area adjacent to the east end of the airport, "despite possible noise and pollution hazards caused by air traffic." The decision to expand residential offerings reportedly was based on increased demand for housing in the area and concerns on the part of Irving officials that their city was being harmed by the growth of the airport. DFW officials, of course, were concerned that unanticipated building close to the airport would hinder expansion plans. When developers announced additional plans for a multi-family residential project on the airport's southwest border in Euless, it seemed that the honeymoon between DFW and its neighbors might be over.

IN THE MIDST OF ALL the development going on around DFW, the industry the airport was built to serve was experiencing incredible changes. Declining passenger loads and higher operating costs were wreaking havoc for the industry and making it increasingly difficult for airlines to survive, much less turn a profit. Fearing that the airlines might be subject to the same fate as the railroads, President Gerald Ford proposed in 1975 that the regulatory scheme of the aviation industry be changed so that the airlines could regulate themselves through "pure competition."

The goal was to deregulate the industry by providing more flexibility in routes and fares—for both airlines and passengers.

The Civil Aeronautics Board agreed in principle that changes were needed and urged Congress to introduce new competition by cutting back the Board's authority and changing the way it regulated. The only real difference in the CAB's proposed solution and Ford's proposal was that the CAB wanted to retain more authority over air fares and routes than the administration had proposed.

The major airlines, on the other hand, feared that the proposals to lessen restrictions on the industry would compromise both the integrity of the air transpiration system and, particularly, air safety. They warned that unchecked competition could ultimately hurt consumers by creating unprofitable rate wars and the elimination of service to many smaller, marginally profitable markets. Additionally, the airlines argued, more congestion would be created at the "already congested" major airports. "Of all the changes advocated by those who seek reform, the concept of free entry and concomitant free exit contains the most potent seeds for the destruction of our nation's air transportation system," concluded a senior official at Delta Air Lines.

Interestingly, the success of Southwest Airlines in Texas was frequently cited to illustrate the potential impact of deregulation. Speaking before the Senate, Senator Edward M. Kennedy argued that successful Texas airlines—those that do not cross state borders and thus are not regulated by the CAB—are good indicators that the industry should be deregulated. Not so, many airline officials responded. Texas International President Francisco Lorenzo told the same audience a week later that "the Texas experience is virtually irrelevant" to the airline industry as a whole. Contending that the low fares are "not related to the free market because there is no transportation market in Texas," Lorenzo urged lawmakers to not give the "Texas experience" more prominence in the debate than it deserved. "Those who support elimination of the federal system of regulation for air transportation have seized upon this experience as the only tangible support for their otherwise esoteric economic theory that a virtually unregulated system of air transportation would produce better service at lower fares than the present federally regulated system."

Southwest officials supported deregulation. Company President Lamar Muse testified before Congress in support of the proposed legislation, saying that his five-year-old airline would begin low-cost flights to several cities outside Texas if the industry were deregulated to allow any airline free entry into the air traffic market and the ability to cut fares to the cost of the service provided. Braniff Chairman Harding Lawrence, on the other hand, called for Congress "to strengthen the concept of regulated competition which has been shown to be in the best public interest."

Despite the opposition of the major airlines, change was inevitable. Commercial aviation was transformed on October 24, 1978, when President Jimmy Carter signed into law the Airline Deregulation Act of 1978. The landmark legislation ushered in a new era for aviation, effectively lessening restrictions on air fares and routes and opening the door to increased competition and a heightened demand for services. Under the law, the CAB's authority could be used only to stimulate competition—not stifle it, as had been the case for nearly four decades. The Board's powers would be phased out over time, and the Board itself dissolved in 1985. The act endorsed the concept of multiple, permissive route awards, providing for airlines to determine whether to begin service to a new destination based on their own analyses of market conditions. Airlines could opt to fly "dormant" routes that were going unserved by other carriers; select one new route a year for the next three years without CAB proceedings (and at the same time protect one route a year from automatic entry); and to expect the CAB to grant applications for new routes unless the Board found that the award was inconsistent with the public interest.

DFW Airport officials described the effect of deregulation on DFW as "both a boon and a bane." "[Deregulation] spawned an unprecedented spate of young, lean-and-hungry upstart carriers and triggered a series of debilitating fare wars. This created a survival-of-the-fittest situation pitting the low-cost upstarts against the major trunk airlines whose cost structures and employee work rules had been established during the time of government regulation by the Civil Aeronautics Board."

The scene outside the CAB just before the new law went into effect really told the tale of deregulation. Airline "representatives" had been camped on the sidewalk outside the office for a week, waiting for the bill to be signed and routes to be made available under the new guidelines. United was first in line, followed by Eastern, American and twenty or so additional carriers to claim open routes not being served by any airlines and dormant routes that were not being used. In what was later dubbed "The Great Air Rush of 1978," a group of people who looked liked concert-goers waiting in line for tickets to a popular show, waited for the doors to open by talking to each other, reading, listening to radios, watching portable TVs or sleeping. As the time to enter approached, the disheveled "stand-ins" were replaced by freshly pressed airline officials and attorneys.

Theoretically, United could have claimed all the routes since the routes were to be awarded on a first-come first-served basis and since there was no limit on how many routes any one airline could have. However, a provision in the new law required that a new carrier begin serving any route claimed within thirty days. Surprising everyone, the company chose only one route—non-stop service between Buffalo, New York, and Orlando, Florida. Like many of the other carriers, United also filed to protect several routes which it had the authority to fly but had not been serving.

AT DFW, THE OPPORTUNITY for more airlines to expand services in and out of the airport also meant continued controversy regarding the use of Love Field. While the U.S. Supreme Court's 1974 decision to not hear the case pitting the two cities against the airline had cleared the way for Southwest to continue operating out of the municipal airport, it did not resolve the issue. Southwest's proposal in 1976 to enter five new Texas markets (Austin, Corpus Christi, Lubbock, El Paso and Midland-Odessa) complicated matters even further. Fearing that the expanded service could have a significant effect on service provided by the major airlines at DFW, the U.S. Department of Transportation asked for "a full report" on the potential impact of the Southwest flights. (Although the Texas Aeronautics Commission had jurisdiction over intrastate flights, a possibility existed that the proposed flights could affect interstate commerce, thus giving the federal government some authority in the matter.)

Around the same time, the DFW Airport Board had adopted a resolution demanding that "all Certificated Air Carrier Services, whether interstate, intrastate or foreign," use the regional airport "to the exclusion of any and all other airports owned and operated by the cities of Dallas or Fort Worth." The resolution was intended to be used as evidence against expanded air service for Southwest. If necessary, Fort Worth officials warned, it would be followed by a lawsuit against the city of Dallas to close Love Field if it becomes "apparent that the big airport here is going to get into financial problems."

In the meantime, Southwest retained the authority to expand its intrastate services, and for the next five years, things were relatively quiet. When the airline announced early in 1979 plans to fly from Houston to New Orleans, however, tempers flared again. The company had applied for authority to fly between Love Field and New Orleans under the "Automatic Entry Provision" of the new airline deregulation law that allowed each airline to choose one new route a year and required the CAB to grant authority unless the airline was not fit, willing and able to fly it. Anticipating CAB approval, House Majority Leader Jim Wright of Fort Worth appealed to Transportation Secretary Brock Adams to help block flights from Love Field to other states and countries. After the CAB issued a tentative order allowing Southwest to begin service to New Orleans on March 17— contingent upon any objections to the plan—DFW officials, city leaders and business groups filed documents with the CAB protesting the planned flights out of Love Field.

Ironically, Henry Newman, the southwest regional director of the FAA who had played such an instrumental role in the development of DFW Airport, reportedly was forced to resign after forty-two years in government service as a result of his role in the controversy. It seemed that his finding that the proposed interstate flights from the Dallas airport would undermine the DFW air traffic system was not well-received. According to media reports, Wright wrote a "blistering" letter to Adams demanding to know why Newman was pushed out. "The fact that he has warned of the danger of mixing general aviation and air carrier traffic at Love Field, a warning based on an intimate personal understanding of the entire situation, simply got him crossways with some would-be policy makers whose professional credentials would not entitle them to carry Hank Newman's briefcase," Wright wrote. Brock responded that Newman's decision to leave "was his own and I have to respect that decision."

The upshot was that the CAB reversed its earlier decision, refusing Southwest's request to fly interstate flights out of Love Field until it had time to determine whether such flights "would cause substantial public harm to the national air transportation system." The CAB approved temporary service of the flights out of DFW instead. Southwest President Howard Putnam said no thanks and threatened to base its interstate flight operation in Houston if the CAB issued a permanent injunction on the flights at Love Field.

In the first day of hearings before the CAB, the judge surprised everybody by instructing the attorneys representing Southwest and DFW Airport, respectively, to try to reach an out-of-court settlement. Early discussions indicated that a compromise might, in fact, be possible if the two cities would drop their opposition to all interstate flights out of Love Field in exchange for an agreement by Southwest to limit long-haul flights. As time wore on, however, it became increasingly clear that the parties would be back in court. After two settlement conferences failed to produce an agreement, a new hearing was set. As the hearing date drew near, homeowners around Love Field who opposed Southwest's expansion asked the CAB to postpone a decision until an environmental impact statement on the matter was completed. The CAB declined and the hearing date was set for May 1979.

In the meantime, Texas legislators had been hard at work on a bill that would give the City of Dallas authority to ban from Love Field any interstate commercial flights to cities more than 600 miles away, while at the same time it would remove the authority of any Texas city with a population of more than 800,000— Dallas and Houston—to deny interstate access to their city-owned airports and give it to the Texas Aeronautics Commission. The bill was designed to clarify the legal powers of local government over the use of the municipal airport. The compromise was acceptable to Southwest, but not DFW airport officials, who maintained that interstate flights of any length into Love Field would take away from the major airlines at DFW the passengers they needed to maintain profitability on interstate and international flights. The bill sailed through the Senate and the House and landed on Governor William Clements' desk.

Almost two weeks later, Governor Clements announced after a closed-door meeting with Dallas and Fort Worth business and city leaders that he would veto the "Southwest Airlines bill" because it violated the original agreement to consolidate commercial air service at DFW Airport. He said, "I am satisfied that it violates the spirit and the letter of the original DFW [Airport] agreements. It also violates the environmental situation that exists around Love Field."

The following month, a CAB judge ruled in the final opinion on the New Orleans case that Southwest should be allowed to fly from Love Field to the out-of-state destination, pending preparation of an environmental impact statement and full CAB approval. In a separate case, however, that involved a request by Air Florida to fly from Love Field to Florida, another CAB administrator ruled against the Air Florida service, noting that DFW was the designated airport for such flights in the North Texas region. Both cases would come before the five-member CAB sometime within the next few months in what many hoped would be the resolution of the Love Field controversy. Interestingly, one of the cases likely would have to be overruled given the related issues involved. As anticipated, the third case involving the earlier ruling granting Southwest the authority to fly into Midway was also joined when the CAB announced that it would render a decision in September. According to Southwest President Howard Putnam, "It's going to be a classic case for deregulation. It's going to be a pretty precedent-setting issue."

On September 13, the CAB voted 3-1 to let Southwest begin flights between Love Field and New Orleans, but withheld action on the other proposals pending the results of a hearing on the environmental impact. Immediately, there were indications that the airport board and the cities would appeal the decision in court. According to Wright, the CAB ignored the intent of Congress and "violated the expressed wishes of local city governments." He hoped the decision would be repealed and reversed.

In fact, Wright stayed involved and introduced an amendment that would ban all interstate flights from Love Field and attached it to two pieces of aviation-related legislation. When both bills stalled because of stiff opposition (primarily from deregulation supporters and Louisiana Senator Russell Long, whose constituents liked Southwest's service to New Orleans), DFW Airport tried to reach a compromise with Southwest that would make DFW the primary airport for the region, while at the same time allowing limited interstate flights for Southwest. Finally, after intense negotiations, the resolution came in the form of new legislation. The "Love Field" · Amendment—or the Wright Amendment as it came to be known in recognition of the bill's primary sponsor—was enacted in February 1980 as part of broader legislation on international aviation policy issues, the International Air Transportation Competition Act of 1979.

The purpose of the Wright Amendment was to limit operations at Love Field to service to cities in Texas or the four states contiguous to Texas (Louisiana, Arkansas, Oklahoma, and New Mexico). Tickets for transportation to destinations outside of Texas and the four contiguous states were prohibited. Airlines could not offer or provide "interline" services—ticketing with other carriers for destinations outside the four states. The limitations and conditions on Love Field service did not apply to the transportation of air cargo, passengers in aircraft with less than fifty-six seats or to charter services.

Of course, the Amendment did not go unchallenged. Opponents of the bill contended that the legislation was unconstitutional because it restricted freedom of travel and freedom of expression. Additionally, there was some question regarding the interpretation of the provision restricting service to carriers that do "not offer or provide any through service or ticketing with another air carrier or foreign air carrier." (An airline interlines if it engages in joint ticketing or baggage handling with other airlines.) As the bill was explained on the floor to the Senate and House when it came up for a vote, Senator Howard Cannon, chairman of the aviation subcommittee of the Senate Commerce Committee, said that the prohibition applied only with respect to a carrier's Love Field service. Only when Texas International sought clearance to fly out of Love Field a few months later, was the full impact of that "explanation" realized. According to the ruling by the CAB, any qualified airline could serve Texas and contiguous states from Love Field.

OTHER LEGAL CONTROVERSIES continued to plague the airport. The long-standing legal battle over SURTRAN's exclusive contract to pick up passengers at the airport was still unresolved with two federal lawsuits pending. One case had been filed on behalf of 2,000 taxi drivers who argued that the contract violated antitrust laws. A second challenge was filed by 200 independent drivers who alleged that the contract between the two cities and SURTRAN had established a "dangerous monopoly." Despite such efforts, the Dallas and Fort Worth city councils voted to extend the SURTRAN contract for five more years. In an effort to resolve the conflict, however, the councils also voted for a resolution that permitted independent cab drivers to pick up passengers if they agreed to pay $1.75 for each fare collected. Cab drivers were not satisfied since SURTRAN's exclusive contract was still in effect. According to the attorney representing the Independent Taxi Drivers Association, the contract required the drivers to pay "a tribute of $1" to SURTRAN Taxicabs, plus a 75-cent fee to the "inefficient, politically-operated" SURTRAN system.

In an effort to better serve passengers, the city councils later expanded service opportunities for independent drivers by allowing them to pick up passengers as well as drop them off. Unfortunately, service still did not always meet demand even with increased participation by "outside" taxi companies. After five years of operation, airport public relations director Jim Street conceded, "Taxi service has been a continuing problem since the airport first opened. We never have had a situation that could be termed good."

Part of the problem, airport officials noted, was that the airport had no control over independent drivers and their desire to work during certain hours. The airport's role in the matter was simply educating drivers about the opportunities for the airport's lucrative business. A particularly troublesome issue was service between the airline terminals. Taxi drivers were reluctant to give up their places in line to take a customer on a trip that would only bring in a couple dollars when the fare into Dallas or Fort Worth would be $20 or more. As a compromise, the SURTRAN Policy Committee approved a $5 fee for the "intra-airport" trips with the hope of stimulating better service.

At the same time, the SURTRAN system was experiencing declining passenger loads. After raising fares from $4 to $5 and later to $7 for service from DFW to a SURTRAN terminal, ridership declined by almost one-half. In an effort to keep SURTRAN in the black, representatives from the two cities met to discuss their options. Some favored the idea of dissolving the existing operating agreement and allowing each city to provide transportation services for their respective areas. Other options included franchising the service to a private operator or getting assistance from the places served, e.g., hotels and chambers of commerce. Another alternative was for the airport to assume control of the system and pass deficit costs along to the airlines. Certainly, something had to be done: service was poor and the system was losing money.

New state laws complicated the taxi situation even further. One law, which ended the regulation of taxi service by the Texas Railroad Commission, specifically excluded the DFW Airport, leaving taxi regulating authority with the Commission. The second law gave airport boards the authority to regulate their own taxi services. SURTRAN officials argued that taxi companies operating at the airport should have to adhere to both laws by seeking a permit from the Railroad Commission in addition to a license from the Airport Board. Taxi operators interpreted the new legislation differently, however, contending that the second law trumped the first, giving the authority at DFW to the Railroad

Commission. The controversy raged on with threats of still more lawsuits simmering.

In August of 1983, Dallas' Consumer Services Department proposed that it become the sole regulatory authority for ground transportation to and from the airport. The move reflected a desire to both reduce inefficiencies and inequities in the service and to preempt the threatened legal actions by Dallas taxi operators. When Fort Worth announced plans to pull out of SURTRAN, the fate of the system seemed decided. At about the same time, a group of taxi companies appeared before the Texas Railroad Commission to ask that the Commission stop regulating taxi services at DFW Airport. Later in the month, the SURTRAN Policy Committee voted to end its contract with the New York-based firm that had managed SURTRAN for two years. Shortly thereafter, the Texas Railroad Commission ruled that the airport board could regulate its own taxicab services, clearing the way for Dallas and Fort Worth to dissolve SURTRAN and assume responsibility for providing transportation services to and from DFW for residents and visitors of their respective cities.

In another legal battle, DFW's status as a good neighbor was tested. In 1981, the airport began test flights on Runway 13L to determine the feasibility of using the runway on a regular basis. Angry residents whose homes were directly in the flight path brought suit against DFW and the FAA to stop the tests. A federal judge denied their request and allowed a sixty-day test of the new flight path, emphasizing that the test was temporary and that permanent use of the flight path would require an environmental impact statement. The Irving City Council voted to appeal the decision both in court and in public hearings held by the airport. In an effort to appease residents, airport officials agreed to construct a $5.3 million taxiway that could cut down on the noise. The issue became moot in the spring of the following year when airport officials decided to suspend flights from 13L in the aftermath of the air traffic controllers' strike and the Braniff shutdown, both of which contributed to a significant reduction in the number of takeoffs and landings at DFW.

POLITICS CONTINUED to play a role in the governing of the new airport. Shortly after the opening, Fort Worth Mayor R.M. Stovall reported that his city had asked Dallas to honor an informal agreement between the two towns to appoint a board chairman from Fort Worth at its first February meeting. Dallas representatives contended, however, that since their city paid higher premiums to support the airport, Dallas should supply the chair. In the midst of this controversy in 1976, J. Lee Johnson III, the vice chairman of the board, resigned, saying simply that he had "occupied a place on the board far too long." This move, of course, weakened Fort Worth's argument since Johnson was the most experienced and logical candidate to assume the chairman's position.

After considerable public debate over the alleged "gentleman's agreement" that the chair's position should be rotated between the cities, Dallas' Henry Stuart, manager of Addison Airport, Inc., was ultimately and unanimously elected chair on February 3, 1976, to serve for one year. Fort Worth's newest member, Paul Mason, chief executive of the First National Bank of Fort Worth— who had been appointed to fill Johnson's unexpired term—was elected vice chairman. In fact, Stuart served for five years until Jack Evans was named chairman in 1980. When Evans resigned to run for mayor of Dallas, Mason became the first representative from Fort Worth to hold the top position on the airport authority. The following year, the title passed to Rodger Meier of Dallas, who had served under Mason as vice-chairman. James C. Fuller of Bell Helicopter Textron became vice-chairman.

Tensions between the two cities were not helped by the fact that the new airport's name quickly had been shortened to just "Dallas" by many people. Airline personnel often welcomed passengers to "Dallas" upon arrival at Dallas/Fort Worth Airport. It reportedly took a chain of correspondence between then U.S. Representative Jim Wright (of Fort Worth) and the chairman of the Civil Aeronautics Board to resolve this problem. Wright formally suggested in early 1976 that the airport's title be shortened to DFW. The CAB concurred that the simpler reference would be useful and agreed to use the three-letter code "in all future references to Dallas/Fort Worth."

LABOR PROBLEMS were common during the airport's first ten years of operation. Airlines experienced many conflicts with pilots, flight attendants, mechanics, machinists and maintenance workers, primarily over wage and benefits packages. It was the Professional Air Traffic Controllers Organization (PATCO) strike that was most damaging to the industry, however. Citing the particular stresses of their work that medically disqualifies many before reaching retirement age, controllers argued that they were underappreciated and underpaid. Unable to agree with the FAA on new contract terms, PATCO members threatened a walk out in the summer of 1981. Although the FAA warned that a threatened strike would be illegal (because controllers are employees of the FAA and strikes by federal employees are prohibited) and could lead to dismissals, controllers scheduled a strike date for June 22. When a vote of PATCO members showed that only 75 percent of the nation's controllers were willing to walk off the job, the strike was called off—or as it turned out, simply postponed.

Negotiations continued and a new package was put on the table. PATCO rejected the new proposal by a huge margin in late July, resurrecting the threat of a strike. Midnight, Sunday, August 3, was the deadline for reaching agreement. In spite of the risk of going to jail for up to a year and paying a $1,000 fine, controllers were prepared to walk off the job at 7:00 a.m. Monday, Dallas-Fort Worth time, if acceptable terms were not offered.

Of course, a walk-out would bring air traffic to a standstill at DFW and other major airports across the country. For that reason, the government put its contingency plan into operation as negotiations continued. The FAA ordered 150 military air traffic controllers to report to civilian airports on Monday morning and asked 550 more to stand by. U.S. President Ronald Reagan applied pressure by threatening "no amnesty" for striking controllers, while the Justice Department promised to prosecute them "to the fullest extent" possible under the law. In spite of such threats, most of the controllers, including 539 local DFW area PATCO members, stood firm. At 4:00 a.m. on August 3, an agreement had not been reached. PATCO officials announced that

81 percent of the nation's controllers had voted to strike, and at 7:00 a.m. the strike began.

President Reagan warned that those who didn't return to work within forty-eight hours would lose their jobs. By mid-morning half the flights at the nation's largest airports—including DFW—had been grounded. Despite additional warnings by the federal government to return to work, only about 29 percent had returned to their jobs by midday. Supervisory personnel filled in for the absent controllers, along with military support. A U.S. District Court judge issued a $2.4 million per day fine on the union, or $100,000 per hour of the walkout.

On the second day of the strike, flights at DFW were functioning at about 75 percent of normal operations (in fact, a much better scenario than had been feared). Airlines still were forced to cut back employees, however, announcing layoffs immediately. The largest carriers lost millions of dollars a day in revenue because of the strike. By the end of the week, the striking controllers had been fired. The FAA said it considered the strike over and was starting to rebuild the nation's flight control system. The effects of the walkout and the government's response were far from over, however. The impact was felt throughout the world in such actions as a boycott of aircraft to and from Canada which temporarily halted air traffic between the two countries. Controllers in other parts of the world also refused to handle planes bound to and from the U.S.

The chief of DFW's control tower somehow managed to keep things running smoothly. In one of what must have been hundreds of media reports on the situation, a Dallas journalist captured his fatigue. "He has spent the day in 'exit interviews' with his former employees—a government procedure requiring an employer to give formal reasons for an employee's dismissal. In the last two weeks he has lost half of his staff, down from 130 to sixty-nine workers. He was tired of talking about the strike and tired of hearing the word stress in conjunction with his employees' jobs. . . And he was getting a little tired of convincing the press and the public that although his ranks were cut by half and the number of flights cut by only 20 percent, flying was safe, because there is more time now between departures, five minutes instead of one or one and a half minutes."

In fact, the solution to the safety issue was just that—greater spacing between planes. For planes that typically trailed each other by about five miles, the norm had become twenty miles. In bad weather, that distance might be doubled. Of course, flight delays were commonplace and passengers were not a happy lot. Nor were airline executives whose airline operations were subjected to FAA-ordered route changes, delayed departures and fare wars.

The situation didn't get any better when half of the first class of post-strike air traffic controller students failed their final exams at the FAA Academy. A report by the House Committee on Post Office and Civil Service on the FAA's plan to rebuild the system concluded that there were serious questions whether the FAA would reach its goal of rebuilding the system by January of 1984. "The only way to lessen the strain on the system is to rehire a substantial number of the striking controllers." The Reagan administration responded to such concerns in December 1981 by allowing the fired controllers to be considered for federal jobs— but not in their old positions with the FAA. The president did go so far as to say that he would consider lifting the ban against strikers. PATCO continued to lobby for just such a ruling that would allow the fired workers to be rehired.

In the meantime, many of the former controllers faced fines and jail time as a result of their participation in the strike. Some of the harshest penalties were handed out in Fort Worth. Noting that there were "consequences for those who break the law," U.S. District Judge Eldon Mahon ordered six former controllers to each pay $750 in fines and sentenced three of the defendants to the maximum one year in prison, suspending all but 90 days of the terms. Within two weeks, the rulings were appealed. The three men's attorney argued both that the statute prohibiting strikes by federal employees was unconstitutional and that the three men had been selectively prosecuted because of their status as PATCO officials and strike leaders. When the 5th Circuit Court of Appeals upheld their convictions, the fired controllers appealed to the U.S. Supreme Court. When the high Court refused to overturn the lower court's decision, it was confirmed that the defendants would serve time in prison. (Ultimately, PATCO would ask a federal bankruptcy judge to dissolve the fourteen-year-old union after court costs, fines and legal fees rendered the organization insolvent.)

While most of the nation's largest airports returned to pre-strike operating levels by early 1982, DFW had to keep operating at more than 15 percent below the previous year's summertime peaks because of a lack of trained air traffic controllers. While the FAA cap on flights at DFW did not hurt the airport financially since 100 percent of DFW expenses were covered by the original airline tenants, the situation restricted the expansion of flight activities. And, of course, the airlines themselves had to watch their competitors at other airports (with more controllers on hand) gain advantages.

A year after the 11,400 controllers were fired, things still weren't back to normal. The FAA became the target of much criticism, particularly in the DFW area, for the limits placed on expansions and the limiting of landing slots. Ironically, the industry essentially deregulated under the Carter administration was now operating under strict guidelines established by another government agency. According to one industry observer, "In a lot of respects, we gave up CAB economic regulation and had to substitute FAA regulation on airport usage."

According to DFW officials, the FAA virtually ignored its need for more flights in a growing region while putting increases in markets showing decreases in market demand. "It's patently unfair, the way we're being treated in this thing," DFW spokesperson Jim Street said. In response, the FAA reported that the agency was "having some severe delay problems at DFW. The number of additional slots reflect what we consider to be the capacity at the airport." Finally, in May 1983, the FAA announced that the slot restrictions at DFW—one of the last airports to be relieved of the regulations—would be lifted September 1, allowing airlines to freely schedule flights in and out of the airport.

IN THE MIDST OF THE TURMOIL created by deregulation and the air traffic controllers' strike, DFW's largest signatory carrier, Braniff, stopped operations and filed for protection under Chapter 11 of the Federal Bankruptcy Act on May 13, 1982. The problems leading to this decision reportedly included an overly ambitious plan to expand services in a deregulated environment, escalating fuel prices and recession-slowed traffic. Deregulation particularly had allowed Braniff to expand at a much quicker pace than would have been possible under the former CAB route approval process. The company had received more new routes than any other airline in the CAB's first action under the new airline deregulation bill. Making DFW its hub, the airline flew coast-to-coast and a lot of places in-between. The strategy was to control the flow of traffic by getting passengers to their final destinations without having to "connect" them with other carriers. Braniff executive John Casey (brother to American's chief executive Al Casey) summed it up, "Why should we feed them if we can feed ourselves?"

Following deregulation, the company quickly added or increased service to thirty-nine U.S. cities and added forty-eight new non-stop routes to its system. It was the first to begin regularly scheduled non-stop service from DFW to Europe. It also was the first to offer Concorde flights between an interior U.S. city and Europe. The company initiated Hawaii as a new destination and announced plans to add "non-stop flights out of DFW to every principal capital in the world." In little more than a year, 627 new pilots were hired and flight attendants were graduating at a pace of sixty a week.

Observers wondered if it was too much too soon. Braniff's strategy was in stark contrast to its competitors, who moved with greater caution into new markets. Which was the better approach? A *Fortune* writer called it "a calculated crapshoot." As if the risks associated with growing an airline so quickly weren't enough, economists at the same time were predicting a slowdown in the nation's economy that would have a direct impact on travel activity. "Despite the stimulus of price reductions, traffic for economic reasons will be slowing." Though some thought Braniff could weather a collapse in traffic by selling off airplanes and taking advantage of its good credit rating, the story did not play out that way. In the first quarter of 1979, the company posted a fall in earnings. The loss was attributed to escalating fuel prices, severe winter weather and start-up costs for new service.

At the same time, however, Braniff maintained its leadership position at DFW. Even after American announced plans in late April 1979 to expand services by 25 percent, Braniff was still the largest carrier at the airport with 176 daily departures (compared to American's 138). Local media headlines predicted continued success. "Braniff reveals new routes." "Braniff outlook is bright." "Braniff growing with deregulation."

By early 1980, the picture had changed, however, just after the company reported a $44.3 million loss for the prior year, followed by an additional loss of $22 million in the first quarter of 1980. Rumors of bankruptcy floated about while the company's chairman continued to defend the airline's strategy and to express optimism for the future. Braniff was still "on course," he insisted. Of course, Braniff was not alone in feeling the pinch of higher fuel prices. Other airlines were experiencing declining profits due to rises in jet fuel, leading some—including Braniff—to attempt to restore profitability through the sale of airplanes, employee layoffs and cutbacks in employee salaries. But Braniff was among those hardest hit. According to a DFW Airport executive administrator, "[Braniff] took a bigger bite of the pie after deregulation and they probably could have done all right if everything hadn't hit at once—fuel price increases, inflation and the economic downturn."

The end seemed near when Braniff posted a record $160.6 million loss in 1981, almost half of which came during the final three months of the year. An accountant's statement was issued stating that the airline might not survive. In early March the company's employees were notified that their paychecks would be cut by 50 percent because of a cash shortage. The company reported additional losses totaling $41.4 million for the first quarter of 1982. The next major announcement was the one most dreaded: the airline was shut down. Hand-printed signs put up at DFW Airport announced the suspension of operations: "BRANIFF is temporarily suspending operations. We apologize for any inconvenience we have caused you. Passengers holding reservations on Braniff should make alternate reservations with other airlines." But that wasn't the final word that people would hear, according to Braniff officials. Chairman and President Howard Putnam said, "We'll be back, whether under the name of Braniff or someone else's."

For DFW Airport, Braniff's bankruptcy meant both a vacancy in the $66 million headquarters complex and a potential loss of up to 325,000 enplaned passengers per month. As it turned out, new carriers moved into the DFW market to fill the void, and by 1982, six new airlines had begun service at DFW—though not all showed up as a result of Braniff's fall. Trans World had begun service earlier, followed (after the bankruptcy) by United, Northwest, Midway, Jet America and Transamerica. At the same time, most of Braniff's routes had been—and would continue to be—served by other DFW-based carriers, lessening the blow for passengers and cargo handlers. The following year, when Continental became the second major airline based in Texas to file for bankruptcy, DFW was impacted only slightly. With only three daily flights at DFW, the losses were much greater at other points in the company's system. For the first time since opening, DFW could boast service by the ten largest U.S. carriers and could claim title to the nation's fourth busiest airport in terms of domestic passengers boarded.

FISCAL YEAR 1983 was characterized by DFW officials as the "Year of Recovery" for the airport. The Braniff bankruptcy, coupled with the recession and traffic controllers' strike, had not boded well for any airport and particularly not for the airline's home base. Braniff had given up one of the airport's four terminals, 150 landing slots, $600,000 a month in landing fees and $21.6 million in rent. Because the airline was in bankruptcy proceedings, the company retained control of its facilities while it reorganized—without having to pay rent.

In the spring of 1983, Chicago-based Hyatt Corporation offered to invest cash in the bankrupt Braniff International Corporation to help the airline re-establish passenger services. In a deal arranged by pilots of the former airline, the hotel company would receive a significant share in the reorganized company in exchange for a sizable investment on Hyatt's part. Given that a fair number of the Braniff fleet already had been liquidated and that airport space and landing rights had been transferred to other carriers, there were many questions regarding the feasibility of the arrangement. Battling an approaching deadline for filing a reorganization plan, Braniff officials labored furiously to work out a deal that would get the grounded airline back in the skies.

After creditors rejected Hyatt's original offer, a second proposal quickly was developed and presented. When the details could not be nailed down, Hyatt withdrew its offer and Braniff filed a reorganization plan which called for the creation of a small ground-service and maintenance concern and the liquidation of the rest of the airline's assets. The door was left open to the possibility of resumed flight operations only if an acceptable offer was made within a specified period of time. In the meantime, DFW officials arranged a plan to assume direct control over Braniff's space at the airport and to lease out the headquarters building, hangar, flight kitchen, cargo building and terminal gate space.

In mid-May, when Hyatt revived its offer to help Braniff become a domestic carrier with thirty planes and about 2,000 employees serving approximately twenty destinations, a sense of hope was restored. On the anniversary of the bankruptcy announcement, Braniff declared that its board of directors had approved a plan under which Hyatt would invest up to $70 million to return the airline to service by October. The agreement came just in time to avoid a deadline in U.S. Bankruptcy Court. When the airline's creditors again refused the proposal, Hyatt sweetened the pot by 20 percent, hoping to gain approval. Following considerable debate among Braniff's creditors and the resignation of the airline's two top officials, the creditors finally reached agreement to go, clearing the way for the company to file an amended plan of reorganization with the Bankruptcy Court. Following the court's approval of the 170-page document, Braniff was ready to resume operations. A new set of "flying colors" was unveiled late in November at a ceremony attended by several hundred people at the company's headquarters where the first repainted jet was christened. Company officials announced that flights would begin in about six weeks.

"A REMARKABLE TEN YEARS" was the theme for the airport's tenth anniversary. Remarkable indeed. DFW had become the second busiest airport in the country (behind only Chicago's O'Hare) and the sixth busiest airport in the world, served by thirty-seven domestic airlines and five foreign-flag carriers. Operating twenty-four hours a day, seven days a week, the airport provided direct access to almost 150 U.S. and more than twenty international destinations on three continents. Passenger traffic had doubled to 23 million, with international traffic up 120 percent. More than 50 percent of all air passengers and 60 percent of all domestic cargo in Texas occurred at DFW Airport.

A tenth anniversary celebration sponsored by the North Texas Commission was held during the week of January 9-14, 1984. The week-long celebration began with a formal ceremony on Monday, followed by special recognitions of air cargo, international travel and airline passenger traffic on succeeding days. A highlight of the ten-year celebration was the creation of the J. Erik Jonsson Aviation Award for "contributions to aviation in the Dallas-Fort Worth Metroplex." The award, of course, was a tribute to its namesake, the former Dallas mayor and co-founder of Texas Instruments Inc. Jonsson had been involved in the development of DFW Airport from the beginning. He was mayor of Dallas in 1964 when the CAB sent the original telegram to Dallas and Fort Worth telling them to select an airport site together. He chaired the interim airport board in the 1960s and later served as the first chairman of the official DFW Airport Board. Through the award, the 82-year-old Jonsson was recognized as "the man most responsible for bringing diverse and competitive interests into a cohesive unit that literally worked miracles in making this airport a reality."

The first award was presented to Henry "Hank" Newman, the former FAA administrator of the Southwest Region who had been instrumental in moving the DFW Airport project forward, particularly in situations involving the federal government. As noted in the ten-year anniversary program, "Through thick and thin as DFW Airport began to take shape, Hank Newman was always there cutting through federal red tape when necessary to help remove obstacles. Or he was making speeches or visiting with local community groups explaining the project and what it would mean to the area. . . Henry L. Newman is the ideal candidate to receive the First Annual J. Erik Jonsson Aviation Award."

TEN

Achieving Greatness

✈

*The strategy was to run the
airport the same way any well-managed
business would be run—putting customers first*

As DFW International Airport entered its eleventh year of operation, some $270 million in construction work was underway on still more expansion and improvement projects. When Executive Director Ernest Dean was asked when the airport would be completely built, his response was, "Probably never." As needs grew, so would DFW. To ensure future growth—and to capitalize on DFW Airport as a premier development asset—the cities and chambers of commerce of Dallas and Fort Worth, the airport board and the North Texas Commission authorized a study for a "DFW Airport Strategy—Year 2000." It was particularly important in a deregulated environment that these entities work together to secure optimum domestic and international airline service for the airport. It was also important to enhance awareness of the public and business community of the significance of aviation to the area's future progress.

DFW's partnership with local business and community leaders was critical in securing access to international markets. Local leaders assisted airport officials in addressing the economic,

For example, negotiations to modify the bilateral aviation agreement between the U.S. and Japan were required before American Airlines could be granted authority to fly between DFW and Tokyo. Congressional representatives worked with airport board members and local business leaders for three years to create the opportunity for the new service, which was finally inaugurated on May 21, 1987. That same sense of teamwork resulted in DFW's selection as one of two new U.S. gateways, providing passengers convenient, time-saving service to the Far East through DFW.

Providing international cargo services also was a priority for these partners in progress. Airport officials worked with the local international trade community to design the DFW Community Cargo System (CCS), an electronic communications network that linked all elements of the trade community. The new system provided shipping information that was available to transportation companies, brokers, importers/exporters and U.S. Customs, expediting deliveries of international cargo shipments. DFW administrators prided themselves on the positive relationships they had developed with local federal inspection agencies because it was those kinds of partnerships that allowed DFW Airport to maintain its reputation as one of the nation's most efficient ports of entry.

As a symbol of DFW's success in becoming one of the finest inland airports in the world and to reflect its changed status, board members voted to change the airport's name from DFW Regional Airport to DFW *International* Airport. According to Dean, the change "acknowledged the preeminence the Airport had attained as a hub for domestic and international trade, as the catalyst in furthering economic prosperity throughout North Central Texas and as a traveler's 'Passport to the World.'"

AFTER A TWENTY-TWO month hiatus, Braniff was back in business in March of 1984 with a 23.4 percent load factor (the number of seats filled) during its first month. To regain customers, the airline gave travel agents free and discounted tickets, removed certain travel restrictions and aggressively marketed cut fares. After three months in the air, the airline was still a long way from the 50 percent capacity the company needed to break even. Industry observers expressed concern that the carrier again was stumbling. Without significant gains in summer traffic, the airline's fate was uncertain.

By September, it was clear that the airline was in trouble. The company announced that it would lay off a quarter of its work force and essentially become a no-frills, low-fare carrier much like Southwest. The following month brought more layoffs, a two-thirds reduction in the fleet of planes, flight cancellations and the release of gates at DFW to other carriers. By the end of its first year back, the airline's survival was still questionable, but there was some hope that it would make it. The smaller size and cost savings that went along with a leaner operating structure allowed the company to hang on in a fiercely competitive business driven primarily by the cost of a ticket.

Things got worse instead of better, however, and in September of 1989, the financially strapped airline again filed for Chapter 11 bankruptcy and laid off more than half of its employees. The airline continued operations on a limited basis, with forty-six daily departures to eleven destinations (compared to a pre-bankruptcy schedule of 256 flights per day to forty destinations). Two months later, Braniff grounded its remaining flights and dismissed most of its employees. As noted in one local media report, "The high-flying Braniff that once opened routes in sixteen cities in one day and served seventy-five cities in nineteen nations at its peak had almost evaporated into the clouds." Though employees remained hopeful that "someone might buy it," this would be Braniff's last breath.

Following Braniff's initial Chapter 11 filing, Delta had become American's chief rival at DFW and announced plans to bid for the leadership position at DFW. While American claimed more than half of DFW's overall passenger activity, Delta was in the midst of a significant expansion program. The airport board had approved the issuance and sale of a $28.8 million special facility revenue bond package that would allow Delta Air Lines to finance the expansion of its hangar, passenger terminal facilities and flight schedules at the airport. In 1986, construction began on a new $18 million satellite terminal that would provide nine additional gates linked by a 650-foot-long underground pedestrian walkway to Delta's Terminal 4E. By 1991, the airline would be operating 254 flights a day at DFW and had begun construction on an $80 million facility to expand its operation.

American also announced expansion plans to meet increasing passenger demands. In 1986, the airline opened a new 11-story, $6 million operations control tower, which allowed the company to consolidate all operations under the same location. (Previously, operations management was handled in separate locations in Terminal 3E.) The new tower—the largest of its kind in the U.S. with the capacity to handle more than 800 operations daily—was part of a $305 million expansion program, which included a new U.S. Customs and Immigration and international baggage claim facility, additional parking space, ticket counters and passenger gates, and a new in-transit lounge. The international service area was the first one-stop Federal Inspection Station in the Midwest.

By 1988, American had established Nashville as its third connecting hub operation (along with Dallas/Fort Worth and Chicago), soon followed by another in Raleigh-Durham and a later one in San Juan. Clearly, the "hub" concept had caught on. The following year, when American celebrated the tenth anniversary of the company's move to DFW, it had a lot to be proud of. The airline was operating more than 2,500 daily flights to 156 destinations around the U.S. and internationally. More than 21,000 of the airline's employees lived and worked in the Dallas and Fort Worth area.

PROBLEMS ENCOUNTERED in the construction of American's new facilities led to one of the darkest moments in the airport's history. The story began when DFW Airport and American Airlines sued John W. Ryan Construction Company, charging that the company's work on projects in American's space in Terminal 2E was defective. Ryan countersued, seeking $150 million in damages and alleging that American and DFW officials interfered with the contractor and misused public bond money. (The suit was later settled out of court.) An internal investigation of the matters surrounding the lawsuit revealed "irregularities" in the administration of both these and other construction contracts.

Allegations of widespread mismanagement and improprieties on the part of airport managers led board members to ask for Executive Director Ernest Dean's resignation. It wasn't long before seven more airport executives stepped down, including the deputy executive director. A special criminal task force investigation ultimately resulted in thirty felony indictments of airport staff members and contractors. Charges included tampering with government documents, falsifying government records, felony theft and related acts. (Though Dean later was arrested on charges of accepting a gift from an airport contractor, he was not indicted.)

When the special auditor's final report was issued after a seven-month investigation, misconduct and mismanagement had been discovered in numerous areas of airport operations. Double payments for the same job, payment for work never performed or for equipment already owned, and consultant fees three times the industry norm were examples of the types of problems identified. Much of the report focused on the planning and engineering department, which was responsible for planning and overseeing construction projects. The special auditor noted "a serious deficiency in the administration" of contracts by individuals in this group. Violations of state laws related to bidding procedures and board approvals also were reported.

Another important finding was that the airport's internal audit was not functioning effectively. It was noted that although an internal auditor previously had identified some of the problems revealed in the report, the findings were ignored in an effort "to get the job done." Some of the staffers who had voiced concerns regarding the improprieties later said they were in the position of knowing about wrongdoing, while working for supervisors who didn't seem to care. "The old audit department was not allowed to be effective," an airport board auditor later said. "Their superiors told them to look at revenue (outside) contracts, and not to look at the airport management."

As the investigation was getting underway, embarrassed board members had to make some quick—and important— decisions regarding the leadership of the airport. Dean's departure had left a significant vacancy in the management ranks that had to be filled. After an emergency meeting, board members asked

Vernell Sturns, then Fort Worth's assistant city manager, to fill the role of interim executive director. Two consultants were brought in to assist Sturns and to examine DFW's financial records. At the same time, the internal investigation was going on, the FAA announced an audit of nearly $70 million in federal money used for construction of the airport since 1982.

Sturns had a big job to do, both in overhauling airport operations and in calming the fears of demoralized staff members who had to continue running the airport. A primary objective was to restore accountability and credibility. Sturns quickly instituted new policies designed to make the airport run more like the public entity that it was. He developed a new policy manual, changed contract procedures to ensure compliance with airport board policy and state laws, and created worksheets to assist board members in their supervision of airport activities.

Sturns later said he viewed his greatest accomplishment as interim director to be restoring the respectability of the airport. But getting there had not been easy. One of the greatest challenges early on, Sturns said, had little to do with the technical aspects of running an airport, but involved the "people" part of his job. Employee morale was a chief concern. Building confidence among airport decision-makers who were uncertain about their own futures was particularly challenging, Sturns later recalled. He offered the example of a young man who was taken from his office in handcuffs (in the presence of his co-workers) because he had not filed a letter that documented a construction transaction—"destroying official documents" in legal terms. Remaining staff members felt that they might be next, Sturns said, so he had to re-establish a sense of being members of a team, "to build trust and comfort in one another" and their ability to get the job done. When something uncomfortable happened, they simply had to take decisive action and move on.

Sturns used what he called "participatory management" to get everyone involved and committed to DFW's future. He held "employee roundtables" that provided employees direct contact with him, and he also spent a lot of time meeting with employees on an individual basis. Once he became knowledgeable as to the issues and problems, he worked with the staff to establish processes that "allowed us to do things in accordance with state law." Ultimately, the integrity of the administration was restored. Though the process had been painful and illegal acts were revealed, in the final analysis, Sturns said, "there was no evidence that anyone profited personally for what was going on." The DFW staff simply tried to accommodate the airlines, he explained. They saved time, he said, but violated state laws in the process.

Along with the airport staff, the airport board members had some soul searching of their own to do. Although the investigation had discovered some deliberate attempts by airport employees to deceive the board, members accepted some blame for the breakdown in airport management. At the time, Board Chair William Weatherford said that before the problems were identified, board members simply "weren't doing a good enough job." Vice Chair Erma Johnson concurred, "The board has to bear some responsibility. We thought we were asking the right questions. There seems to have been an attempt to lie to the board. Nevertheless, that doesn't let us off the hook." Acknowledging that members didn't question the truthfulness of staff reports, another board representative explained, "You don't question success." Still another said that while board appointments had been viewed by some as "political patronage jobs" with little work involved, that would have to change. A new system of checks and balances obviously was needed with board members taking a more active role.

Weatherford led the way in terms of working with the police in a year-long investigation of contract mismanagement at the airport and in redefining the board's role, making it "more responsible overnight." He later said that he insisted that board members know what was going on, rather than simply showing up once a month for votes. "That's how we got in trouble in the first place." After order was restored, Weatherford's colleagues on the board and other airport officials praised him for his commitment to the airport, to which he reportedly often devoted more time than to his own business, one of the state's largest insurance companies. He received no compensation for his work on behalf of DFW.

246 From Prairie to Planes ✈

ONE OF THE MOST IMPORTANT steps in ensuring the future success of the airport was the board's selection of a new executive director. As the interim chief, Sturns became a candidate for the top job. But in a 6-5 split along city lines, Dallas representatives outvoted Fort Worth to select Oris Dunham Jr., then deputy general manager of airports for Los Angeles. Dunham's extensive experience in airport management was cited as a critical need by those voting for him. Sturn's supporters, on the other hand, argued that even though he lacked experience in airport management, he should have a chance to continue what he had accomplished as interim director.

But there was more involved than the question of airport experience. The ever-present (though often subdued) rivalry between Dallas and Fort Worth reared its head during the deliberations over the new executive director. When Sturns was rejected, Fort Worth members were irked. So was the Fort Worth African-American community, which expressed concern that the vote had been based on race because Sturns was black and Dunham was white. The decision also drew the attention of city officials, leading a Fort Worth City Council member to mount an unsuccessful attempt to change the board's voting procedures to give Fort Worth representatives a greater voice.

In the meantime, Sturns faced a big decision. He had a job waiting for him back in the Fort Worth city manager's office, while DFW officials had made it clear to him that they would like him to remain at DFW under Dunham's leadership. Helping to finish the job he was hired to do at DFW was the choice Sturns ultimately made. He resigned his position with the City of Fort Worth and became deputy executive director at DFW International Airport on May 1, 1986.

Coming to DFW had not been an easy decision for Dunham either—particularly in light of the circumstances. He was in line to become the top executive in Los Angeles, and he had initially declined to be considered for the DFW job. But the assurances of support from DFW board members finally convinced him to consider a move east and ultimately persuaded him to accept the position. When Dunham took over, only five of the ten or so people in key management positions were still at DFW. The others had resigned as a result of the investigation. But Dunham was not to be deterred. Though he acknowledged the significant impact of the inquiry on the airport, his primary goal was rebuilding. He would do this, he said, by getting construction back on track and letting people know that DFW was still "one of the top airports in the world."

Dunham was aided in that effort by a resilient group of leaders from the two cities who had built the port on the plains in the first place. In fact, it was that very sense of spirit and enthusiasm that attracted Dunham to DFW. Early after his arrival, he noted the "can-do" attitude of his new Texas associates. "When I come up with something that fifty people in LA would tell me I couldn't do, here it's 'sure, let's get it done.' I love it. I would never get that kind of support in LA."

One of Dunham's first steps was to request and receive board approval for a review and audit of the airport's administrative structure and policies. When completed, the comprehensive management audit laid the foundation for a new structure designed to carry DFW into the next century. Notwithstanding the conflicts over Dunham's selection, the cities of Dallas and Fort Worth again had pulled together to help DFW International Airport weather the storm and emerge even stronger. According to the 1986 Annual Report, "Not since the cities of Dallas and Fort Worth teamed up to construct what is currently the fourth busiest airport in the world have airport board members and staff displayed such intense mutual interest in the future development of DFW Airport."

Despite the controversy surrounding Dunham's appointment, the two men seemed to make a good team. In announcing Sturns' new post, Dunham said that he had promised to teach Sturns everything he knew about airports if Sturns would teach him everything he knew about Texas. In fact, the partnership continued until 1990, when Dunham stepped down and Sturns was named executive director.

IN ADDITION TO SHARING the task of rebuilding the credibility of the airport, Sturns and Dunham—during their respective terms —shared the experience of heading the airport during the two most serious air disasters in the history of DFW. The first occurred on August 2, 1985, shortly after Sturns assumed the director's post. "It was 6:02 p.m." Sturns later remembered. Almost everybody had gone home and Sturns was in the process of leaving the office. A call came in from someone who simply said, "We just had an L-1011 go down." Sturns jumped in his car and drove down to the Department of Public Safety where rescue operations were already in place.

Delta Flight 191 had crashed just short of the runway while attempting to land in a severe thunderstorm. It was Texas' worst air disaster and the first major disaster to occur at DFW. Wind shear, inadequate pilot training in wind shear conditions and delayed warnings ultimately were determined to be the causes of the tragedy, which took the lives of 137 people. Federal safety investigators reported that the crew and passengers on the L-1011 jumbo jet had little warning of its perilous position. Survivors later recalled that the last words from the cockpit were "We are OK'd for landing."

In fact, the subsequent investigation showed that a DFW air traffic controller did urge the Delta crew to abort the landing. "Delta, go around," the frantic controller ordered after seeing Flight 191 emerge from the thunderstorm. But the command was not acknowledged and seconds later the plane hit the ground. (Delta later sued the U.S. government, arguing that meteorologists and air traffic controllers did not provide adequate warnings about the weather conditions. The airline asked that the government be held responsible for part of the more than $100 million Delta had paid to victims' families.)

The airport's response team received high marks for its handling of the crash. The eleven years of practicing emergency techniques in simulated disasters paid off when the time came to respond to a real one. In spite of a few glitches, including some angry media representatives who were not afforded what they viewed as adequate access to the crash site, DFW officials later reported satisfaction with how staff members handled the myriad of tasks associated with the disaster. Internal evaluations found that the alarms sounded almost immediately, bringing police and fire crews to the scene within two minutes. The thirty-one injured passengers received immediate care. On the down side, identification of the victims took longer than usual because of the extensive burns on some of the bodies. Additionally, traffic jams created problems on State Highway 114, just north of the crash scene, resulting in police and fire units from the surrounding area being delayed until traffic was re-routed to mitigate the tie-ups.

An official investigation of the airport's crash preparedness was conducted by a team of federal experts who focused on detection and reporting of weather conditions, possible physical obstructions to aircraft and the execution of emergency plans. The safety evaluation team visited DFW a week after the crash, finding that the airport met or exceeded all federal safety standards. Overall, the airport's ability to respond to emergencies was rated as "excellent." At the same time, the National Transportation Safety Board noted that some communications problems identified during its investigation of the crash should be corrected.

The recommended adjustments were made and tested just three short years later. On August 31, 1988, Delta Flight 1141 crashed at DFW at 9:03 a.m. Nineteen of the ninety-seven passengers and crew of seven were killed. Just after takeoff the plane crashed back to the runway, split in two and exploded into flames before sliding to a stop in a field just north of West Airfield Drive on the airport's southwest side. An exhaustive study by the National Transportation Safety Board concluded that the aircraft had been improperly prepared for takeoff.

This time, the DFW emergency response team did a "magnificent" job handling the disaster, according to crash investigators. An eleven-member fire and rescue committee, organized by the National Transportation Safety Board, left the scene with the chair of the committee praising workers for "one of the best rescue operations I've ever seen." DFW's Department of Public Safety and selected officers later were honored with the American Association of Airport's Executives' Award for Valor and the International Association of Fire Chiefs' Benjamin Franklin Award for extraordinary lifesaving and heroism associated with the crash of Flight 1141.

The airport's Public Information unit also was recognized for effectively managing crisis communications and for helping the news media report the story of the crash. Reporters from outside the area were particularly impressed with their efforts. "You hear about how friendly Texans are," an aviation reporter who had flown in from Germany said shortly after his arrival at the crash scene. "That has been certainly true to helping the media report on this accident." Airport staff members ran shuttle buses for reporters to the crash site, set up mobile phone lines, and provided refreshments and sun shelters. An ABC affiliate noted, "We do disasters all over the country. Rarely do you find people this prepared and this organized. On a scale of one to ten, I'd give this a nine."

Because DFW was one of only two major U.S. airports to suffer multiple air disasters involving commercial jetliners, airport officials were concerned that DFW's reputation for safety would be diminished by the second crash. But aviation experts reportedly viewed the occurrence of the two incidents at DFW to be unrelated to the airport. At the same, these and other air disasters raised concerns nationally about the need for enhanced radar systems that would provide earlier warnings of hazardous weather conditions and thus reduce the risk of accidents.

Following the crash of Flight 191, DFW Airport was listed among fifteen national facilities approved to receive a Doppler radar system. However, the new technology would not be installed until 1992 and even then, there were many other airports that wanted the systems but would not get them because of cuts in the federal budget for air traffic safety systems. When combined with concerns about inexperienced and overworked air traffic controllers, the picture of air safety was a bit bleak. The more crowded skies created by deregulation put safety high on the list of issues claiming the attention of airport operators.

Preparing for such a monumental disaster as a commercial airplane crash is, of course, incredibly difficult because of the unpredictable nature of such things. Len Limmer, the director of public safety, had had no previous experience himself with airplane crashes. Nor, he found, could he hire anyone who did. Airplane crashes are such rarities that few professionals who have spent a life-long career in aviation ever have had occasion to deal with them. "I was hiring twenty-year people who had never experienced a plane crash," Limmer later recalled.

Searching for a way to remedy this inexperience, Limmer found an answer when shortly after assuming his position at DFW a commercial airplane crashed with great loss of life at Logan International Airport in Boston. Limmer suddenly realized that he should hurry to Boston himself to see how officials there reacted to the situation. He was there by pre-dawn hours on the day following the crash. When he returned to Dallas he felt far more confident in developing an emergency plan for DFW. And he also realized that his other security personnel should have the same experiences. To achieve this, Limmer identified a series of "go-teams"—small teams of individuals under his supervision who would be prepared to drop whatever they were doing at whatever time and visit the site of the next commercial air crash in the United States. Through this procedure, over the years DFW's security and rescue officers achieved considerable experience at the sites of airplane crashes.

Limmer's experience led him to a further step. He realized that the possibility of an airplane crash—in the unfortunate chance that one should happen—just off the airport property rather than on the property was high. As a result, he began a series of annual disaster drills with the four adjoining cities—Euless, Irving, Grapevine, and Coppell—so that all parties would be prepared for such a disaster.

Projections that DFW could become the first U.S. airport to top one million takeoffs and landings annually led the FAA to begin construction on two new control towers at DFW in 1991. When the two new towers were dedicated three years later, DFW became the only airport in the world with three control towers. The new facilities enabled DFW's east and west runway systems to operate like separate airports, enhancing overall safety while expanding capacity.

Congestion at DFW also was relieved with the development of Alliance Airport, a city-owned industrial airport, which opened in Fort Worth in 1989. Operated by The Perot Group, it was the first major airport in the world designed solely for business and industrial aviation. The 400-acre airport was a public/private partnership, with land and infrastructure provided from private sources and most of the equipment and technical support provided by the U.S. government. Designed as a center for commercial and industrial development, the airport was to be surrounded by office towers, manufacturing complexes and residential neighborhoods.

Soon after the facility's opening, AMR Corp., the parent of American Airlines, announced that it would build a new $480 million maintenance base at Alliance—another giant step, many believed, toward Dallas and Fort Worth becoming the nation's aviation capital. By the end of its first year of operation, Alliance had become a model for other industrial airports. With an international airport nearby, a major highway on one side and a railroad distribution center on the other, Alliance offered quicker and greater access to air transportation services than traditional air cargo operations. The new facility, along with Addison Airport, a general aviation center located just north of Dallas, played an important role in relieving traffic congestion at DFW.

INTERNATIONAL PASSENGER traffic grew along with the airlines, with international demand expected to drive DFW Airport's future growth. With a trend toward more open travel policies in an increasing number of nations, things could only get better, it seemed. As a sign of DFW's growing importance as an international hub, the U.S. Department of Transportation selected American Airlines as the third U.S. airline to serve Australia. The company inaugurated service to Sydney, Australia, and Auckland, New Zealand, in February of 1990. The DOT also authorized American to fly between DFW and Calgary, Edmonton, and Alberta, Canada.

Following the demise of Eastern and Pan Am, American picked up many of the routes left vacant and quickly became a dominant player in the Latin American market as well. In 1994, with American's new service to Sao Paulo, Brazil, Metroplex passengers gained direct access to South America. The number of international destinations served by DFW more than doubled between 1990 and 1995, reaching a total of thirty-three. Mexico remained the number one destination for travelers at DFW, followed by Europe, Canada, Central and South America and the Far East.

By 1997, the number of international destinations had climbed to thirty-eight, with DFW's foreign flag carriers increasing flight frequencies to major international centers of world commerce. Future priorities in the international market included direct access to London's Heathrow and expanded routes to Japan, Taiwan, mainland China and new locations in Mexico and Canada. In addition to upgrading international travel offerings, the new services would yield significant economic benefits for the North Texas economy. For example, the addition of a non-stop flight between DFW and London's Heathrow by a foreign flag airline would contribute an estimated $200 million annually to the region's economy. One new route to Japan could generate more than $700 million additional economic activity per year.

DFW's Foreign Trade Zone was expanded from 200 to 2,500 acres, placing it among the top airport zones in the world. By 1992, the zone was processing $110 million worth of domestic and international merchandise with the help of 4,000 employees. The later ratification of a free trade agreement between the U.S., Mexico and Canada meant even greater activity. No entity stood to gain more from the North American Free Trade Agreement (NAFTA) than the Dallas-Fort Worth area, which was the center of a new $6 trillion market including 360 million consumers. Not only was the NAFTA Labor Secretariat headquartered in Dallas, but the NAFTA Center that facilitated trade among NAFTA partners was located at DFW Airport. As a result of the agreement, DFW became a premier hub of distribution to Mexico.

DFW's intermodal distribution benefits placed it among the top centers of distribution in the nation. Specifically, a total of 98 percent of the U.S. population can be reached via truck or rail from DFW within forty-eight hours; area rail lines connect with many North American cities and an expanding number of Mexican markets; the area is served by major highways, rail lines and general aviation and reliever airports; and the airport offers service to all major North American markets in less than four hours.

In 1995, almost two-thirds of all Texas cargo passed through DFW, with the airport claiming 30 percent more in total cargo volume than the next five airports in Texas combined. Japan remained DFW's top trading partner, with a 25 percent share of the airport's total trade. DFW's top trading commodities included electrical machinery, nuclear machinery, medical equipment, aircraft and spacecraft, chemical products, precious metals and stones, clocks and watches, pharmaceutical products, base metal products, toys, games and others. After international market growth was forecast to outpace domestic U.S. market growth, DFW officials began to plan for a new international cargo facility.

As an international gateway and one of the busiest airports in the world, DFW had to deal with myriad problems resulting from millions of people moving through the facility every year. Drug raids were necessitated by the increasing amounts of drug trafficking. In 1984, a nationwide campaign was launched by the U.S. Customs Service to help combat the growing problem. Drug-sniffing dogs and more frequent searches were part of the effort to reduce drug trafficking through the airport. In subsequent years, the efforts of DFW's Department of Public Safety, working with Drug Enforcement Task Forces, would result in numerous arrests, the confiscation of millions of dollars worth of drugs and the seizure of cash and other assets associated with illegal drug traffic.

Drugs weren't the only thing people attempted to smuggle through the airport. For example, in 1984, DFW led the nation in the number of travelers caught carrying concealed guns, with 391 guns confiscated during the year. At the same time, an increasing number of terrorist threats throughout the world raised concerns regarding airport safety and led to stepped-up security efforts at airports worldwide. After a 1985 episode in which a lapse in security surrounding a visit by then U.S. President Ronald Reagan led to the resignation of DFW's chief public information officer (who released information on the location of the President's plane), security measures at the airport were fine-tuned. When the Prince of Wales arrived at the airport the following year for a four-day visit to Texas, security was tight. Press credentials and equipment were thoroughly checked before media representatives were admitted to an area from which they could witness the Prince's arrival in a Royal Air Force Queens Flight—the British version of Air Force One.

A spate of international airplane hijackings had occurred a few months before DFW's opening in 1974, and at that time the Federal Aviation Agency had begun requiring airports to station a uniformed officer at all checkpoints. Limmer, as public safety director, had suggested a different approach which the FAA accepted and which soon became standard for all airports. Instead of posting uniformed officers at the many checkpoints, he installed cameras and microphones that could be activated when necessary and a central monitoring room in each terminal. From this monitoring point officers could view all checkpoints simultaneously and be alert for unusual situations. Silent alarms were concealed at various locations. It was a more effective approach that permitted an effective use of personnel. DFW became the first airport in the nation to have such a system.

An incident at DFW in early 1987 demonstrated that even the most sophisticated security measures cannot prevent all problems, however. One afternoon in early January, a gunman grabbed a young boy at a ticket counter—an unsecured area open to the public—pulled a gun, forced his way through security, and demanded a plane to Egypt. After holding the boy hostage for eight hours, the gunman released him unharmed and surrendered to officials. Because of the monitoring system, officers were able to see the situation promptly and to respond simultaneously as a unit.

Even so, airport officials continued to work with tenant airlines to improve security both in the airport and on flights in and out of DFW. Following the TWA Flight 800 explosion in 1996, the FAA ordered airports to adopt new measures to help ensure passenger safety. At the same time, the White House Commission on Aviation Safety and Security recommended the installation of more effective bomb detectors, additional "sniffer" dogs, improved passenger "profiling" (to help identify "high-risk" passengers), and enhanced security screening and bag matching (to prevent unaccompanied bags from staying on planes). One result from such procedures was that passengers were spending more time in airports before departures—especially on international flights.

TO ENSURE THE AIRPORT'S long-term success, DFW officials were challenged to find ways to reduce spending while at the same time improve operations. The strategy was to operate the airport the same way any well-managed business would be run— putting customers first. The focus at DFW was on enhancing air service, encouraging business development, expanding international opportunities and building the airport's reputation as the "Aviation Gateway to the 21st Century and beyond."

Technological improvements helped make it happen. For example, a new computerized pavement maintenance management system upgraded DFW's airfield operations. A state-of-the-art automated access control system provided tighter security throughout terminal facilities by preventing unauthorized entries into aircraft operations areas. And a new computerized parking control system, which tied license plate numbers to ticket numbers, improved customer service by making it easier to accurately assess. Additionally, new curbside signage and intra-airport telephones assisted travelers in locating ground transportation services and parking facilities. Later, the introduction of a new state-of-the-art air traffic control system, which coincided with the opening of a seventh runway, helped reduce air traffic delays—and save DFW air carriers millions of dollars in the process.

In other efforts to reduce costs, the airport board authorized a refinancing of outstanding joint revenue tax-exempt bonds, allowing DFW to save millions of dollars in interest payments. For example, in just one transaction, new bonds were issued at a lower fixed rate that saved the airport $57 million. Some of that savings was passed on to DFW's airline partners in the form of lower operating costs. The airport board also created the non-profit Airport Facility Improvement Corporation (FIC), which could issue tax-exempt bonds for financing airport improvement projects. The FIC was involved in the financing of such projects as American Airlines' expansion of Terminals 2E and 3E.

Another innovative cost-cutting initiative involved the reorganization of the Airport Development Department. The new approach allowed DFW to involve more local and Disadvantaged Business Enterprise companies while at the same time reducing contract costs. This new approach also demonstrated board members' commitment to promote cultural and racial diversity throughout the organization. Erma Johnson, who in 1987 became the first woman and the first African-American woman to serve as chairman of the airport board, played an instrumental role in enhancing opportunities for woman and minorities at DFW. Johnson, who was vice chancellor of human resources for the Tarrant County Junior College, led an effort to improve minority representation through the establishment of an annual minority and female business enterprise workshop designed to provide opportunities for contractors and suppliers to become familiar with the airport and its operating procedures.

One financial matter than befuddled airport managers involved intra-airport transport. Although AIRTRANS reliability had increased significantly over time, ridership had experienced a steady decline, falling 50 percent in the five years from 3 million passengers to 1.5 million. By 1984, airport officials were worried enough to hire outside consultants who, they hoped, could figure out why people were opting for other transportation alternatives. One factor, they knew, was the "hub and spoke" system many airlines had set up at DFW, allowing them to keep passengers (instead of delivering them to other carriers) until they reached their final destinations, thus reducing the need for transfers within terminals.

In 1986, airport board members decided to drop the 50-cent charge to ride AIRTRANS. Although cost didn't seem to be a big factor in declining ridership, it had been the subject of numerous complaints from airport visitors. In fact, it ranked right up there with the dollar-bill changer in terms of complaints received. The fee also did little to offset the loss of $800,000 that was generated by AIRTRANS each year. After the fee was dropped, the airlines agreed to a modest increase in landing fees to help cover the approximately $1 million a month operating cost of the system.

MANAGING CHANGE—the "buzzword" of the business world in the 80s and 90s—certainly was an overriding theme for the aviation industry. A quote from DFW's 1990 Annual Report characterized the operating environment and captured the mood in Dallas and Fort Worth: "Today, airports exist in a world of change: innovation in the transportation industry, national and international events, deregulation, new trade alignments, mergers of airlines, fluctuating fuel prices, air traffic congestion, shifting passenger and security demands, and environmental concerns." The result of all this was one of the toughest times ever in aviation history.

Deregulation particularly had created a competitive environment that forced airlines to reduce fares and make flying more affordable for more travelers. It also created a change in how airlines—and airports—operated. After launching its first official "hub" operation at DFW in 1981, American had changed the face of passenger traffic at DFW. An airport that had been designed primarily to serve local passengers suddenly was serving far more connecting passengers. While the hub concept allowed the airlines to increase market share, it also required changes in airport facilities to accommodate passenger needs to move quickly between flights. The long terminals at DFW that had been designed to allow local passengers to park close to their gates had become inconvenient at best for connecting passengers who often had to walk long distances between gates and sometimes to another terminal.

At the same time, passenger traffic was growing at almost incredible rates. In the ten years from 1978 to 1988, passenger boardings had increased from 275 million to 450 million. Increased flight delays and stepped-up demands for runway space challenged airport officials to assuage airline executives who complained that the system was growing too slowly to accommodate their needs. While DFW was affected less than most major airports, initially because of ample runway space with still more under construction, the writing was on the wall. If DFW officials didn't start planning for the future, they soon would encounter the record delays already being reported at some of the country's busiest airports. It was clear that the master plan developed for DFW in 1967-68 would require significant updating. Airfield development became a priority, including the construction of additional runway and taxiway complexes, roadway infrastructures and real estate development.

As interim director, Sturns had started the ball rolling. Since the airport's opening, there had been so much attention on finishing the projects outlined in the original plan, he said, that little attention had been paid to reviewing—and revising—the master plan for airport development. Sturns recognized that it was time for a new "master plan" to accommodate the changing conditions brought about by deregulation, and he initiated discussions with the FAA about updating DFW's facilities. Dunham continued this work and, very soon after he arrived at DFW, asked the airport board to update the master plan. The result was a new Airport Development Plan (ADP) that would serve as the foundation of DFW's future development, with built-in flexibility that allowed for changes as required by operating conditions and new regulations.

In brief, the plan called for a $3.5 billion expansion that included two new runways, a new terminal and lots of other improvements. The stated mission was "to plan, provide, maintain, operate and regulate airport facilities to promote the growth of the Metroplex economy, and the development of the airport to its maximum potential, accommodating future changes and providing for future passenger needs." Funding for the ADP would come from five existing sources, including Federal Grants-in-Aid; internal cash flow; Joint Revenue Bonds; Special Facilities Revenue Bonds; and Airport Facilities Improvement Corporation (FIC) Bonds. No local tax dollars would be required to implement the new plan.

The FAA's involvement in DFW's expansion indicated that the airport was expected to play an important role in the future of aviation. FAA Chief of Staff Michael T. Goldfarb said, "DFW is in the forefront of airport development in the United States, and quite frankly, the FAA's interest in DFW stems directly from the fact that Dallas/Fort Worth Airport ranks. . . Number One in terms of its impact on the national aviation system. That means the effect of Dallas/Fort Worth on the national air transport system could not be greater." Fortunately for DFW, the FAA put its money where its mouth was and committed $100 million from future budget authority for the purpose of constructing a major taxiway and terminal apron system on the west side of DFW airport. This award represented the largest discretionary commitment of funds in the history of the FAA.

Phase I of the ADP study addressed the terminal facility needs of American Airlines, then DFW's largest carrier and accounting for more than 60 percent of the airport's enplanements. The report recommended developing a new west side terminal and relocating American Airlines to the west side, along with the renovation and expansion of existing terminal space. Other Phase I projects included a new aircraft rescue and firefighting facility; the construction of an East Air Traffic Control Tower; the expansion of American's maintenance complex and expanding the cargo area.

Phase II examined airspace, airfield, terminal, ground transportation, land use, environmental and financial concerns for the future needs of DFW. The plan provided the foundation and direction for planned developments, which included new runways, new terminal buildings, new underground "people-movers," redesigned parking facilities and new access highways. The plan specifically addressed the need for additional runway capacity to accommodate increased flight frequency resulting from both the use of smaller aircraft and a hub-and-spoke system of operation. By 2010, passenger enplanements at DFW were expected to double. To meet the anticipated increases in passenger demand, the Plan proposed two additional north-south air carrier runways that would provide capacity for 330 operations an hour in visual conditions and 240 operations an hour during bad weather. Runway 16/34 East would be 8,500 feet long and located 5,000 feet to the east on the existing east side runway. Runway 16/34 West would be 9,760 feet long and located 5,800 feet west of the existing west side runway.

The ADP also called for significant improvements in the existing passenger terminals used by DFW's two major "hubbing" airlines—American and Delta. The airside terminal functions would be separated from the landside functions, providing for aircraft parking on both sides of the terminal concourses. As proposed, this reconfiguring would require two complete terminal complexes on the east and west sides, respectively. Each complex would accommodate up to 62.8 million passengers annually with about 100 gates.

The ADP also predicted an increase by 2010 of 10,100 more vehicles visiting DFW during peak hours, more than doubling the peak-hour demands in 1990. Recommendations included adding one lane each way for International Parkway and improving off-airport highways. In fact, the State Department of Highways and Public Transportation already had approved the construction of two major improvements near DFW. State Highway 360 would be extended to the west of DFW and State Highway 161 would be constructed on the east. DFW proposed a new east-west connector freeway that would provide additional airport access from the surrounding area while at the same time ease traffic congestion on existing roadways.

The proposed airport expansion would take place in three phases. Phase I, from 1991-1995, would include the new east side runway and the west side terminal development. Phase II, from 1996 to 2000, would include the west side runway and begin expansion of the east side terminal. Phase III, from 2001 to 2010, would include runway extensions and the completion of terminal projects.

AS DFW CONTINUED to expand, it was important to work with the surrounding communities, which had grown increasingly concerned about the environmental impact of increased activity at DFW. Officials in nearby towns also were troubled by fears that the airport would develop the land around it for non-aviation-related purposes and, thereby, encroach on the tax base of neighboring communities. In fact, a consultant's study commissioned by the North Texas Commission to examine the issues that would influence development of the airport by the year 2000 concluded in 1984 that the airport's future could be marred by escalating noise levels and a worsening relationship with its neighbors. Going so far as to suggest that a new airport might be needed before the end of the century, consultants addressed four primary issues of concern: (1) increasing aircraft noise; (2) limited growth potential and incompatible land use in surrounding towns; (3) poor coordination between the board and cities; and (4) cumbersome decision-making processes.

Hoping to avoid such problems, airport officials worked closely with local residents and businesses to ensure that everyone affected by the airport's expansion had an opportunity to express their views regarding the impact on the environment and the region. An Airport Community Committee was established to serve as the information resource on airport developments for the surrounding cities. Working with American Airlines and the North Texas Commission, DFW officials also established the DFW Action Center to respond to public correspondence and inquiries from neighboring communities. As might be expected, most of the correspondence focused on environmental issues, including the forecasts for new runways and noise.

Under the National Environmental Policy Act of 1969, the airport was required to assess the environmental impact of the proposed development and to prepare an Environment Impact Statement prior to any action. Public hearings and an FAA review also were required. The process included a presentation by airport officials of a "mitigation plan" for compensating those adversely affected by the changes. The plans included options ranging from the acquisition of homes in certain areas to the soundproofing of homes in places less affected to "aviation easements"—a one-time payment of a percentage of the home's fair market value in exchange for the right to fly over.

Even before the new development plan was officially announced, however, airport officials had run into problems with their neighbors in the community of Southlake. The problem was primarily created by revised traffic projections caused by deregulation. When Runway 13 Right-31 Left was conceived, it was based on the airport's 1974 Environmental Impact Statement, which reported that the runway would be used only 10 percent of the time. After deregulation, however, airport officials had to revise those estimates up to meet increased needs created by deregulation. The bottom line was that instead of less than 200 flights per day, more than 500 flights per day could take off and land over the Southlake area, which lay four miles from the end of the runway. Not surprisingly, residents were not happy about what they perceived to be increased risks to health and safety. One particularly sensitive issue was that three schools lay directly in the flight paths.

As the date for opening the new runway drew near, the conflict escalated. Residents requested that restrictions be placed on the types of planes that could use the runway; airport officials argued that restricting the use of the runway would diminish its purpose. Southlake sought a court order to restrict the use of the runway until an environmental impact study could be completed. The U.S. district judge who heard the case found that residents had failed to show "an immediate harm" while the airport had demonstrated that a greater public good would be served with the additional runway, which would relieve runway congestion. The runway opened on December 4, 1986, as the case was being appealed in the courts. The lawsuit finally was resolved in 1988 with a settlement agreement that provided DFW full use of the runway as long as noise was held within guidelines set forth in the airport's 1974 Environmental Impact Statement. In exchange, Southlake would drop the suit and restrict further residential development within the flight path to the runway.

Things seemed relatively quiet after that until DFW officially announced the proposed new expansion program. In fact, the perceived quiet turned out to be simply a lull in the storm, during which opposition forces were being formed. In anticipation of the formal announcement of the Airport Development Plan, the Mid-Cities had hired an environmental attorney experienced in fighting airport expansion. City officials in Grapevine, Irving, Euless and Coppell went so far as to pass ordinances allowing them to fine the airport if it developed land in their cities without official approvals. Airport officials responded by filing suit in state court asking that the ordinances be overturned. Dallas and Fort Worth, as well as the airlines, stood in support of DFW, with all contending that the Texas Municipal Airports Act, which created the DFW airport board, gave the authority to decide how the airport would be developed to Dallas and Fort Worth. (Because the airport itself was not a municipality, it had no formal zoning authority.)

Airport officials also reminded people that the development of the airport had been "on the books" since the facility opened, noting that the original "Master Plan" included nine runways, three of which had not yet been built. The Friends of DFW, composed of former airport board members and organized to assist the airport in expansion, supported the airport's position on this issue. "I have no sympathy for those towns because the people who are shouting about it were people who moved into a place where they ought to have known better than to build a house too close to the airport," said former Board Chairman Willard Barr.

R.M. Stovall echoed those thoughts. "I can't see that they have any justification for complaining at all," he said. Particularly Irving. At the time land was being acquired to build the airport, Stovall recalled, Irving's mayor sent him a letter saying that the city of Irving wouldn't acquire the land by the airport and that it would be zoned to be compatible with the airport. "We backed off and didn't buy it. He backed off and didn't rezone, and that's why we're having the litigation today." His biggest regret, Stovall said, was that airport officials hadn't acquired more land for the airport early on. If they had done so, he said, "we wouldn't be in the squabble we are having now."

Additionally, while noise pollution was a very real concern for residents and DFW officials, the airport's impact on the area's booming economy had to be considered—particularly the consequences of *not* building. Some viewed the expansion of the airport as the "single-most important issue facing North Texas—in terms of economic growth and prosperity." If the airport stopped growing, so too would the Metroplex, many feared. The North Texas Commission released a study that showed that if the expansion were stifled, the area would lose up to 31,000 jobs and $9 billion in wages by 2010.

When public hearings were held in the early 1990s to discuss the airport's expansion, local residents were more interested in the issues of quality of life and property values than new jobs. Tempers flared during meetings that lasted up to twelve hours, with hundreds of people standing in line for microphones. Some of the opponents argued that they had planned their communities on the basis of "a good faith understanding that DFW would not violate the plans that were indicated in the airport's 1967 master plan." Others contended that the proposed new runways simply were not needed and that excess traffic could be rerouted to the area's other airports. Still more said that a new regional airport was the best solution to the increasingly crowded skies.

DFW officials argued that if the expansion was blocked, DFW would lose its reputation as a preeminent air transportation facility and would cease to serve as the economic engine that fueled the area's growth. The airport's position in this land-use fight was supported by increasing delays in flight times at DFW. For example, in just one year from 1988 to 1989, delays had increased 38 percent. Though weather had to be factored into such figures, airport congestion was becoming a real problem. In testimony before the House Aviation Subcommittee, DFW Executive Director Oris Dunham addressed the critical shortage of national airport capacity. "Airport capacity is now emerging as the weakest link in the national air transportation system and is the major constraint on the growth of our nation's air system today."

In the meantime—while DFW was embroiled in a fight with the surrounding communities—American Airlines was bulging at the seams with increased passenger traffic expected to double by the year 2000. Anticipating an indefinite delay in the proposed airport expansion, the airline announced a temporary solution to its space problem. It would spend $276 million to add ten new gates, construct a satellite American Eagle facility, build a parking garage, and make improvements to existing facilities. The two-year program gave American exclusive use of fifty-five gates in terminals 2E and 3E and the ability to add more than 100 daily flights to its current schedule of around 400. The company said it was putting the decision about a new terminal on hold until the land-use issue was resolved and the new runways approved.

That proved to be a wise call as the situation became even more contentious. Hundreds of news reports chronicled the continuing controversy between city and airport representatives.

When work actually got underway on the east-side runway site, Irving officials responded to what they perceived as a challenge to their authority by asking for an injunction to stop the activity. Just a few weeks later, city officials decided to drop the injunction suit in favor of a formal request to DFW officials to stop work on the runway. The airport board denied the request in a letter from Executive Director Sturns to Irving Mayor Roy Brown.

Sturns spelled out the airport's view on the two issues in contention: "The issue of who has the authority to regulate land use and control airport operations is non-negotiable." With respect to the second issue—whether the compensation offered property owners to mitigate the environmental impacts associated with airport development was adequate—Sturns said that while the board's mitigation proposal exceeded federal standards, he and other DFW officials stood ready to negotiate with representatives of the City of Irving on this issue. In conclusion, Sturns wrote: "The airport board cannot and will not allow the region's single most important economic asset to be held hostage and in the process place the economic future of all of North Texas at risk. The viability of our economy, the lives of the individual homeowners and the entire national air transportation system is at stake." In response, the City of Grapevine, in which DFW's four terminals were located, along with Euless and Irving, changed their respective cities' zoning from "DFW Airport District" to "GU"— government use—which effectively gave zoning authority back to the cities. DFW appealed, and while the airport's challenge to the zoning changes was pending, DFW officials presented to the FAA the reports of an environmental impact study on the two proposed runways. After reviewing all the documents, including residents' objections to the plan, the FAA approved the proposal, clearing the way for the airport to begin initial site preparation and to begin implementation of the mitigation program. Soon thereafter, however, the state district judge who heard the appeal on the zoning issue ruled that the Texas Municipal Airports Act did not clearly empower the airport board to zone its own property.

DFW officials appealed once again, this time asking the Texas Legislature to clarify the Act and specifically to determine whether the state had intended to give the cities authority over another state-created institution when the Act was written and approved by the Legislature in 1947. As written, the wording of the Act was: "The joint board shall have the power to plan, acquire, establish, develop, construct, enlarge, improve, maintain, equip, operate, regulate, protect and police any airport, air navigation facility, or airport hazard area to be jointly acquired." (Article 46d-14(c)) "Any resolutions, rules, regulations or orders of the joint board shall have the same force and effect in the territories or jurisdictions involved as the ordinances, resolutions, rules, regulations or orders of each public agency would have in its own territory or jurisdiction." (Article 46d-14(d)(5). Senator Ike Harris from Dallas sponsored new legislation, introducing Senate Bill 348 which would give DFW Airport the right to proceed with expansion plans, overriding zoning ordinances in the surrounding cities. If passed, the new legislation would amend the Texas Municipal Airports Act by prohibiting municipalities from enacting or enforcing ordinances regulating land owned by the airport. Then Executive Director Vernell Sturns noted the significance of the issue before the Texas lawmakers: "After 20 years of operation, the cities of Irving, Grapevine and Euless have passed three zoning ordinances that would—if they are not overturned in court or here in the Legislature—hamstring DFW forever—and stifle economic growth in the process. . . it simply is not workable for the world's second busiest airport to be subject to varying zoning ordinances from multiple jurisdictions."

The DFW official in charge of the lobbying effort to amend the act was Jeffrey P. Fegan, then director of planning and engineering. It was a "gut-wrenching experience," Fegan later would recall. The stakes were high, of course. Without the new legislation, there would be no further development at the airport. The lawmakers had the power to decide whether DFW would maintain control of airport property or, as Fegan put it, "be subject to small-time politics for the rest of our existence." The DFW lobbying team, which included DFW attorney Kevin Cox, talked to every legislator in the state. When the bill finally came up for vote, it was a dramatic time. Soon it was clear, however, that DFW's lobbying efforts had paid off. The measure passed the Senate with an overwhelming margin and received the same wide-spread support in the House.

Five years after the controversy began, then Texas Governor Ann Richards signed into law a bill amending the Texas Municipal Airports Act, giving airports—not the cities in which they are located—the authority to make developments. Changes would still be subject to the approval of the FAA. Almost before the ink was dry, DFW went to work on the construction of the first new runway, which was expected to take three years and $300 million to build. (After the passage of the new law, the state Supreme Court set aside the lower court's ruling on the zoning issue and told the court to reconsider its decision in light of Senate Bill 348. The ruling came in early 1995, with the judge finding that the law giving the airport authority to zone land on its property and expand without the cities' approval was constitutional.)

As runway development continued, DFW provided affected residents with what was believed to be the most generous mitigation program in aviation history. Airport officials also introduced programs to protect the environment, including a recycling effort, the development of new wetlands in areas disrupted by construction, and a unique soil-cleaning program to extend the use of airport property. An innovative noise-monitoring system designed to monitor aircraft operating in the Dallas/Fort Worth area also was installed. The new technology helped airport managers monitor noise levels in the area and address residents' concerns.

Ironically, just when DFW was ready to get going, the airline industry was slowing down. Operating in an increasingly competitive environment, carriers were struggling to keep up with expenses, not the least of which were airport fees for rent, landing and other costs. Although DFW enjoyed generally good relations with the airlines and particularly its largest carrier American, it had to consider the impact of asking its tenant airlines to assume debt for the 1997 $5.5 billion expansion program. The real question was whether the plan developed six years earlier—when the airlines were more profitable—was too ambitious in the new market. If the airport didn't keep growing, it could lose business. If it grew too fast, it could be strapped for cash. As airport officials pondered their options, it was clear that plans for the new west terminal intended for American would not be revived any time soon. The terminal construction was put on hold, as were other expansion projects. As a result, the $3.5 billion expansion plan was revised to reflect a more conservative $1.2 billion budget.

ELEVEN

Open Skies Ahead

✈

DFW: The world's airport of choice.
Jeffrey P. Fegan

The year 1995 brought DFW a new executive director and a new flight plan. When Vernell Sturns announced he was stepping down in February of 1994, the airport board chose Jeffrey P. Fegan, the young but already experienced aviation expert, to take the helm. Fegan had joined DFW ten years earlier as chief planner. Ironically, planning was something Fegan didn't do a lot of for a while because his appointment came just six months before the criminal investigations got under way. With airport officials' attention focused on resolving the crisis at hand, planning was not a priority. As a result, Fegan's early work for DFW involved primarily monitoring progress on the original master plan.

Fegan quickly moved up at DFW, holding positions in Planning and Programming and Planning and Engineering, before being named deputy executive director of finance and administration. When he succeeded Sturns as executive director, he had the opportunity to develop a plan that would take DFW into the 21st century. After presenting his vision for DFW at a board retreat, airport board members gave him a standing ovation. His plan was called "DFW Airport: The World's Airport of Choice." As Fegan said, "DFW will be the airport of choice by creating a positive, competitive environment that exceeds our customers' expectations."

The primary objectives were to (1) drive costs down, (2) expand capacity, (3) create an excellent operating environment, and (4) enhance customer services. The overriding goal was to secure DFW International Airport's place as the undisputed leader in the global aviation community. The specifics included the creation of an exciting, congenial environment for travelers, complete with retail shops and national-brand restaurants; the development of effective cost-containment measures geared at encouraging expanded air travel services at DFW; and the pursuit of non-airline related, revenue-generating opportunities designed to reduce operating costs. The objective was to move up one notch to become the world's busiest airport by the year 2000. The strategy for getting there was unchanged: to support the continuing growth of business and economic opportunities benefiting the cities of Dallas and Fort Worth. By helping to grow the area, DFW would grow, too.

Jobs was one major ingredient which DFW Airport continued to provide the local economy. The Dallas and Fort Worth Metroplex had become the economic center of the Southwest, with the nation's third highest concentration of Fortune 500 corporate headquarters. Since the airport's opening, the Dallas/Fort Worth area had attracted the attention of business executives who identified the area as one the best places in the U.S. to conduct business. J.C. Penney, GTE Telephone Operations, Fujitsu America and MCI were just a few of the organizations that in recent years had chosen the Metroplex as the site of new facilities, with all noting the proximity to a major international airport as one of the principal factors in their choice of a business location. Even more recently, high-tech companies such as Intel, Nokia, National Semiconductor and Primeco started moving into the area. A 1996 study by Arthur Anderson & Co. listed both Dallas and Fort Worth among the top three cities for foreign relocations.

In 1994, United Parcel Service had completed a new $21 million regional cargo hub at DFW. The new 250,000-square-foot facility, which was capable of handling 25,000 packages per hour, created new jobs for hundreds of workers. The next year, Emery Worldwide opened a new 55,000-square-foot freight terminal at DFW, significantly increasing opportunities in cargo. In 1997, UPS began a $7.8 million expansion program to accommodate projected growth and enable the company to almost double its processing capacity, handling up to 67,000 packages hourly—and creating still more employment opportunities at DFW.

By 1998, DFW was the largest employment center in the area, generating more than 200,000 jobs and contributing a staggering $11.2 billion annually into the region's economy. The airport's aggressive outreach to minority and women-owned businesses— which generated more than $240 million in professionals services, construction, procurement and concession contracts being awarded to M/WBE firms in 1997—was recognized at both the local and national level. Airport officials accepted the North Texas Minority Enterprise Development Committee's Outstanding Governmental Agency Award and the FAA's National DBE Program Award.

BECOMING THE "Airport of Choice" meant a primary focus on customers at DFW. Toward that end, Fegan created an airport concessions department and hired an outside professional to direct the new department on how to improve customer relations. DFW representatives also visited airports with excellent concessions to get some ideas for enhancing customer services at DFW. By 1996, more than a hundred shops and restaurants were located throughout the airport, which would later claim title to the "largest kitchen in Texas." Brand names such as T.G.I. Fridays, McDonald's, Pizza Hut and other popular eateries became commonplace at DFW. Menus ranged from "Tex-Mex" to Italian to Chinese. Specialty stores offered fine wines, designer accessories, sports memorabilia and more. Expanded coffee shops and news stands added convenience and increased customer options. The best news for customers was that the new food and beverage offerings were priced within 10 percent of "street prices." Though perhaps not the "envy of area shopping malls," as Fegan predicted, the new services were well-received by DFW passengers.

Ground transportation and parking services also were upgraded. In 1996, an additional 3,000 parking spaces were opened with the completion of a new $16.5 million, five-level parking garage located at American Airlines' Terminal 3E. In 1997, a second parking structure worth $16.2 million was opened, bringing the total number of parking spaces at DFW to more than 35,000—more than any other airport in the world. Additional shuttle parking at the north and south entrances also was added. At the same time, DFW assumed management of the airport's taxi service.

New passenger information, multilingual signage and curbside attendants also improved customer services. Helpful information about Dallas and Fort Worth greeted the more than 160,000 travelers passing through DFW every day. And, in 1996, DFW went "on-line," offering the most comprehensive airport web site in the world at http://www.dfwairport.com. Internet and e-mail access became available to passengers in every terminal via GTE Internet cyberbooths—a first-of-its-kind service.

Airport officials worked closely with the tenant airlines in their efforts to better serve customers. For the most part, the partnerships were effective. However, one customer service program (begun prior to Fegan's appointment as executive director) that ultimately did more harm than good was a project spearheaded by DFW's lead tenant, American Airlines. With the idea of better serving passengers' needs for flight information, American erected eight large dynamic signs on International Parkway at the entrance of the airport to display the airline's arriving and departing flights. This made things easier and quicker for passengers to locate their gates. Even before the signs went up, however, there were concerns that the gate information signs could cause accidents. After receiving a lengthy airline-funded report that the electronic billboards would be safe, however, then Executive Director Sturns approved the project (over the objections of both the airport's head of public safety and its chief building official).

Within a year, airport police said the signs had been the cause of nine multi-car accidents that had injured thirteen people. In each incident, drivers reported that they had been distracted by the signs. The official response from American was that the signs were a public service whose safety had been thoroughly tested. After a serious accident in late 1993 involving two California restaurant executives, airport officials urged that the signs be turned off. They were not, but airport officials put flashing warning lights just outside the toll plazas, along with caution signs and "rumble strips" in the pavement. In 1994, the two executives sued American and the airport for negligence, seeking $50 million in damages. The judge ruled that DFW was not liable for any damages because it is a governmental entity and is protected by sovereign immunity. The case against American went to trial in the fall of 1996. American Airlines also indemnified the airport.

After a six-week trial, the civil jury found American negligent for erecting the signs, and ordered the airline to pay $9.6 million in actual damages and $10 million in punitive damages to the restaurant executives. The motorist who contributed to the accident also was ordered to pay about $4.6 million. It was a program built on good intentions, but one seemingly doomed from the start. Following the verdict, the signs came down.

THE LONG-AWAITED east-side Runway 17L/35R opened in 1996, increasing landing capacity at DFW by nearly 50 percent and sending DFW on its way to becoming the busiest airport in the world. The new runway opened with a special "Run the Runway" 5K race that attracted more than 4,500 participants who traveled the runway distance to help DFW celebrate the newest addition to its airfield. The official ribbon-cutting— accomplished by the propeller of a Fina 300 Extra flown by DFW board member and veteran aerobatics pilot Jan Collmer—was followed by the first commercial landing on the runway. Dignitaries and guests welcomed Captain P.J. Kelly and her crew as American Airlines Flight 486 from Las Vegas touched down.

The added capacity made possible by the new runway meant improved air services for travelers to Dallas-Fort Worth, and it even brought a 15 percent reduction in airspace delays nationwide as well as greater efficiency in helping passengers and cargo reach their destinations. It also brought considerable savings for DFW's tenant airlines. Combined with other cost-cutting efforts, the new runway allowed DFW to reduce the cost per enplaned passenger to a quite remarkable $2.46 per person—one of the lowest rates in the nation. Over the next twenty years, the increased capacity and efficiency was expected to yield more than $5 billion in savings for DFW airlines and their passengers.

A week before the opening of the new runway, the FAA introduced a new DFW Metroplex Air Traffic System Plan that made DFW the first airport in the world capable of landing four aircraft simultaneously during good weather conditions. Designed exclusively for DFW, the new FAA system included a $40 million Terminal Radar Approach Control facility that enabled air traffic controllers to handle increased traffic more efficiently, thus reducing flight delays nationwide. It was the largest navigational system change in U.S. aviation history.

DFW's enhanced capabilities did not go unnoticed outside the Dallas-Fort Worth area. Officials in the Chicago area particularly were watching closely, concerned that DFW soon would dethrone O'Hare as the busiest airport in the world. With the added capacity provided by the new runway, DFW was one step closer to claiming the title. It seemed only a matter of time. As reported by Chicago's aviation commissioner himself, "There's no question that DFW is breathing down our neck."

BY 1997 THE AIRLINES had regained their health, with public demand for air travel at an all-time high. "Open skies" agreements with other countries, coupled with an expanded list of domestic destinations called for the internationalization of services and increased airport capacity. At year end, DFW had begun the expansion of Terminal 2W, with the intention of adding five new gates and renovating seven others. (In November 1998 Terminal 2E became Terminal A, 2W became B, 3E became C and 4E became E.) Plans for a brand new terminal also were revived, along with plans for a new state-of-the-art people mover that would link existing terminals with the new one. An eighth runway and extensions on three existing runways also were on the table.

In the same year, total operations (takeoffs and landings) at DFW reached over 850,000. In terms of passenger traffic, DFW ranked third in the world, serving more than 60 million passengers. Overall, DFW had twenty carriers offering service to nearly 200 destinations worldwide. Cargo had reached an unprecedented 894 million tons.

More important, however, as airport officials looked to the future, were the predicted increases in these numbers. By the year 2015, aircraft activity at DFW was expected to increase 63 percent to nearly 1.4 million. Passenger traffic was expected to nearly double, with more than 100 million passengers traveling to or from DFW Airport every year. Operations were estimated to reach 1.4 million annually, with cargo approaching two million tons.

To accommodate such growth, DFW officials had begun working on yet another plan—the "1997 Airport Development Plan Update"—which would guide DFW's growth and development well into the 21st century. The goal of the $5.5 billion expansion program was to unite the airport's vision—to become the world's Airport of Choice—with an on-going, strategic planning process. The update, which called for an increase in gate capacity by 100 percent within the next twenty years, set the stage for continued growth and prosperity at DFW—and confirmed once again what airport planners had said a long time ago: "DFW must be built to grow."

The new development plan called for major long-term improvements to the airport, plus the addition of runways, taxiways and terminals. Highlights of the expansion program were an eighth runway, a new terminal for DFW's largest tenant, American Airlines, and a people-mover train system that would transport passengers from one end of the airport to the other.

ONE ISSUE that had the potential to stifle such growth at DFW was the same issue that had troubled DFW officials since the airport's opening—Love Field. The conflict seemed never-ending. In 1986, the Department of Transportation had approved the request of Continental Airlines to fly out of Love Field, but with the stipulation that the airline be subject to Wright Amendment restrictions. Lawsuits followed, and two years later, the Texas Supreme Court upheld the ruling that Continental was entitled to use Love Field (subject to the restrictions) and said Dallas must provide the airline space to operate. This decision made no one happy. Dallas thought the courts had usurped their authority to control activities at the city-owned airport. Fort Worth was concerned that an expansion of services at Love Field would continue to drain revenue from DFW. Southwest Airlines feared the potential impact of a new competitor in the market. (Unspoken was the recollection of what had happened to Fort Worth's Greater Southwest in the 1950s and early 1960s after its very promising opening.) And Continental said it would not move to Love Field unless it could serve destinations beyond those stipulated under the Wright Amendment.

The Love Field debate reached Washington late in 1989, where a proposal to repeal the Wright Amendment was being debated in Congress. U.S. Representative Dan Glickman from Kansas had introduced a bill to repeal the amendment, arguing that the law was unconstitutional and unfairly restricted airline competition. While the proposal was still being debated in Congress, Glickman asked the FTC to study the situation, which he argued unfairly harmed his constituents in Kansas who were subjected to inflated fares as a result of the Amendment. When issued in mid-1992, the FTC's report caused quite a stir. It concluded that a weakening or repeal of the Wright Amendment would "result in more service, more competition, lower fares, and more traffic" for the region. Although the report had no direct impact on any Congressional action, it did serve as additional support for changing the law.

Needless to say, the report was not well-received by either the airlines or the airport that stood to lose the most if Love Field services were expanded. Airport spokesperson Joe M. Dealey Jr. stated, "It is the board's position that any person or organization that favors modification or repeal of the Wright Amendment is guilty of abdicating or surrendering—take your pick—DFW International Airport's leadership role and continuing emergence as an international aviation crossroads and center for economic development."

The significance of this issue to not only Dallas/Fort Worth but to the nation was captured in the report of a hearing before the House of Representatives Subcommittee on Public Works and Transportation. Committee Chairman James L. Oberstar explained the drama that had surrounded the legislation since its enactment twelve years earlier: "The subject of today's hearing is less sweeping in nature than those heard by the subcommittee earlier this year on international aviation policy, nor does it have the national policy implications of the hearings we held on the retreat of competition in this age of deregulation. But what the subject of Love Field may lack in national or international glitter, it certainly makes up for in intensity of feelings, economic consequences, and in regional and local drama. In fact, this "tale of two cities" could well have been written and scripted by Victor Hugo for all the intrigue, plots, and subplots it has spawned throughout the last several years."

While the debate continued in Washington, the cities of Dallas and Fort Worth were involved in yet another battle over the future of Love Field. When Dallas officials decided to hold public hearings on whether to ask Congress to modify the Amendment, Fort Worth filed a lawsuit to stop the action, reminding its cross-town rival that such a move would violate the original commitment of the cities to the 1968 agreement that established DFW Airport and provided the airport board with the authority to make decisions regarding commercial air carriers. The issue was resolved when the Dallas City Council agreed to reaffirm its commitment to the Amendment.

For the next few years, DFW and Love Field operated relatively peacefully. Although the Wright Amendment continued to be the topic of debate both in Texas and Washington, no action was taken to significantly affect operations at the two airfields. In 1997, however—just after DFW officials announced the development plan update and eighteen years after the Wright Amendment was first passed—the situation changed dramatically. New Congressional legislation eased flight restrictions out of Love Field, adding Alabama, Kansas and Mississippi to the list of destinations open to Love Field carriers. The new law also provided that large jets could fly anywhere from Love Field as long as they had fifty-six or fewer seats.

The city of Fort Worth immediately responded with a lawsuit in district court against the City of Dallas, DFW Airport and others, once again charging that if Dallas allowed the expanded service it would be in violation of the cities' original agreement to support the growth and development of DFW to the exclusion of other airports. City officials asked the district judge to order Dallas to enforce flight limitations at Love Field. Dallas countersued, arguing that it could not override federal law. American Airlines, which later joined Fort Worth in the suit, launched a multimillion dollar advertising campaign criticizing lawmakers for the changes and announced that its proposed $2 billion terminal was on hold until the dispute was resolved. At the same time, American also said it would begin service out of Love Field if forced to do so to remain competitive. If Dallas allowed long-haul service out of Love Field, American argued, it would breach the original DFW bond covenants, freeing it to move some flights to Love Field. DFW Airport board members said that the airport expansion program—which was designed primarily to serve American's needs for new space—was postponed indefinitely.

When marathon mediation sessions failed to resolve the dispute by the summer of 1998, American requested that the U.S. Department of Transportation change its airline certificate to allow it to fly anywhere permitted by federal law from Love Field. The airline also asked Dallas officials to provide gate space at Love Field so it could begin operations. Some thought American was bluffing about operating out of Love Field. Others viewed the possibility of American moving back to the Dallas airfield as the beginning of the eventual erosion of DFW's position in market.

On August 31, twenty-four years since American had moved all its operations from Love Field to DFW, the airline played its hand. A ribbon-cutting ceremony launched American's new Love Field service, offering fourteen daily flights to Austin. It was the "first step to destroying the hub at DFW," according to Fort Worth Mayor Barr.

Just prior to American's move to the municipal airport, the Department of Transportation had announced that it would attempt to resolve the Love Field expansion dispute by determining whether federal law pre-empted the City of Dallas' right to limit commercial air service there. Fort Worth, joined by American Airlines, responded with a request that the federal agency not get involved. The city argued that while the DOT could join in the existing litigation as a party or by filing a brief with the court, it was an unconstitutional intrusion by the executive branch of government for the agency to issue a ruling on the matter. At the same time, start-up Legend Airlines (based at Love Field) sought to have the Fort Worth lawsuit delayed until the DOT could complete its review. On September 14, State District Judge Bob McCoy refused to postpone a decision, ruling that the DOT's actions would have no bearing on the legal questions before the Court.

The complex legal battle seemed never-ending. Where it would all lead, no one knew. To those who had followed DFW Airport's progress from the beginning, the rhetoric sounded very familiar. But who could have anticipated that the same issues that clouded the opening of the airport twenty-five years earlier would continue to linger overhead? Amidst the uncertainty created by the dispute, however, DFW officials had an airport to run. With the silver or twenty-fifth anniversary just ahead, it was time to celebrate past successes and anticipate a future in which DFW was expected to become the world's busiest airport.

THAT SILVER anniversary celebration on September 22, 1998, was arranged by the person who for more than a decade had been the airport's most visible spokesperson, Joe M. Dealey Jr., director of the Public Affairs Department, who on this day was behind the scenes. At the noon-day event, held at Founders Plaza where the granite monument held the names of the first board members, three different speakers addressed separate topics—"The Past," "The Present," and "The Future." J. Lee Johnson III, a founding board member, recalled that he personally—and some of the others as well—had spent twelve years of work and planning before the airport actually opened in January 1974. Betty Culbreath, the second woman to serve as chair of the DFW Airport Board, emphasized that success had been achieved through the hard work and dedication of both Dallas and Fort Worth residents. And Jeffrey P. Fegan, executive director, spoke excitedly of the year 2015 when more than 100 million passengers would be passing through the airport each year. A vice president

DFW Airport Board Chairs

1965-1968 (interim board)	J. Erik Jonsson
1968-1975	J. Erik Jonsson
1976-1979	Henry Stuart
1980	Jack Evans
1981	Paul W. Mason
1982-1983	Rodger Meier
1984	Bob Bolen
1985-1986	William Weatherford
1987	Erma Johnson
1988-1989	Pete Schenkel
1990	Louis J. Zapata
1991-1992	William E. Cooper
1993	Bert C. Williams
1994-1995	David R. Braden
1996	Robert I. Fernandez
1997-1998	Betty J. Culbreath

J. Erik Jonsson Aviation Award Winners

Henry L. Newman	Robert S. Folsom
George Haddaway	Albert Casey
Rodger R. Meier	Bayard H. Friedman
Thomas M. Sullivan	Najeeb E. Halaby
Willard Barr	J. Lee Johnson III
R.M. Stovall	Bob Bolen

of American Airlines, Peggy Sterling, unveiled a sculpture her company had commissioned especially for the plaza, "Share the Dream," which depicted three children pretending to fly.

The statue seemed perfect for the occasion since twenty-five years ago many of Fort Worth's and Dallas' aviation pioneers had contemplated what then was called the "impossible dream." The idea of turning prairie land into a world-class air transportation center was beyond comprehension for many in those days. But the founders persevered, and by working together they and other Dallas and Fort Worth leaders turned that dream into reality. If those visionaries could be rounded up today for a visit at Founder's Plaza, one can only wonder what they would say about the incredible transformation that has taken place. It seems very likely that by listening closely as the Texas breezes carried their voices away, one just might hear them say, "We never imagined anything so great."

Notes

(Page numbers and key phrases are followed by sources for information)

Chapter One
2. "with room to spare" - DFW soon was superseded as the world's biggest airport by Montreal's airport and in the early 1990s by Denver's airport. By 1998 DFW was the world's third largest airport.
6. "business at Denver International" - *New York Times*, March 18, 1998.

Chapter Two
8. "would he ever stop?" - Roger Bilstein and Jay Miller, *Aviation in Texas*, (Austin: Texas Monthly Press, 1985), 10; Mark Sullivan in *Our Times, The United States, 1900-1925*, II, (New York: Charles Scribner's Sons, 1927), 554.
9. "never recovered from the humiliation." In 1915 Glenn Curtiss rebuilt the Aerodrome, fitted it with a bigger engine, and managed to fly it. In 1924 the Smithsonian Institution put the Aerodrome on display and declared it to be the first heavier-than-air machine that had been capable of flight.
10. "wings while in flight." The claim appears in *The WPA Dallas Guide and History*, written from 1936 to 1942, as part of the Works Projects Administration. The manuscript, edited by Gerald D. Saxon and Maxine Holmes, was published in 1992 by the Dallas Public Library, Texas Center for the Book, and University of North Texas Press. A description of McCarroll's aviation accomplishments appears on page 147.
10. "by 50,000 Britons" - Bilstein and Miller, *Aviation in Texas*, 13-14.
10. "took to the air" - "Aviation" entry, *The New Handbook of Texas*, I, 319.
10. "first day of the meet" - *The Dallas Morning News*, March 3, 1910.
11. "their admission fees" - Payne, *Dallas: An Illustrated History*, 140, 143.
11. "they wanted more" - *The Dallas Morning News*, March 6, 1910.
11. "New York, last Oct." - *The Dallas Morning News*, Dec. 22, 1910
12. "subject to heart failure" - ibid.
12. "ride back to Fair Park" - ibid., Jan. 9, 1911.
12. "three extra days" - ibid., Jan. 8, 1911.
13. "summarizing the situation" - Ibid., Jan. 9, 1911.
13. "two-day meet in Fort Worth" - Ibid. and *Fort Worth Star-Telegram*, June 4, 1967.
13. "after leaving Dallas" - Ibid. and *Fort Worth Star-Telegram*, June 4, 1967.
13. "customary way—by rail" - *The Dallas Morning News*, Jan. 9, 1911.
13. "there would be no pay" - Ibid., Jan. 11, 1911.
14. "for another meet" - Ibid.
14. "on-lookers watched" - *Fort Worth Star-Telegram*, June 4, 1967.
14. "behind the pilot" - *The Dallas Morning News*, March 24,1912, as cited by Judy Culbertson, "Birdmen, Barnstormers, and Bootleggers: Early Aviation in Dallas,

1910-1927," 13, a paper prepared for a course taught by the author in the Southern Methodist University Master of Liberal Arts Program.

15. "lost their lives" - *The Dallas Morning News*, Jan. 2, 1911.

15. "delivered to Fort Worth" - Oliver Knight, *Outpost on the Trinity* (Norman: University of Oklahoma Press, 1953), 181-82.

15. "in a landing cartwheel." - Nancy Wiley, *The Great State Fair of Texas* (Dallas: Taylor Publishing Co., 1984), 69.

16. "in a crash in California." - Henry Ladd Smith, *Airways: The History of Commercial Aviation in the United States* (New York: Alfred A. Knopf, 1942), 53-54.

16. "monoplane in times of war." - *Daily Times Herald*, March 23-31, April 1, 1912.

16. " 'make his vertical drop each day.' " - "Memorandum of Agreement," Sept. 17, 1914, between the State Fair of Texas and Lincoln Beachey, Inc., Special Collections, McDermott Library, The University of Texas at Dallas.

16. "climb out of the wreckage" - Smith, *Airways*, 35, and *The Dallas Morning News*, Oct. 23, 25, and 27, 1914, as cited by Culbertson, "Birdmen, Barnstormers, and Bootleggers," 8-9.

16. "the last flight of each day." - Contract, 1915, between Art Smith and the State Fair of Texas, ibid.

17. "without permission of the board." - *Daily Times Herald*, Oct. 20, 22, 1915.

17. "Texas, Oklahoma, and Arkansas." - *Fort Worth Star-Telegram*, June 7, 1942, and June 4, 1967.

17. "bent an axle in his landing." - ibid.

18. "for Fort Worth bearing gifts." - *Daily Times Herald*, Jan. 2, 1917.

18. "and many other items." - Ibid., Jan. 2, 8, 1917.

19. "only twenty-one minutes." - Ibid., Jan. 9, 1917.

19. "the purchase of army aircraft." - Smith, *Airways*, 38-39.

19. "the entire nation, as well." - Roger Bilstein and Jay Miller, *Aviation in Texas* (San Antonio: Texas Monthly Press, Inc., and The University of Texas Institute of Texan Cultures, 1985), 51.

19. "south of the city." - Ibid., 52.

20. "joined the Canadian forces." See individual entries for these fields in *The New Handbook of Texas*; also *Fort Worth Press*, Dec. 2,1962.

20. "at Fort Worth's training facilities" - *The Dallas Morning News*, Nov. 25, 1917.

20. "near the scene of the crash." - *Fort Worth Star-Telegram*, June 4, 1967.

20. " 'fly very low and very slow.' " - Ibid.

21. "most important military aviation center." - Ibid. and *The Dallas Morning News*, Nov. 30, 1917.

21. "for a suitable landing field." - "Above the Dallas Skyline," *Dallas*, Aug. 1925, 10.

21. "with an option to buy." - Ibid.

21. "San Diego, California, in 1913." - Ibid., Nov. 27, 1917, Dec. 20, 1917; Love Field entry in *The New Handbook of Texas*, IV, 306.

22. "in a public statement." - *The Dallas Morning News*, Nov. 25, 1917.

22. "assembled before flying." - "Westward—Dallas' Love Affair," *Dallas Times Herald* supplement, July 15, 1984, page 18, as cited by Culbertson in "Birdmen, Barnstormers, and Bootleggers," 18-19.

22. "returning to his home base." - Ibid.

22. "air at one time." - Ibid., Dec. 20, 1917.

22. "and half for evening." Ibid., Nov. 27,1917.

23. "had passed the test." - Ibid. and Nov. 29,1917.

23. "having aviation fields." - Ibid., Dec. 15, 1917.

23. "selected and marked." - Ibid.

23. " 'within a short time.' " - Ibid., Dec. 4, 1917.

23. "in the United States." - *The Dallas Morning News*, Dec. 2, 1917.

23. "for his own private use.)" - Ibid., Dec. 8, 1917.

24. "spoil their surprise attack." - Frontiers of Flight Exhibit, Love Field, as cited by Culbertson, "Birdmen, Barnstormers, and Bootleggers," 18.

24. "official recognition as an Ace." - *Aircraft Yearbook, 1919* (New York: Manufacturers Aircraft Association, Inc., 1919), 295.

24. "in front of the spectators." - Sam Acheson, *Dallas Yesterday* (Dallas: SMU Press, 1977), 290-92.

25. "in the coming years." - Smith, *Airways,* 40.

25. "transferring right away to Dallas." - Dallas *Daily Times Herald*, Jan. 2, 1919.

25. "Kelly Field in San Antonio." - Ibid. and Bilstein and Miller, *Aviation in Texas,* 54.

26. "industrial district at the site." - "Above the Dallas Skyline," 9.

26. "as a municipal flying field." - Ibid.

26. "was one of them." - Long is featured at Love Field's Frontier of Flight Museum.

26. "Dallas Aviation School at Love Field." - Culbertson, "Birdmen, Barnstormers, and Bootleggers," 21.

26. "Charles A. Lindbergh." - Ibid.

26. "a Love Field building." - Ibid., 22.

26. "just before crashing." - *Aircraft Yearbook, 1923* (New York: Aeronautical Chamber of Commerce of America, Inc., 1923), 113.

26. "mother of Love Field." - Julie Tipps, "The Early History of Love Field, 1917-1926," 5-6, an unpublished paper prepared for Southern Methodist University's Master of Liberal Arts program, Nov., 1997.

27. "on a mileage basis." - "Above the Dallas Skyline," 9.

27. "instructions for the school." - James E. White, "Aviation in Dallas, 1919-1939," 4, an unpublished paper prepared for Southern Methodist University's Master of Liberal Arts program, Sept., 1983.

27. "in Texas and Oklahoma." - *Aircraft Yearbook, 1923,* 40-41.

27. " 'We go wherever there is air.' " - "Above the Dallas Skyline," 9.

27. "wind and weather conditions." - "The Flying Center of Texas," *Dallas*, June 1926, 31.

27. "can be found at the field." - Ibid.

28. "within the next two years." Above the Dallas Skyline, 9.

28. "forty states and four foreign countries." - Ibid.

28. "cheered him at Love Field." - Culbertson, "Birdmen, Barnstormers, and Bootleggers," 23; "World Flyers Visit City," *Dallas*, Oct. 1924, 10.

29. "had become their passion." - undated clipping, *Fort Worth Press*, in W.G. Fuller Files, B46, F11, University of Texas at Dallas Aviation Collections.

29. "Woods Flying Service." - Ibid.

29. "American Airlines, was another." - *Fort Worth Star-Telegram*, June 4, 1967.

30. "starred Robert Redford." - Ibid., and Bilstein and Miller, *Aviation in Texas,* 42.

30. "in the same year it began." - *Fort Worth Star-Telegram*, June 4, 1967.

30. "Kelly Field in San Antonio." - Typescript of interview with W.G. "Bill" Fuller, "Air Transportation in Texas," B38 F1, W.G. Fuller Papers.

30. "to take care of the details." - Ibid.
31. "for him to work in." Ibid.
31. "for the remainder of his life." - Card entitled "Fort Worth Municipal Airport,"
B38, F2, and ibid..
31. "returned to San Antonio." - "William Gardiner Fuller," typescript chronology of
Fuller's career, B38, F1; and Lt. Bennett E. Meyers to Whom It May Concern, July 2,
1920, B39, F2; W.G. Fuller Papers.
32. "Mayor H.C. Meacham." - Fuller to H.S. Burwell, Dec. 7, 1926, and card entitled
"Fort Worth Municipal Airport," B38, F2, W.G. Fuller Papers.
33. "with a batch of mail." - Chas. B. Braun, "Two Years of Air Mail in Texas,"
Dallas, May 1928, 9.
33. "from all parts of the state." *Fort Worth Star-Telegram* clipping, [May 1926],
B46, F4, Fuller Papers.
33. "by New York and Chicago." Card, "Fort Worth Municipal Airport," B38, F2,
Fuller Papers.
33. "air transportation company." - Col. Paul Henderson, "Dallas Moves North!"
Dallas, May 1926, 7, 20, 21; Payne, *Big D*, 117.
34. "National Air Transport, and others." - Fred Pruter, "America's First Aerial Good
Will Tour," Dallas, April 1926, 8, 24, 25, 26.
34. "the loss of a single letter." - Charles B. Braun, "The New Transportation," ibid.,
June 1927, 19.
34. "and no time is lost." - National Air Transport, Inc., advertisement, ibid., June,
1927, 15; Chas. B. Braun, "Two Years of Air Mail in Texas," *Dallas*, May 1928, 9,
20.
35. "Texas, Oklahoma, Louisiana, and Arkansas." - (Dallas) *Daily Times Herald*,
June 23, 1927.
35. "aviation needs for years to come." - Ibid., June 24, 1927.
36. "in Oak Cliff at Steven's Park." - Ibid., July 1, 1927.
36. "to buy the facility." - Ibid., July 13, 14, 1927.
36. "new age of transportation." - Ibid., July 8, 1927.
37. "a prominent presence, too." - Payne, *Big D*, 118-19.
37. "never to be heard from again." - Ibid., 120.
38. "holiday for the occasion." - *The Dallas Morning News*, Sept. 27, 1927.
38. "until Fords have wings?" - (Dallas) *Daily Times Herald*, Sept. 28,1927.
38. "ranged from seven to fifty acres." - Ibid., March 27, 1928.
38. " 'Class A' status." - Ibid., March 16, 1928; Payne, *Big D*, 117.
38. " 'beautifully laid out for airports.' " - *Daily Times Herald*, March 17, 1928.
39. "one of the best in the nation." - Ibid., March 16, 1928.
39. "used as a training site." - Ibid., March 29, 1928.
39. "air lines and airplane factories." - Ibid., March 23, 1928.
39. "existing airports in the nation.)" - *Aircraft Yearbook*, 1930.
39. "with indecision," they warned." - (Dallas) *Daily Times Herald*, March 23, 1928.
39. "to locate at Meacham Field." - Ibid.
39. " 'enough for several years.' " - Ibid., March 30, 1928.
40. "and a free-for-all race." - "Airports and Airways," *Aviation*, April 16, 1928,
1105-1106.
40. "for the use of his office." - Ibid., May 14, 1928, 1416.

40. "five other investors." - Judith Singer Cohen, *Cowtown Moderne: Art Deco Architecture of Fort Worth, Texas* (College Station: Texas A&M University Press, 1988), 32.

41. "the brochure boasted." - A copy of the brochure is in B38, F23, Fuller Papers. See also Capt. W.H. Scott, "Texas Air Transport," *Aero Digest*, March, 1929, 62; and "Air Transportation in Texas," typescript of an interview with W.G. Fuller, B38, F1, Fuller Papers.

41. "the eventual American Airlines." - Henry Ladd Smith, *Airways: The History of Commercial Aviation in the United States* (New York: Alfred A. Knopf, 1942), 150.

42. "glider flight in the world." - *Fort Worth Star-Telegram*, June 4, 1967.

42. "in Cleveland surpassed them." - *Aircraft Year Book for 1930* (New York: D. Van Nostrand Co., 1930), 148-150.

42. "to Chicago was $96.80" - Edwena Harris, "An Air Mail Vacation," *Dallas*, Sept. 1927, 7.

42. "just a nuisance." - Ibid.

Chapter Three

43. "business center of the city." - *American City*, May 1929, 130, and April 1931, 85.

44. "transport and industrial pilots." - *Dallas*, July 1930, 8.

44. "said to be $750,000." - "Aviation in Dallas," 32, and "Status of Airports and Landing Fields," *American City*, May 1935, 13.

44. "midway airport in 1930." - Aviation Department Report, *Dallas*, Dec. 1930, 10.

44. "5:30 a.m. train to Fort Worth." - *The Dallas Morning News*, Oct. 17, 1941. "Official Routes of the Five Air Mails Now Serving Dallas," *Dallas*, July 1934.

44. "jumped to 30,000 miles." - Alvin M. Josephy Jr., editor, *The American Heritage History of Flight* (n.p. American Heritage Publishing Co., 1968), 267.

45. "with 11,053 flights." - undated card entitled "Fort Worth Municipal Airport," B38, F2, Fuller Papers.

45. "to be built until 1946." - "New Planes to Speed Up Air Travel," *Dallas*, June 1935, 6.

46. "rest rooms and baggage rooms," - Josephy, editor, *The American Heritage History of Flight*, 245.

47. "to provide the best facilities." - "New Hangar Completed," *Dallas*, March 1932, 9.

47. "providing the best possible facilities for airlines" - "Aviation Department, City of Dallas," 1952, Love Field clippings file, 1962, Dallas Public Library; and "Fort Worth Municipal Airport," [1937], B38, F2, Fuller Papers.

47. "between 1934 and 1938" - "Analysis of Municipal Airport Profit and Loss Statements," Meacham Field, B38, F30, and undated card entitled "Fort Worth Municipal Airport," B38, F2, Fuller Papers; "The Future of Airports in Cities," *American City*, May 1939, 81.

47. "barracks for enlisted men." - "Aviation," report of Dallas Chamber of Commerce aviation committee, *Dallas*, Dec. 1932, 11.

48. " 'if you never came back,' " - Carter to Weddington, March 24, 1931, B38, F2, Fuller Papers. See also the letter dated April 5, 1928, in which Carter agrees to pay for Weddington's gasoline.

48. "sent out over the air waves." - Smith, *Airways*, 283, and unidentified clipping, Sept. 14, 1930, B46, F5, Fuller Papers.

49. "Vice President John Nance Garner" - Oliver Knight, *Fort Worth: Outpost on the Trinity* (Norman: University of Oklahoma Press, 1953), 223-24.

49. " 'I speak for Fort Worth!' " - Jerry Flemmons, *Amon: The Life of Amon Carter, Sr. of Texas* (Austin: Jenkins Publishing Co., 1978), 359.

49. "true pioneers of American aviation." - Ibid., 254.

50. "only air-cooled one in the nation." *Fort Worth Star-Telegram*, June 20, 1937.

50. "Maintenance and Inspection office" - "Fort Worth Municipal Airport," [1937], B38, F2, Fuller Papers.

50. "to achieve this purpose." - Ibid., April 25, 1939.

50. " 'finest airport terminal west of New York.' " *Dallas Journal*, Oct. 4, 1940, Love Field clippings file for 1940, Dallas Public Library.

51. "278 acres with thirteen hangars." - Holmes and Saxon, editors, *The WPA Dallas Guide and History*, 389; *Dallas Times Herald*, Jan. 17, 1958..

51. "as well as surrounding areas" - *Fort Worth Star-Telegram*, Aug. 19, 1962.

52. "*Fort Worth Star-Telegram* headline." - Oct. 1, 1940.

52. "New York and Latin America." - *The Dallas Morning News*, Oct. 2, 1940.

52. "Dallas and Tarrant County line." - Ibid.

52. "proposed midway field." - Ibid., Oct. 3, 1940.

53. "at a mid-cities location." - Ibid.

53. "solely for military purposes." - Fritz-Alan Korth, "A Tale of Two Cities," senior thesis, Princeton University, April 19, 1961, page 8-9. A copy of this thesis is in the Fort Worth Public Library.

53. "from 3,500 feet to 4,500 feet." - Ibid., 11.

54. "construct the landing fields." - *The Dallas Morning News*, Oct. 17, 1941.

55. "to achieve that number." - Bilstein and Miller, *Aviation in Texas*, 94-95.

56. "before the war ended." - Ibid., 95.

56. "learned to fly the B-24 there." - Carswell Air Force Base entry, *New Handbook of Texas*, I, 997.

56. "would not be direct." - *Fort Worth Star-Telegram*, March 21, 1943.

57. "others in Dallas believed." - Newspaper articles in Feb. and March, 1943, thoroughly explore this situation. Also see Payne, *Big D*, 208-210, for a general discussion.

57. "would definitely be impacted." - *The Dallas Morning News*, March 5, 1943.

57. " 'any road now reaching Dallas.' " - Ibid., Feb. 28, 1943.

57. "it was the CAA's plan, not his." - Telegram from Carter to Woodall Rodgers, reprinted in the *Fort Worth Star-Telegram*, Jan. 11, 1943.

57. "had requested the change." - *Dallas Times Herald*, March 23, 1943.

58. " 'go home if you don't.' " - *The Dallas Morning News*, March 23, 1943.

58. "to change existing runways." - *Dallas Times Herald*, March 23, 1943.

58. " 'in after married life.' " - Dallas Morning News, March 23, 1943.

59. " 'we just don't have the answers.' " - Ibid.

59. " 'for the protection of our patrons.' " - Ibid., March 26, 1943.

59. "the committee members reported." - Ibid.

60. "Love Field to that size." - Ibid., April 1, 1943.

60. "50 percent of the benefits." - Ibid.

61. "post-war boom in aviation." - Payne, *Big D*, 211.

61. "Houston, San Antonio, and Fort Worth." - *Dallas Times Herald*, Feb. 16, 1942.

61. "2,172 acres at the site." - *The Dallas Morning News*, Feb. 15, 1948.

62. "Rock Island Railroad on the south." - *Fort Worth Star-Telegram*, Oct. 29, 1947.

62. "in funding the project." - Ibid.

63. "transcontinental flights to Midway." - *The Dallas Morning News*, Oct. 30, 1947.

63. " 'east side of Fort Worth.' " - Ibid.

64. "international flights would land." - Ibid.

64. " 'every means available to us.' " - *Dallas Times Herald*, Nov. 5, 1947.

64. "projected Midway Airport." - Ibid.

65. "development of the new airport." - *The Dallas Morning News*, Dec. 13, 1947.

65. "Tom C. Gooch as members." - *Dallas Times Herald*, Nov. 5, 1947.

65. "to abandon Love Field." - *The Dallas Morning News*, Oct. 31, 1947.

65. "what developments will be." - Ibid.

66. " 'rapid development of aviation at Dallas.' " - *Dallas Times Herald*, Feb. 11, 1948.

66. "all airlines stops at Midway." - Ibid.

66. " 'a public park into a seaplane base.' " - Ibid.

66. " 'stop the plan from being carried out.' " - Ibid.

67. "shifted to the Midway project." - Ibid.

67. "headquarters in Washington, D.C." - *The Dallas Morning News*, Feb. 15, 1948.

67. "Dallas was unsuccessful." - Ibid., Feb. 19, 1948.

67. "local funding of $11 million." - *Daily Times Herald*, March 1, 1948.

67. "since being completed in 1940." - Ibid., Feb. 22, 1948.

68. "of improvements for Love Field." - Ibid., Feb. 9, 1948.

68. "on a mission over the South China sea." - William A. Ware, "Aviation," *Dallas*, Dec. 1949, 43.

68. "the huge aircraft aloft." - "Horace S. Carswell, Jr.," *New Handbook of Texas*, I, 997.

69. "and patrolling high-tension wires." - Bilstein and Miller, *Aviation in Texas*, 134.

69. "as he handed over the commemorative spade." - *Dallas Times Herald*, March 17, 1974.

69. " 'twice this many people to serve.' " - "The President's Report," *Dallas*, Dec. 1950, 29.

69. "metropolitan area in the South." - Ibid.

70. "to pacify its fears of anything." - Ibid.

70. "room enough for both." - *The Dallas Morning News*, Feb. 4, 1951.

70. "would go to Midway." - Ibid.

70. "come in on the airport." - Ibid., April 7, 1952.

70. "rejected the offer outright." - Ibid., June 26, 1951.

71. " 'in the next 10 years.' " - Ibid.

71. "and Fort Worth, 50,375." - *Dallas Times Herald*, July 6, 1951.

72. "would be ahead, too." - Ibid., Aug. 15, 1951.

72. "a joint authority existed." - *The Dallas Morning News*, April 14, 1951.

72. "Love Field would be essential." - *Dallas Times Herald*, Aug. 8, 1951.

72. Carpenter's proposal was hostile." - Aug. 15, 1951.

73. "openly disagreed with him." - Ibid., Aug. 8, 1951.

73. " 'move for the City of Dallas.' " - Ibid., Aug. 15, 1951.

73. "had contributed nothing." - Ibid., Aug. 6, 1951.

74. "8,500 feet long on the other side of the field." - Ibid., Aug. 6, 1951.

74. "without hampering those of Dallas." - Ibid., Aug. 8, 1951.

74. "65 percent of that traffic." - *The Dallas Morning News*, April 7, 1952.
74. " 'aviation business to Fort Worth.' " - *The Dallas Morning News*, April 7, 1952.
75. "with its master plan." - Ibid., May 5, 1952; "Aviation," *Dallas*, Dec. 1952, 13.
75. "in the Love Field area." - *The Dallas Morning News*, Jan. 28, 1953.
75. "without affecting Dallas' area service at all." - Ibid., Jan. 29, 1953.

Chapter Four
76. "of little consequence." - Flemmons, *Amon,* 253.
77. "his own airport" - Pamphlet entitled "Airport" in B41, F19, Fuller Papers.
77. "the publisher replied." - Ibid., 251-53.
77. " 'one of the outstanding airports in the world.' *Fort Worth Star-Telegram*, April 26, 1953.
78. " 'and time to Mexico City.' " - Ibid.
78. "past the speaker's stand." - Ibid.
78. " 'dream come true.' " - Ibid.
78. "was placed at $106,000." - Wayne W. Parrish, "Amon Carter Field: One of World's Finest," *Fort Worth Star-Telegram*, May 17, 1953.
79. "Dallas, he said, " 'would have to take a back seat.' " - Ibid.
79. "Dallas passengers to be a success." - Flemmons, *Amon,* 254.
79. "the regional headquarters offices." - *Dallas Times Herald*, April 19, 1953.
80. "Eastern, Braniff, and Delta." - *The Dallas Morning News*, May 3, 1953.
80. "far-reaching master plan." - "Dallas Stages 'All-Out' Fight for Air Services," *Dallas*, Dec. 1953, 25.
80. "flight offerings there." - *Dallas Times Herald*, Oct. 20, 1954.
81. "same quarter a year earlier" - *The Dallas Morning News*, Oct. 7, 1954.
81. "compared to $4.25 at Love." - Ibid.
81. "passed with plenty to spare." - *Fort Worth Star-Telegram*, Nov. 21, 1954.
81. "passengers on 5,101 flights." - *The Dallas Morning News*, Dec. 31, 1954.
81. "control center in Fort Worth." - Ibid., Aug. 19, 1954.
81. "in developing the mid-cities airport." - Ibid.
82. "their present white elephant." - Ibid.
82. "debt service of $235,731." - "Amon Carter Field, Profit and Loss Statement," B41, F35, W.G. Fuller Papers.
83. " 'will be greatly appreciated.' " - The letter is reprinted in *The Dallas Morning News*, Nov. 14, 1954.
84. "the Fort Worth officials concluded." - Ibid.
85. " 'financial success of its airport.' " - Ibid.
85. "the program expanding Love Field." - Ibid.
85. " the entire North Texas area.' " - Ibid., Nov. 21, 1954.
85. " 'neighbor is pitted against neighbor.' *Fort Worth Star-Telegram*, Dec. 5, 1954.
85. " 'whim and fancy of a group in another city.' " - *The Dallas Morning News*, Nov. 21, 1954.
85. "prejudice in favor of Fort Worth." - Ibid.
86. " 'as it has always been—my best.' " - *Fort Worth Star-Telegram*, Nov. 23, 1954.
86. " 'or for their elected representatives.' " - Ibid.
88. "to our respective cities." - *The Dallas Morning News*, Nov. 30, 1954.

88. "influence fellow board members." - Ibid., July 22, 1955.
89. "to support Dallas' wishes." - Ibid., July 23, 1955.
89. "its busiest month to date." - *Fort Worth Press*, [June 1954], clipping in B45, F1, Fuller Papers.
90. "the penalty in the long run." - *Fort Worth Star-Telegram*, March 10, 1955.
90. "the finest air terminal in the world." - *Dallas Times Herald*, Jan. 14, 1955; *The Dallas Morning News*, Oct. 29, 1955; *Dallas Times Herald*, July 7, 1957.
90. "a new $1.5 million facility." - *The Dallas Morning News*, April 14, 1957.
90. " 'hemmed-in and overcrowded Love Field.' " - *Fort Worth Press*, July 7, 1957.
91. "to America's various bases." - *Fort Worth Star-Telegram*, Nov. 17, 1957.
91. "the airport at $2,500 a month." - *Fort Worth Press*, July 7, 1957.
91. " 'might produce some other revenue,' " - *Fort Worth Star-Telegram*, July 12, 1960.
91. "as many crew members as passengers." - Ibid., July 26, 1960.
92. "lost our battle to save Carter Field." - Ibid.
92. " 'to or from this airport?' " - Ibid., July 28, 1960.
92. "double in 1965 to 2,782,010." - "Historical Domestic Airline Traffic Origination, 1960-1967," CAB/FAA Airport Activity Statistics of Certified Route Air Carriers; *Fort Worth Star-Telegram*, April 1, 1959..
92. "two direct European flights daily." - *The Dallas Morning News*, April 11, 1962.
92. "by avoiding duplication." - *Fort Worth Star-Telegram*, April 19, 1962.
93. " 'centralizing their schedules at Love Field, Dallas.' " - The letter was quoted months later when it became available in the *Dallas Times Herald*, Sept. 12, 1962.
93. "sat idly nearby." - *Dallas Times Herald*, Sept. 30, 1962.
94. " 'of the two metropolitan communities.' " - Ibid., Aug. 19, 1962.
94. "decisions of this nature." - Ibid.
94. "Amon Carter's son-in-law." - Ibid., Aug. 20, 1962.
94. "and determined opposition." - *The Dallas Morning News*, Aug. 22, 1962.
95. "such talks would be fruitless." - *Dallas Times Herald*, Aug. 23, 1962.
95. "petitioned for such a hearing." - *The Dallas Morning News*, Aug. 22, 1962.
95. " 'development of the North Texas area.' " - *Dallas Times Herald*, Oct. 5, 1962.
95. "prior to that time." - *The Dallas Morning News*, Aug. 26, 1962.
96. "other general aviation airports." - *Dallas Times Herald*, Aug. 30, 1962.
96. "so many area interferences." - Ibid.
96. "regional leader in air service." - *The Dallas Morning News*, Aug. 22, 1962.
96. "Carter Field as the regional airport." - Ibid., Sept. 5, 1962.
97. " 'costing the Dallas taxpayers anything.' " - *Dallas Times Herald*, Sept. 6, 1962.
97. " 'Southwest part of the United States.' " - *Fort Worth Star-Telegram*, Nov. 2, 1962.
97. " 'on any shanty in Fort Worth.' " - *Dallas Times Herald*, Nov. 6, 1962.
97. "and Truce Field." - *Fort Worth Star-Telegram*, Nov. 2, 1962.
97. "upcoming airport hearings." - Ibid., Jan. 30, 1963.
98. "income of $1,426,719." - *Dallas Times Herald*, March 2, 1963; *The Dallas Morning News*, Dec. 27,1963, Oct. 7, 1962.
98. "decision could be expected." - *The Dallas Morning News*, Dec. 11, 1963.
98. "He criticized both cities and airports." - *The Dallas Morning News*, April 8, 1964.
99. " 'at the best possible site.' " - Ibid.

99. " 'in the Dallas-Fort Worth area.' " - Ibid.
99. "most significant sentence in the report." - Ibid., April 9, 1964.
99. " 'the creation of regional airports.' " - Ibid.
100. "drop its appeal of Newmann's decision." - *Dallas Times Herald*, May 6, 1964.
100. " 'for years to come.' " - Ibid., May 8, 1964.
100. "a good image with the CAB." - Ibid., May 25, 1964.
100. " 'We should come out all right.' " - *The Dallas Morning News*, June 13, 1964.
101. "completed on Sept. 15." - Ibid., Sept. 16, 1964.
101. " 'cargo and passenger services.' " - *Dallas Times Herald*, Oct. 1, 1964.
101. "buildings from its pathway." - Ibid., Nov. 26, 1964.
101. "no more favorable to Fort Worth." - Ibid.
102. "not be tolerated by taxpayers." - Interview with Erik Jonsson, Nov. 18, 1993.
102. "Love Field cannot be it." - Ibid.
102. "H.B. Fuqua represented Fort Worth." - Ibid., Nov. 3, 1964.
102. "all sides of the questions." - Interview with Bayard Friedman, May 15, 1998, and J. Lee Johnson III, May 6, 1998.
102. "In a productive fashion." - Interview with Erik Jonsson, Nov. 18, 1993.
103. "before the CAB deadline." - *The Dallas Morning News*, Dec. 21, 1964.
103. "New Year's eve meeting." - *Dallas Times Herald*, Dec. 31, 1964.

Chapter Five
105. "immediately, and cost efficiency." - *The Dallas Morning News,* June 9, 1965.
105. "a book, *Airport Planning*." - *Fort Worth Star-Telegram*, June 4, 1967.
106. "up to about 18,000 acres." - Interview with J. Lee Johnson III, Jan. 13, 1994, on audiotape, DFW Public Affairs Department.
106. "insufficient highways." - Ibid.
106. "for the final decision." - Larry Upshaw, "Superport I," undated publication, [Jan. 1972], scrapbook, DFW Archives.
106. "from nearby communities." - Ibid.; audiotape interviews with Erik Jonsson, Dec. 13, 1993, and R.M. Stovall, Nov. 23, 1993, DFW Public Affairs Department.
107. "to the board for expenses." - *Dallas Times Herald*, Sept. 26, 1965.
107. "a power of eminent domain." - *The Dallas Morning News*, Sept. 28, 1965. The contract between the two cities was signed on Sept. 27, 1965.
107. " 'truly a new era.' " - *Dallas Times Herald*, Sept. 26, 1965.
108. "sales for a month. " - Ibid., Sept. 29, 1965.
108. "large parcels of property." - Ibid.
108. "land that was necessary.)" - DFW Airport Board minutes, May 3, 1967.
108. "hospitals, and schools." - DFW Airport media kit, Sept., 1973.
108. " 'put the airport somewhere else.' " - Ibid., Oct. 4, 1965.
108. "worth $10,000 an acre." - Upshaw, "Superport I," 20.
109. "plesiosaur was discovered." - Associated Press dispatch, May 12, 1972, scrapbook, DFW
109. "by a Grapevine man." - *Fort Worth Press*, Nov. 26, 1971.
110. "viewed the site as 'absolutely ideal.' " - Audiotape interview with Willard Barr, Nov. 22, 1993, DFW Public Affairs Department.
110. "the world's biggest airport." - "Site Selection Study," TAMS, Dec. 15, 1965, DFW Airport Archives.
110. "with FAA and air-carrier approval." - Two other TAMS partners working with Prokosch were James H. Stratton and Thomas J. Fratar. Theodore A. Bork was project

manager and Eugene W. Friedrich was assistant project manager. Consultants included Forrest and Cotton and Carter Burgess, associate engineers; Freese, Nichols & Andress and Redy and Associates, consulting engineers; Mason-Johnston & Associates, soils survey; Bruce & Gunn, mapping; and John F. Gill, aeronautical.

111. "by 1975 to 8.3 million." - A copy of the document, "Airport Layout Plan," TAMS [July 1966], is in the DFW Airport Archives.
111. "to 113,500 in 1980." - Ibid., 3
112. "and 6,000 sightseers." - Ibid., 5.
112. "journey to San Francisco." - Ibid., 7.
112. "areas such as concessions." - Ibid., 31.
113. "hopelessly optimistic." - "Airport Layout Plan."
113. "rapid transit facilities." - Upshaw, "Superport I," 19.
114. "voters turned down the proposition." - *Dallas Times Herald*, June 7, 1967.
114. "four days away." - Ibid.
114. "Fort Worth would carry on alone." - Ibid.
114. "the authority of the board.)" - Interview with Friedman, May 15, 1998.
115. "nor had organized labor." - *Dallas Times Herald.*, June 9, 1967.
115. "based on relative populations." - Minutes, Dallas-Fort Worth Regional Airport Board, June 10, 1967.
116. "sold out their own city." - Bill Leader, "Story of DFW International Airport really begins in 1926," *DFW People*, Jan. 27, 1994, 8.
117. "would retain a 6-5 voting edge." - Audiotape interview with Erik Jonsson, Dec. 13, 1993, DFW Public Affairs Department.
117. "was entirely satisfactory to them." - Interview with Bayard Friedman, May 15, 1998.
117. " 'was building the airport.' " - Leader, "Story of DFW International Airport really begins in 1926," 9-10.
118. "no more than ten minutes." - Interview with Len Limmer, Sept. 30, 1998.
118. "upset the progress being made." - Interview with Bayard Friedman, May 15, 1998.
118. "Their job descriptions" - "The Over-All Preliminary Plan for Construction of the Dallas-Fort Worth Regional Airport," Dallas-Fort Worth Regional Airport Board Report to the City Councils of Dallas and Fort Worth, Sept. 1968, DFW Archives.
120. " 'years of future requirements.' " - Ibid.
120. "from 329,900 square feet to 446,910." - "Airport Master Plan," TAMS, Dec. 22, 1967, introductory letter.
120. " 'first benchmark of airport planning.' " - Ibid., 50.
121. "nearly 60 percent to 8.35 million." - Ibid., 13.
121. " 'primary criteria of airport planning' " - Ibid., 50.
121. "helicopter landing facilities." - Ibid., 28-29, 30.
121. " 'the new breed of aircraft.' " - Sullivan, "Dallas-Fort Worth Regional Airport, 'First of the Jumbo Jets,' " *Planning and Development*, undated, DFW Archives.
121. "and 410,000 tons in 1985." - "History of the Development of the Dallas/Fort Worth Regional Airport," DFW Archives.
122. "his conclusions about it." - Sullivan to Dean, June 19, 1968, correspondence files, DFW Archives.
122. "both of them in New York." - *The Dallas Morning News*, July 2, 1968; Al Foster, "Hallmark of Quality," *St. Louis Commerce*, Nov. 1971, 41-43.
122. "The board agreed with Sullivan." - *The Dallas Morning News*, July 2, 1968.

122. "The board agreed with Sullivan." - *The Dallas Morning News*, July 2, 1968.
122. " 'should have brought my press clippings.' " - Ibid.
123. " 'who did the architectural work.' " - *Fort Worth Star-Telegram*, July 3, 1968.
123. "management and coordination." - DFW Airport media kit, Sept., 1973.
123. " 'charming as can be.' " - Transcript, "Airlines Top and Technical Meeting," July 16, 1968, correspondence files, DFW Archives.
123. "Cranbrook Academy of Arts at Detroit." - Foster, "Hallmark of Quality," 42; *Dallas Times Herald*, Sept. 22, 1973.
123. "given them by Sullivan." - Transcript, "Airlines Technical Meeting," Aug. 1, 1968, ibid.
124. "airlines and airport operations." - Untitled two-page memo by Sullivan, July 10, 1968, ibid.
124. "and/or economic construction." - Stanford to Schrader, July 22, 1968, ibid.
125. "ultimate capacity of the runways." - Transcript of "Airlines Top and Technical Meeting," July 16, 1968, correspondence files, DFW Archives.
125. " 'we had a brand new plan.' " - Ibid.
125. "159 operations per hour." - Ernest E. Dean to Ross I. Newmann, Aug. 30, 1968, correspondence files, DFW Archives.
126. "fact and fiction was Tom Sullivan." - Hailey, *Airport* (Garden City, N.J.: Doubleday & Co., Inc.), 417.
127. "trans-Atlantic fares as low as $69.)" - Speech to North Dallas Chamber of Commerce, June 27,1968, correspondence files, DFW Archives.
127. "experiences gained through travel." - Speech dated June 21, 1968, ibid.
127. " 'crossroads of the nation.' " - Speech to North Dallas Chamber of Commerce, June 27, 1968, ibid.
127. " '7,000 miles per hour.' " - Quoted in Jim W. Jones, "Rocket Craft Predicted for Airport," *Fort Worth Star-Telegram*, April 4, 1973.
127. "when it came to pass." - Speech to Dallas Lions Club, July 19, 1968, correspondence files, DFW Archives.
128. "the desired speed and convenience." - Ibid.
128. " 'much of the unpredictable.' " - Ibid.
128. "right up to each gate." - *Dallas Times Herald*, Sept. 23, 1973.
129. "less than the Prokosch terminal." - *The Dallas Morning News*, Sept. 29, 1968.
129. "three New York airports combined." - Thomas E. Sullivan, "Dallas-Fort Worth Regional Airport, 'First of the Jumbo Hubs,' Significant Facts and First Phase Development," rev. Aug. 24, 1970, DFW Archives.
129. "rail system linking all terminals." - Ibid.
129. "steel plants and coal mines." - *Dallas Times Herald*, Sept. 29, 1968.
129. " 'We'll be getting more for less.' " - *Fort Worth Star-Telegram*, Sept. 28, 1968.
129. "would be ready by late 1972." - *Richardson Daily News*, Oct. 1, 1968.
130. " 'revolutionary new airport concept.' " - *The Dallas Morning News*, Sept. 29, 1968.
131. "and Laurel Land Memorial Park" - *Dallas Times Herald*, Sept. 26, 1971.

Chapter Six
132. "show her hand or throw in." - *Fort Worth Press*, Oct. 2, 1968.
132. " 'sly, clever Fort Worth plot.' " - Ibid., Oct. 4, 1968.

132. "that the property was needed." - Associated Press, Oct. 5, 1968.

133. " 'That's the $64 question right now.' " - *The Dallas Morning News*, Nov. 27, 1968.

133. "open for business in late 1972." - *Irving Daily News*, Nov. 29, 1968.

133. "input on the terminal structures." - Sullivan to Erik Jonsson and other board members, Aug. 7, 1969, correspondence files, DFW Archives.

134. "Savings bond as his reward.)" - Thomas M. Sullivan to Gillem, Jan. 13, 1969, DFW Correspondence Files.

134. "Jonsson's first airplane ride." - *Fort Worth Star-Telegram*, Dec. 12, 1968.

134. " 'for residence in an asylum.' " - United Press International, Dec. 13, 1968.

134. " 'valuable transportation services.' " - *The Dallas Morning News*, Dec. 12, 1968.

134. " 'to take the first step.' " - *Fort Worth Star-Telegram*, Dec. 12, 1968.

134. " 'I just won't do for Fort Worth.' " - Bill Rives, "Views," *Denton Record-Chronicle*, Dec. 15, 1968.

135. "for three weeks afterwards." - Thomas M. Sullivan to E. Paul Burke of Frontier Airways, Feb. 14, 1969.

135. " 'Airport Costs Spiral.' " - *Dallas Times Herald*, Jan. 28, 1969.

135. "recent cocktail conversation." - *Ibid.*, Jan. 30, 1969.

135. "business in closed sessions." - *The Dallas Morning News*, Feb. 1, 1969.

135. "but the purchase of the land." - *Fort Worth Press*, Jan. 29, 1969.

135. " 'he is 100 percent for the airport.' " - *Fort Worth Star-Telegram*, March 26, 1969.

135. "joint appearances." - *The Dallas Morning News*, April 4, 1969.

136. "twelve million gallons of water.)" - *Dallas Times Herald*, Sept. 12, 1973.

136. "pounding of huge airliners." - *Fort Worth Star-Telegram*, Feb. 2, 1969.

136. "job was on schedule!" - *Dallas Times Herald*, March 15, 1970.

137. "investment of $601 million." - *Fort Worth Star-Telegram*, Feb. 5, 1969.

137. " 'a vast project.' " - *Dallas Times Herald*, Feb. 4, 1969.

137. "would be for land." - *Irving Daily News*, Feb. 5, 1969.

137. "at nearly $50 million." - *Dallas Times Herald*, July 1, 1969.

137. "for its land purchases." - *The Dallas Morning News*, April 30, 1969.

137. "$1,415 for 6,000 acres." - Ibid., May 6, 1969.

137. "that had been predicted." - Ibid., Dec. 24, 1970.

137. "36 million passengers a year." - *The Dallas Morning News*, Feb. 21, 1971.

138. "an automated system." - Ibid., July 2, 1969.

138. " 'within the terminal complex.' " - Mettler to John Richter, Jan. 13, 1969, DFW correspondence files.

138. "supplies, mail, and trash." - *The Dallas Morning News*, Feb. 21, 1971.

138. "and Dashaveyor of Venice, California." - *Arlington Daily News*, April 4, 1970.

138. "airline or parking lot." - *The Dallas Morning News*, March 31, 1970.

138. "80 to 90 miles per hour." - *Fort Worth Star-Telegram*, Jan. 20, 1971.

139. "bid was for $48.5 million." - *The Dallas Morning News*, Feb. 21, 1971.

139. "the AIRTRANS system." - *Fort Worth Star-Telegram*, March 5, 1971.

139. "No, assured Ernest Dean." - *The Dallas Morning News*, March 3, 1971.

139. "1,750 new local jobs." - *Irving News-Texan*, July 14, 1971.

140. "ready until July 1973." - *Fort Worth Press*, July 14, 1971.

140. "were expected to be operational." - *Grand Prairie News*, July 15, 1971.

140. "8.5 miles wide." - *Dallas Times Herald*, April 13, 1970.

140. "thirty-five miles long." - *Orlando* (Florida) *Sentinel Star*, May 9, 1973.

141. "airport with easy access." - Interview with Len Limmer, Sept. 30, 1998.

141. "by combining the functions." - Ibid.

142. " 'and inspection space requirements.' " - Thomas M. Sullivan to Dr. Herman J. Abs, Deutsche Lufthansa Aktiengesellschaft, Koeln, Germany, Feb. 3, 1969, DFW correspondence files.

142. " 'and any points of softness.' " - Thomas M. Sullivan to Toru Akiyama, Feb. 4, 1969, ibid.

142. "airline to come to DFW." - *The Dallas Morning News*, Sept. 28, 1971; *Hurst and Mid-Cities Daily News*, Oct. 3, 1971.

142. "partner for the area." - *The Dallas Morning News*, March 5, 1972.

143. " 'attract international airlines.' " - *Fort Worth Star-Telegram*, Feb. 2, 1969.

143. " 'airport of real significance.' " - *Dallas Times Herald*, March 15, 1970.

143. "were followed is not known." - Stanford to Sullivan, April 7, 1969, ibid.

144. "a TAMS report showed." - *The Dallas Morning News, Fort Worth Star-Telegram, Dallas Times Herald*, May 11, 12, 1971, and *Arlington Daily News*, July 11, 1971.

144. " 'would offer more revenue.' " - *Fort Worth Star-Telegram*, July 16, 1971.

144. " 'to outmoded standards.' " - Associated Press, July 19, 1971.

144. "biggest and heaviest aircraft." - Ibid.

144. "would be hauled." - *Richardson Daily News*, July 19, 1971.

145. "an increase in its price." - *The Dallas Morning News*, July 20, 1971.

145. "to be supplied DFW." - *Dallas Times Herald*, July 30, 1971.

145. "airport and Oklahoma City." - *Grand Prairie Daily News*, Oct. 27, 1971; Fort Worth Star-Telegram, Dec. 11, 1971.

145. "with a layer three feet thick!" - Associated Press dispatch, April 14, 1972.

145. "in Dec. 1971." - *Dallas Times Herald*, Nov. 24, 1971; Fort Worth Star-Telegram, Dec. 8, 1971.

145. "SST and its sonic boom." - Associated Press, Aug. 8, 1971.

146. "to purchase the Concorde." - Frederick C. Ford to J. Erik Jonsson, July 2, 1973, correspondence files, DFW Archives.

146. "to housing developments." - *Dallas Times Herald*, July 25, 1971.

146. " 'will make it the finest.' " - Sullivan to William F. McKee, Aug. 8, 1969, correspondence files, DFW Archives.

146. "about $255,000 annually." - *The Dallas Morning News*, Aug. 4, 1971.

146. "and not hazardous." - Jonsson to W.W. Petts, Feb. 1970, correspondence files, DFW Archives.

147. "maximum capacity of 8 million." - *Houston Chronicle*, Jan. 21, 1973.

147. "suspended in the main lobby." - Associated Press, Aug. 8, 1971.

147. "simply had to be done." - Ibid., Nov. 21, 1971.

147. "a shortage of hangar space." - *Fort Worth Star-Telegram*, Dec. 4, 1968.

148. " 'We will be affected.' " - *Dallas Times Herald*, Sept. 26, 1971.

148. " 'destination only 250 miles away.' " - Ibid., Jan. 13, 1972.

148. "was expanding rapidly." - Ibid.

148. " 'could be used as a backup.' " - Ibid., June 1, 1972.

148. " 'commuter flights at Love Field.' " - Associated Press, Oct. 8, 1971.

149. "were very appealing." - Kevin Freiberg and Jackie Freiberg, *Nuts!
SouthwestAirlines' Crazy Recipe for Business and Personal Success* (Austin: Bard
Press, 1976), 20-23.
149. "agreement was too open-ended." - Charles W. Cronin to Jonsson and board
members, Feb. 12, 1970, correspondence files, DFW Archives.
149. "airport was operational." - Sullivan to file, Feb. 6, 1970, ibid.
149. "confessed a Delta Airlines official." - *The Dallas Morning News*, undated
clipping, DFW scrapbook.
150. "operations out of Love Field." - *The Dallas Morning News*, Nov. 6, 1971;
Dallas Times Herald, Nov. 5, 1971.
150. "permit others to follow." - *Dallas Times Herald,* Nov. 5, 1971.
150. "another airline, Texas International." - *The Dallas Morning News*, Oct. 20,
1972.
150. "move to a new facility." - Ibid., Feb. 7, 1973.
150. "lost its battle in court." - *The Dallas Morning News*, June 8, 1972.
150. " 'another competitive experience,' " - Ibid., Feb. 7, 1973.
151. "whisky or ice chest." - *Houston Chronicle*, Feb. 6, 1973.
151. "order their transfer to DFW." - *The Dallas Morning News*, March 25, 1973.
151. "that created the new airport." - *Fort Worth Star-Telegram*, March 27, 1973.
151. " 'a 23 percent diversion of passengers,' " -*Dallas Times Herald*, March 29,
1973.
152. "if Southwest were permitted to stay." - *Fort Worth Star-Telegram*, April 12,
1973.
152. "to exclude Southwest." - Ibid., April 30, 1973.
152. " 'a victory for the commuter.' " - *Dallas Times Herald*, May 1, 1973.
152. "$3.65 million a year." - *Fort Worth Star-Telegram*, May 1, 1973.
152. "accomplished the impossible." - "Little Airline That Could?" *Financial Trend*,
June 24, 1973.
152. "paid $100,000 in fines.)" - Freiberg and Freiberg, *Nuts!* 24-25.
153. "if he were bypassed." - *Dallas Times Herald*, Jan. 27, 1972.
153. "were disappointed." - Ibid.
153. "passed along to Fort Worth." - *The Dallas Morning News*, Jan. 28, 1972.
154. "responsible for $5 million." - Ibid., Feb. 6, 1972; *Fort Worth Star-Telegram*,
Feb. 5, 1972.
154. "headlined *Business Week* in the spring." - "The land boom at a Texas airport,"
Business Week, March 11, 1972, 116.
154. "impact on real estate values." - *Dallas Times Herald*, March 26,1972.
155. "would continue for many years." - *New York Times*, April 9, 1972.
155. "cost of $1.48 million." - *Grand Prairie Daily News*, April 13, 1972.
155. "the Air-Trans people mover." - *The Dallas Morning News*, July [n.d.] 1973,
DFW Archives scrapbook.
156. "residents was higher." - Ibid., Dec. 3, 1972.
156. "commissioner-general." - Ibid., Jan. 4, 1973.
156. "at major American airports." - *Christian-Science Monitor*, Jan. 12, 1973.
157. "international airports combined." - Guy Ryan, Copley News Service,
Philadelphia Bulletin [n.d.], DFW clippings.
157. "on its original time schedule." - *Dallas Times Herald*, Feb. 5, 1973.
157. "Roy Orr on the airport." - *Hurst Mid Cities Daily News*, May 18, 1973.

157. "railroad to Chicago's development." - *The Dallas Morning News*, July 18, 1973.
158. " 'fulfill its purpose.' " - Ibid.
158. "Delta-Continental terminal." - *Grand Prairie Daily News*, [May 1973]
158. "last-minute changes." - *Dallas Times Herald*, April 15, 1973.
158. "still was on target." - *The Dallas Morning News*, June 7, 1973; *Fort Worth Press*, June 7, 1973.

Chapter Seven
160. "south end for the winter." - *Kilgore News-Herald*, Sept. 9, 1973.
160. "In frequent references..." - *Time, Inc.*, 1972, Walter McQuady, reprint, DFW Archives.
160. "how pleasant a jetport can be." - *The New York Times*, as reprinted in the *Palm Beach Post*, June 20, 1973.
161. "fulfill this destiny." - *Irving Daily News*, Feb. 5, 1969.
161. "impact the entire region." - *Cleburne Times-Review*, Sept. 21, 1973.
162. "land at our airport as a first." - News release, Aerospatiale of France/British Aircraft Corporation, Sept. 17, 1973, The Braniff Collection, Box, 1, Folder 7, UTD Aviation Special Collections.
162. "at supersonic speeds over the U.S." - *The Dallas Morning News*, July 21, 1973.
162. " 'flying from any other.' " - *Concorde Bulletin*, No. 10 newsletter, Aug. 24, 1973.
162. " 'airport of tomorrow.' " - *Dallas Times Herald*, Sept. 21, 1973.
163. "Johnson had said." - J. Lee Johnson III, July 16, 1973, correspondence files, DFW Airport Archives.
163. "Concordes from British Airways." - *The Washington Post*, July 25, 1973.
163. " 'the world of aviation.' " - *Fort Worth Star Telegram*, Sept. 21, 1973.
164. " 'or standing in doorways.' " - *The Dallas Morning News*, Sept. 22, 1973.
164. " 'cars to the planes.' " - *Fort Worth Star Telegram*, Sept. 21, 1973.
164. " 'a lot to learn from this airport.' " - Ibid.
164. " 'Concrete must be cheap around here.' " - *The Dallas Morning News*, July 21, 1973.
164. " 'very lost for a long time.' " - "Aviation's Future Down in Texas,"*Business Week*, July 29, 1973.
164. " 'functional simplicity.' " - *Fort Worth Star Telegram*, Sept. 21, 1973.
165. "outside of Washington and New York." - *Dallas Times Herald*, Sept. 19, 1973.
166. " 'midst of formal splendor.' " - *Kennedale News*, Sept. 27, 1973.
166. "from valet parking." - *Dallas Times Herald*, Sept. 22, 1973.
166. "took a bus home." - *Fort Worth Star Telegram*, Sept. 23, 1973.
167. "the 'impossible dream.' " - Stanley H. Scott and Levi H. Davis, *A Giant in Texas: A History of the Dallas-Fort Worth Regional Airport Controversy, 1911-1974* (Quanah: Nortex Press, 1974), 75-77.
167. " 'something of a miracle.' " - *Dallas Times Herald*, Sept. 23, 1973.
167. " 'of Dallas and Fort Worth.' " - *Fort Worth Star Telegram*, Sept. 23, 1973.
167. " 'airport and community planning.' " - Ibid.
167. " 'history of transportation.' " - Scott and Davis, *A Giant in Texas*, 66.
168. "in the years ahead." - *Fort Worth Star Telegram*, Sept. 23, 1973.
168. " 'airport and community planning.' " - Ibid.

168. " 'the sky is the limit.' " - Ibid., Sept. 22, 1973.
168. " 'unity of purpose, cannot achieve.' " - Ibid.
169. " 'in the show's finale.' " - *The Dallas Morning News*, Sept. 23, 1973.
169. " 'to both men and women.' " - Recorded in the *Fort Worth Star Telegram*, Sept. 23, 1973.
169. "the dedication weekend." - *Texas Metro*, Sept. 1973.
170. " 'improvement in quality of life.' " - *Dallas Times Herald*, Sept. 23, 1973.
170. " 'of this great region.' " - Scott and Davis, *A Giant in Texas*, 72.
170. "a world aviation center." - *Dallas Times Herald*, Sept. 23, 1973.
171. "in the region's economy." - *Fort Worth Press*, Sept. 11, 1973.
171. " 'centers of the country.' " - *The Dallas Morning News*, Sept. 15, 1973.
172. "continued economic growth of Dallas." - Arthur D. Little, Inc. Report, UTD Special Aviation Collection, 1973.
172. "in approving the request." - Minutes, DFW Airport Board, Aug. 2, 1973.
172. "regularly scheduled monthly meeting." - Ibid., Sept. 9, 1973.
173. "new facility and equipment." - *Dallas Times Herald*, Sept. 21, 1973.
173. "good reasons for their request." - *Dallas Times Herald*, Oct. 1, 1973.
174. "over Southwest flights." - *The Dallas Morning News*, Jan. 23, 1973.
175. "still announced cutbacks." - Ibid., Dec. 29, 1973.
175. " 'when published the next.' " - *Fort Worth Star Telegram*, Dec. 30, 1973.
175. "58 operations, respectively." - Ibid., Dec. 20, 1973.
176. "14 percent in landing fees." - *Irving Daily New*, Jan. 2, 1973.
176. "ready for occupancy." - *Fort Worth Star-Telegram*, Jan. 8, 1974.
176. "and ground movement." - Ibid., Jan. 11, 1973.
176. " 'a very special occasion.' " - *Irving News*, Jan. 11, 1974.
176. "by flat bed trucks." - *Fort Worth Star Telegram*, Jan. 14, 1974.
177. "Public Safety Director Limmer recalled." - Interview with Len Limmer, Sept. 30, 1998.
177. " 'during the Christmas holidays.' " - *Dallas Times Herald*, Jan. 13, 1973.

Chapter Eight
179. "150 more operations daily." - 1974 Dallas/Fort Worth Airport Annual Report.
179. "into new facility." - *Arlington Urbanite*, Jan. 17, 1974.
179. "disseminate flight information." - DFW Airport Report, Dec., 1973.
180. "and ticketing machines." - Braniff news release, Sept. 20, 1973, UTD Aviation Special Collections.
181. " 'prosperity for the Metroplex.' " - *Dallas Times Herald*, Sept. 23, 1973.
181. "150 million pounds of freight a year." - Ibid.
181. "additional freighter aircraft." - *Fort Worth Star Telegram*, Sept. 23, 1973.
182. "residents to the airport.)" - *The Dallas Morning News*, Jan. 9, 1974.
182. "also cost $1.50 a day." - *Fort Worth Press*, Jan. 18, 1974.
182. "cost $17.00 - $20.00" - *The Dallas Morning News*, Jan. 23, 1974.
182. "greater access to the airport." - *Fort Worth Press*, March 31, 1974.
183. " 'brought to reality.' " - *Arlington Citizen-Journal*, Jan. 17, 1974.
183. "operational by July 1974." - Minutes, DFW Airport Board, Jan. 8, 1974.
183. "and 6,000 sightseers." - Airport Layout Plan, TAMS, July 1966.
184. " 'the size of Wichita Falls.' " - *Dallas Times Herald*, Sept. 9, 1973.
184. "in Washington, D.C." - *Fort Worth Star Telegram*, July 23, 1973.
185. "the airport complex." - Ibid.

183. "visitors to the airport." - Ibid.

183. "of state and other VIPs." - Minutes, DFW Airport Board, Jan. 5, 1973.

183. "with four chairs each." - *Fort Worth Star Telegram*, July 23, 1973.

185. "had not been received." - Ibid.

186. "DFW Regional Airport." - *Irving Daily News*, Jan. 22, 1974.

186. "to their departure gates." - *The Dallas Morning News*, Jan. 17, 1974.

187. " 'smallest things imaginable.' " - Ibid., Jan. 22, 1974.

187. " 'and value depreciation.' " - *Dallas Times Herald*, Jan. 28, 1974.

187. "as originally allowed." - *Fort Worth Star Telegram*, Feb. 24, 1974.

188. " 'most nearly perfect airport in the country.' " - "Airport for 2001," *Time*, Sept. 24, 1973.

188. " 'other airports in the nation.' " - *Longview Journal*, July 23,1973.

189. " 'airport design and construction.' " - 1975 Dallas/Fort Worth Airport Annual Report.

189. "$15 million." - *Fort Worth Press*, Jan. 9, 1974.

189. "and supporting personnel." - 1974 Dallas/Fort Worth Airport Annual Report, 1974.

190. " 'no plans' to step down." - *Fort Worth Star Telegram*, Jan. 18, 1974.

190. " 'the time was not right.' " - *The Dallas Morning News*, Feb. 6, 1974.

190. "first black appointed to the board." - Ibid.

190. "the operations committee." - *Irving Daily News*, Feb. 6, 1974.

190. "the privately owned machines." - Minutes, Dallas/Fort Worth Airport Board Meeting, April 1974.

191. "on which the airport was built." - DFW Airport Guide, DFW Airport archives.

191. "between $200 and $300 million." - 1974 Dallas/Fort Worth Airport Annual Report.

191. " 'exciting industry in the region.' " - *Fort Worth Star Telegram*, Sept. 23, 1973.

191. " 'this decade for this region.' " - Ibid.

191. "for Fort Worth and Tarrant County." *Fort Worth Press*, Feb. 3, 1974.

191. "to be better in 1974." - Ibid.

191. "attracting businesses and industries." - *The Dallas Morning News*, Feb. 5, 1974.

192. "opening of DFW Airport." - 1974 Dallas/Fort Worth Airport Annual Report.

192. "in international trade." Ibid.

192. "level of 'healthfulness.' " - *Dallas Times Herald*, Sept. 23, 1973.

192. "air service into DFW." - *Denton Record-Chronicle*, Sept. 19, 1973.

192. "expansion of flights at DFW." - *Dallas Times Herald*, Sept. 23, 1973.

192. "smaller than it actually was." - Ibid.

193. "considered most lucrative." - *Fort Worth Press*, Jan. 20, 1974.

193. "to thwart the plan." - *The Dallas Morning News*, Feb. 24, 1974.

193. " 'flights to DFW.' "- *Fort Worth Star-Telegram*, Jan. 21, 1974.

193. " 'operate from the new facility.' " - *Fort Worth Press*, Feb. 22, 1974.

193. "could close Love Field." - *Fort Worth Star-Telegram*, Feb. 23, 1974.

194. "by supporting DFW." - Ibid., March 15, 1974.

194. " 'maximum extent possible.' " - *Airport News Advertiser*, March 24, 1974.

194. "delay the ruling a year." - *Dallas Times Herald*, Feb. 23, 1974.

194. " 'this is certainly bad.' " - *Arlington Daily News*, April 19, 1974.

194. "service flights from Austin." - *Fort Worth Star-Telegram*, March 2, 1974.

195. "would never happen." - *The Dallas Morning News*, March 12, 1974.
195. "to Austin the next month." - *Fort Worth Star-Telegram*, March 13, 1974.
195. "good faith from the facility." - Ibid., March 19, 1974.
195. "use DFW exclusively." - *Fort Worth Press*, March 20, 1974.
195. "jurisdiction in the case." - *The Dallas Morning News*, March 27, 1974.
196. "was also questioned." - *Fort Worth Star-Telegram*, April 2, 1974.
196. "from the municipal airport." - *Dallas Times Herald*, April 17, 1974.
196. "thereby sharing in the costs." - *Fort Worth Star-Telegram*, April 2, 1974.
197. "out of Love Field." - Ibid., April 5, 1974.
197. "use the new airport." - *The Dallas Morning News*, April 6, 1974.
197. "the airport of the region." - Ibid., April 7, 1974.
197. " 'in its class anywhere' " - Ibid., March 17, 1974.
198. " 'nationally and internationally.' " - *Fort Worth Star-Telegram,* April 24, 1974.
198. " 'through a single regional airport.' " - Ibid., April 30, 1974.
198. " 'various interests concerned.' " - Ibid.
199. " 'in the same direction.' " - *The Dallas Morning News*, March 24, 1974.
199. " 'of the Southwest Metroplex.' " - *Dallas Times Herald*, April 24, 1974.
199. "was running smoothly." - *The Dallas Morning News*, Feb. 7, 1974.
199. "early retirement." - *Dallas Times Herald*, April 8, 1974.
199. " 'two cities come true.' " - *Fort Worth Star-Telegram,* April 9, 1974.
200. " 'to make it happen.' " - "A Remarkable Ten Years," DFW Airport press kit, 1984.

Chapter Nine
202. "in the world today." - 1974 DFW Airport Annual Report.
202. "transferring passengers." - Ibid.
202. "New York's LaGuardia." - "A Remarkable Ten Years." DFW Airport press kit, 1984.
202. " 'to go to Dallas for a stopover first.' " - *Dallas Fort Worth Business*, June 4, 1979.
202. " 'first in safety.' " - *The Dallas Morning News*, Feb. 8, 1982.
203. "followed by Great Britain." - 1979 DFW Airport Annual Report.
203. "promoting 'price innovation.' " - *The Wall Street Journal*, Dec. 22, 1977.
203. "dictated by [politics]." - *Dallas Times Herald*, Dec. 22, 1977.
204. " 'attention on Dallas-Fort Worth.' " - *The Dallas Morning News*, Jan. 12, 1979.
204. " 'without any problems.' " - *Fort Worth Star-Telegram*, Aug. 9, 1978.
204. "the speed of sound." - Braniff Files, Box 29, File 1, UTD Aviation Special Collections.
205. "radiation from the sun." - *Fort Worth Star Telegram*, Jan. 8, 1976.
205. "have disastrous consequences." - *Dallas Times Herald*, Jan. 18, 1976.
205. " 'the Concorde as well.' " - Ibid.
206. " 'down a side street.' " - *The Dallas Morning News*, Jan. 22, 1976.
206. "during the trial period." - *Fort Worth Star Telegram*, Feb. 5, 1976.
206. "transports at Kennedy." - *Dallas Times Herald*, Feb. 24, 1976.
207. "noise and air pollution." - *Fort Worth Star Telegram*, March 18, 1976.
207. " 'might become a hazard?' " - *Dallas Times Herald*, Feb. 22, 1976.
207. "overturn Coleman's decision" - *The Dallas Morning News*, Feb. 26, 1976.

207. "at least six months." - *Fort Worth Star-Telegram*, May 20, 1976.

207. "U.S. treaty obligations." - *Airport Highlights* (a publication of the Airport Operators Council International, Inc. in Washington, D.C.), March 22, 1976.

207. "from all U.S. airports." - *Fort Worth Star-Telegram*, March 26, 1976.

207. "commercially to the U.S." - Ibid., May 20, 1976.

207. "Caribbean and Europe." - Ibid.

208. " 'port of entry in the world.' " - *Dallas Fort Worth Business*, Aug. 10, 1979.

208. "subject to U.S. duties.)" - *A Remarkable Ten Years*, 1974.

209. "Gatwick Airport to October." - 1980 DFW Airport Annual Report.

209. " 'attained that greatness.' " - Ibid.

209. "air routes for the airport." - *A Remarkable Ten Years*, 1974.

210. " 'planned and sought after.' " - *Dallas Fort Worth Business*, June 4, 1979.

210. "behind American and Delta." - *A Remarkable Ten Years*, 1974.

210. "cut back or frozen." - *Fort Worth Star-Telegram*, Jan. 21, 1982.

211. "on June 1, 1980." - *Dallas Times Herald*, April 20, 1980.

211. "heavy traffic periods." - 1983 DFW Airport Annual Financial Report.

212. "computers and recreation." - News release, Braniff International Corporation, Jan. 6, 1976. UTD Aviation Special Collection, Box 2, File 3.

212. "$142,000 in ground rent." - *Dallas Times Herald*, July 28, 1976.

213. " 'we knew lay ahead.' " - Al Casey, *Casey's Law: If Something Can Go Right, It Should* (New York: Arcade Publishing, 1997), 192-3.

213. "new headquarters facility." - *The Dallas Morning News*, Oct. 5, 1978.

213. "to make the move." - Ibid., 195.

213. "applying retroactively." - *Dallas Times Herald*, Dec. 30, 1978.

213. "by tax-free bonds." - Ibid., 201.

214. "small Fort Worth-based carriers." - *Fort Worth Star-Telegram*, Nov. 19, 1978.

214. "followed in 1970." - Ibid.

215. " 'good for everyone's business.' " - *Dallas/Fort Worth Business*, April 16, 1979.

215. "two nine-story towers." - *The Wall Street Journal*, June 18, 1983.

215. "almost 400 in 1978." - *Dallas Times Herald*, Dec. 16, 1978.

216. "2,500 people upon completion." - *Dallas Times Herald*, Aug. 2, 1979.

216. "other area of the country." - *The Banner*, Jan. 15, 1979.

216. " 'operate it for the year.' " - 1981 DFW Airport Annual Financial Report.

217. "would soon follow." - *The Dallas Morning News*, Feb. 9, 1983.

217. " 'caused by air traffic.' " - *The Wall Street Journal*, Feb. 16, 1983.

217. "hinder expansion plans." - *Fort Worth Star-Telegram*, March 9, 1983.

217. "neighbors might be over." - Ibid., May 18, 1983.

217. "through 'pure competition.' " - *Dallas Times Herald*, Jan. 27, 1976.

218. "administration had proposed." - *The Dallas Morning News*, April 10, 1976.

218. "marginally profitable markets." - *Dallas Times Herald*, April 25, 1976.

218. "official at Delta Airlines." - Ibid.

218. "impact of deregulation." *Dallas Times Herald*, April 13, 1976.

219. "federally regulated system." - *The Dallas Morning News*, April 14, 1976.

219. " 'in the best public interest.' " - *Fort Worth Star-Telegram*, May 18, 1976.

219. "inconsistent with the public interest." - Ibid., Nov. 1, 1978.

220. "officials and attorneys." - *Fort Worth Star-Telegram*, Oct. 25, 1978.

220. "had not been serving." - Ibid.

221. "of the Southwest flights." - *The Dallas Morning News*, May 8, 1976.

221. " 'of Dallas or Fort Worth.' " - *Fort Worth Star-Telegram*, June 3, 1976.
221. " 'get into financial problems.' " - Ibid.
221. "and able to fly it." - *The Dallas Morning News*, March 7, 1979
221. "other states and countries." - Ibid., March 6, 1979.
221. "out of Love Field." - *Fort Worth Star-Telegram*, March 8, 1979.
221. " 'was not well-received.' " - *Dallas Times Herald*, March 7, 1979.
222. " 'I have to respect that decision.' " - Ibid.
222. "said no thanks." - *Fort Worth Star-Telegram*, March 22, 1979.
222. "flights at Love Field." - *Dallas Times Herald*, April 25, 1979.
222. "out-of-court settlement." - *Fort Worth Star-Telegram*, March 29, 1979.
222. "to limit long-haul flights." - *The Dallas Morning News*, March 31, 1979.
222. "the matter was completed." - Ibid., May 1, 1979.
223. "and international flights." - *Dallas Times Herald*, May 5, 1979.
223. "service at DFW Airport." - *The Dallas Morning News*, June 13, 1979.
223. " 'exists around Love Field.' " - *Fort Worth Star-Telegram*, June 13, 1979.
223. "in the North Texas region." - *Dallas Times Herald*, June 28, 1979.
223. "related issues involved." - Ibid., June 28, 1979.
223. " 'precedent-setting case.' " - *The Dallas Morning News*, June 29, 1979.
224. "decision in court." - Ibid., Aug. 4, 1979.
224. "repealed and reversed." - *Fort Worth Star-Telegram*, Aug. 14, 1979.
225. " 'a carrier's Love Field service.' " - *Dallas Times Herald*, Aug. 7, 1980.
225. "a 'dangerous monopoly.' " - *The Dallas Morning News*, Sept. 12, 1978.
225. "was still in effect." - Ibid., Aug. 3, 1978.
225. "SURTRAN system." - *Fort Worth Star Telegram*, Dec. 8, 1978.
226. "airport's lucrative business." - *Dallas Times Herald*, April 30, 1979.
226. "stimulating better service." - *The Dallas Morning News*, May 23, 1980.
226. "by almost one-half." - *Fort Worth Star-Telegram*, Sept. 3, 1980.
226. "and chambers of commerce." - *Dallas Times Herald*, Aug. 28, 1990.
226. "along to the airlines." - *Fort Worth Star-Telegram*, Sept. 3, 1980.
227. "Railroad Commission." - Ibid., June 22, 1983.
227. "Dallas taxi operators." - *Dallas Times Herald*, Aug. 3, 1983.
227. "services at DFW Airport." - *The Dallas Morning News*, Aug. 17, 1983.
227. "their respective cities." - Ibid., Aug. 19, 1983.
227. "cut down on the noise." - Ibid., Aug. 30, 1983.
227. "and landings at DFW." - Ibid., May 8, 1981.
228. "first February meeting." - *Dallas Times Herald*, May 27, 1982.
228. " 'references to Dallas-Fort Worth.' " - *Fort Worth Press*, Jan. 15, 1973.
229. "under-appreciated and underpaid." - *Fort Worth Star-Telegram*, March 20, 1976.
229. "the threat of a strike." - *The Dallas Morning News*, May 30, 1981.
229. "acceptable terms were not offered." - *Fort Worth Star-Telegram*, May 30, 1981.
229. "possible under the law." - *The Dallas Morning News*, Aug. 3, 1981.
230. "with military support." - Ibid., Aug. 3, 1981.
230. "because of the strike." - *The Wall Street Journal*, Aug. 4, 1981.
230. "flight control system." - Ibid., Aug. 7, 1981.
230. "to and from the U.S." - *Fort Worth Star-Telegram*, Aug. 8, 1981.
231. " 'one and a half minutes.' " - Ibid., Aug. 11, 1981.
231. " 'the striking controllers.' " - *Dallas Times Herald*, Aug. 30, 1981.

231. "the ban against strikers." - *Fort Worth Star-Telegram*, Nov. 5, 1981.
231. "90 days of the terms." - Ibid., Dec. 9, 1981.
231. "officials and strike leaders." - Ibid., Dec. 19, 1981.
232. "serve time in prison." - Ibid.
232. "the organization insolvent." - *Dallas Times Herald*, June 28, 1983.
232. " 'on airport usage.' "*Fort Worth Star-Telegram*, July 2, 1982.
232. " 'capacity at the airport.' " - *Houston Post*, Aug. 2, 1982.
232. "in and out of the airport." - *The Dallas Morning News*, Aug. 1, 1982.
233. "and recession-slowed traffic." - Ibid., May 25,1983.
233. " 'we can feed ourselves?' " - *Fort Worth Star-Telegram*, Sept. 25, 1983.
233. " 'every principal capital in the world.' " - *Fortune*, March 26, 1979.
233. "pace of sixty a week." - *Dallas Times Herald*, Jan. 7, 1979.
233. " 'a calculated crapshoot.' " - *Fortune*, March 26, 1979.
233. " 'reasons will be slowing.' " - Ibid.
234. "for new service." - *Dallas Times Herald*, Jan. 7, 1979.
234. "compared to American's 138)." - *Grapevine News-Advertiser*, April 26, 1979.
234. " 'on course,' he insisted." - *The Dallas Morning News*, May 4, 1980.
234. " 'the economic downturn.' " - *Fort Worth Star Telegram*, July 17, 1980.
234. "might not survive." - *The Dallas Morning News*, Feb. 26, 1982.
234. "of a cash shortage." - Ibid., March 2, 1982.
234. "first quarter of 1982." - Ibid., May 1, 1982.
235. " 'other airlines.' " - *Fort Worth Star-Telegram*, May 13, 1982.
235. " 'of Braniff or someone else's.' " - *The Wall Street Journal*, May 14, 1982.
235. "in the company's system." - *Dallas Times Herald*, May 8, 1983.
235. "domestic passengers boarded." - *Fort Worth Star-Telegram*, May 13, 1982.
235. "$21.6 million in rent." - *Dallas Times Herald*, May 8, 1983.
235. "re-establish passenger services." - Ibid., April 8, 1983.
236. "feasibility of the arrangement." - *The Wall Street Journal*, April 11, 1983.
236. "developed and presented." - *The Dallas Morning News*, April 18, 1983.
236. "within a specified period of time." - *The Wall Street Journal*, April 20, 1983.
236. "terminal gate space." - *Fort Worth Star-Telegram*, April 22, 1983.
236. "with the Bankruptcy Court." - *The Dallas Morning News*, June 24, 1983.
237. "in about six weeks." - *Fort Worth Star-Telegram*, Nov. 29, 1983.
237. "traffic on succeeding days." - *Fort Worth Star-Telegram*, Ibid., Dec. 14, 1984.
237. " 'making this airport a reality.' " - "A Remarkable Ten Years," 1984.
237. "first annual J. Erik Jonsson Aviation Award." - Ibid.

Chapter Ten
239. " 'Probably never.' " - 1983 DFW Airport Annual Report.
239. "the area's future progress." - "A Remarkable Ten Years, " 1984.
240. "on May 21, 1987." - 1986 DFW Airport Annual Report.
240. "Far East through DFW." - Ibid.
240. "international cargo shipments." - Ibid.
240. "most efficient ports of entry." - Ibid.
240. "Passport to the World." - 1984 DFW Airport Annual Report.
240. "marketed cut fares." - *The Wall Street Journal*, April 18, 1984.
241. "airline's fate was uncertain." - *The Wall Street Journal*, May 31, 1984.
241. "much like Southwest." - *Fort Worth Star-Telegram*, Sept. 6, 1984.
241. "at DFW to other carriers." - Ibid., Oct. 25, 1984.

241. "per day to forty destinations)." - *Dallas Times Herald*, Nov. 12, 1989.
241. " 'evaporated into the clouds.' " - Ibid.
241. "schedules at the airport." - *Fort Worth Star-Telegram*, April 6, 1983.
242. "expand its operation." - 1991 DFW Airport Annual Report.
242. "and other construction contracts." - 1985 DFW Airport Annual Report.
243. "areas of airport operations." - *Fort Worth Star-Telegram*, Feb. 4 and 21, 1986.
243. "in this group." - *Dallas Times Herald*, Feb. 3, 1986.
243. " 'get the job done.' - Ibid., Feb. 4, 1986.
243. "didn't seem to care." - *Fort Worth Star-Telegram*, Feb. 4, 1986.
243. "look at the airport management." - *The Dallas Morning News*, July 13, 1986.
244. "action and move on." - Interview with Vernell Sturns, May 6, 1998.
245. "state laws in the process." - Ibid.
245. " 'a good enough job.' " - *Fort Worth Star-Telegram*, Feb. 5, 1986.
245. " 'let us off the hook.' " - *The Dallas Morning News*, Feb. 5, 1986.
245. " 'question success.' " - *Fort Worth Star-Telegram*, Feb. 5, 1986.
245. " 'in the first place.' " - Ibid., Feb. 19, 1987.
245. "on behalf of DFW." - Ibid.
246. "and Dunham was white." - Ibid., Jan. 24, 1986.
246. "a greater voice." - *Dallas Times Herald*, Feb. 17, 1986.
246. "Dunham's leadership." - *Fort Worth Star-Telegram*, April 16, 1986.
247. "result of the investigation." - *The Dallas Morning News*, May 18,1986.
247. "top airports in the world." - Ibid.
247. " 'support in LA.' " - Ibid.
247. "development of DFW Airport." - 1986 DFW Airport Annual Report.
247. "he knew about Texas." - Interview with Sturns, May ???, 1998.
248. "were already in place." - Ibid.
248. " 'OK'd for landing.' " - *The Dallas Morning News*, Aug. 4, 1985.
248. "plane hit the ground." - *Fort Worth Star Telegram*, Aug. 5, 1985.
249. "were rated as 'excellent.' " - *The Dallas Morning News*, Sept. 28,1985.
249. "should be corrected." - Ibid., July 15, 1986.
249. " 'I've ever seen.' " - *Dallas Times Herald*, Sept. 7, 1988.
249. "crash of Flight 1141." - 1988 DFW Airport Annual Report.
250. "arrival at the crash scene." - *Dallas Times Herald*, Sept. 3, 1988.
250. " 'I'd give this a nine.' " - Ibid.
250. "a Doppler radar system." - *The Dallas Morning News*, March 28, 1986.
251. "Limmer later recalled." - Interview with Len Limmer, Sept. 30, 1998.
251. "sites of airplane crashes." - Ibid.
251. "for such a disaster." - Ibid.
252. -"residential neighborhoods." - *Fort Worth Star Telegram*, March 18, 1990
252. "nation's aviation capital." - *Dallas Times Herald*, Nov. 17, 1989.
252. "air cargo operations." - *Fort Worth Star Telegram*, Dec. 17, 1990.
252. "and Alberta, Canada." - 1989 DFW Annual Report.
253. "in Mexico and Canada." - 1996 DFW Airport Annual Report.
253. "economic activity per year." - Ibid.
253. "distribution to Mexico." - 1996 DFW Airport Activity Report.
253. "in less than four hours." - Ibid.
254. "international cargo facility." - Ibid.
254. "through the airport." - *Dallas Times Herald*, June 18, 1984.
254. "guns confiscated during the year." - *Mid Cities Daily*, Jan. 1, 1985.

255. " to have such a system." - Interview with Len Limmer, Sept. 30, 1998.

255. "simultaneously as a unit." - *The Dallas Morning News*, Jan. 7, 1987.

256. "on international flights." - *USA Today*, Nov. 27, 1996.

256. " '21st Century and beyond.' " - Ibid.

256. "lowering operating costs." - 1992 DFW Annual Report.

257. "its operating procedures." - *Fort Worth News-Tribune*, June 29, 1984.

257. "transfers within terminals." - *Dallas Times Herald*, May 21, 1984.

257. "complaints received." - *Fort Worth Star-Telegram*, Feb. 5, 1986.

257. "operating cost of the system." - Ibid., Feb. 6, 1986.

258. "ever in aviation history." - 1991 DFW Annual Report.

258. "275 million to 450 million." - *The Dallas Morning News*, Oct. 23, 1988.

258. "accommodate their needs." - *Fort Worth Star-Telegram*, June 9, 1984.

258. "country's busiest airports." - *The Dallas Morning News*, June 15, 1984.

259. "future passenger needs." - 1990 DFW Annual Report.

259. "implement the new plan." - Ibid.

260. " 'could not be greater.' " - 1988 DFW Airport Annual Report.

260. "history of the FAA." - Ibid..

260. "Northwest's cargo area." - 1990 DFW Annual Report.

260. "during bad weather." - Ibid.

261. "with about 100 gates." - 1990 DFW Airport Annual Report.

261. "on existing roadways." - Ibid.

262. "decision-making processes." - *Fort Worth Star-Telegram*, Sept. 5, 1984.

262. "new runways and noise." - 1989 DFW Annual Report.

263. "relieve runway congestion." - *The Dallas Morning News*, Nov. 26, 1986.

263. "flight path to the runway." - *Fort Worth Star Telegram*, March 2, 1988.

263. "ordinances be overturned." - *Fort Worth Magazine*, Winter 1990-91.

263. "Dallas and Fort Worth." - *Dallas Times Herald*, Feb. 7, 1990.

264. "Board Chairman Willard Barr." - Interview with Willard Barr, Nov. 22, 1993.

264. " 'having the litigation today.' " - Interview with R.M. Stovall, Nov. 23, 1993.

264. " 'squabble we are having now.' " - Ibid.

264. "$9 billion in wages by 2010." - *Fort Worth Magazine*, Winter, 1990-91.

265. " 'nation's air system today.'" - *The Dallas Morning News*, Feb. 7, 1990.

265. "new runways approved." - *Dallas Times Herald*, Feb. 7, 1990.

266. "to stop the activity." - *Fort Worth Star Telegram*, Aug. 15, 1992.

266. " 'is non-negotiable.' " - *Irving News*, April 7, 1992.

266. "is at stake." - Ibid.

266. "mitigation program." - News release, DFW Airport, April 7, 1992.

267. "'the rest of our existence.'" - Interview with Jeffrey P. Fegan, Sept. 18, 1998.

268. "and $300 million to build." - *DFW People*, May 13, 1993.

268. "Senate Bill 348" - *Fort Worth Star Telegram*, Oct. 2, 1993.

268. "approval was constitutional." - *Irving News*, Jan. 22, 1995.

268. "address residents' concerns." - 1995 DFW Airport Annual Report.

Chapter Eleven

271. "exceeds our customers' expectations." - DFW marketing brochure.

271. "of a business location." - *Dallas Times Herald*, May 8, 1989.

271. "started moving into the area." - *Fort Worth Star-Telegram*, Nov. 14, 1996.

272. "for hundreds of workers." - 1992 DFW Airport Annual Report.
272. "employment opportunities at DFW." - 1996 DFW Airport Activities Report.
272. "National DBE Program Award." - 1997 DFW Airport Annual Report.
272. "well-received by DFW passengers." - News release, DFW Airport, May 11, 1995.
273. "first-of-its-kind service." - 1996 DFW Airport Annual Report.
273. "chief building official." - *The Dallas Morning News*, March 29,1994.
274. " 'rumble strips' in the pavement." - Ibid.
274. "to the restaurant executives." - *The Dallas Morning News*, Nov. 23, 1996.
274. "from Las Vegas touched down." - 1996 DFW Airport Annual Report.
275. "lowest rates in the nation." - Ibid.
275. "flight delays nationwide." - 1996 DFW Airport Activities Report.
275. " 'is breathing down our neck.' " - *Chicago Tribune*, March 27, 1994.
276. "approaching two million tons." - 1997 DFW Airport Annual Report.
277. "restricted airline competition." - *The Dallas Morning News*, Oct. 13,1989.
277. " 'more traffic' for the region." - *Fort Worth Star-Telegram*, July 12, 1992.
277. " 'for economic development.'" - *DFW People*, July 16, 1992.
278. "throughout the last several years." - Hearing Before the Subcommittee on Aviation of the Committee of Public Works and Transportation, House of Representatives, One Hundred Second Congress, First Session on H.R. 858, Sept. 24, 1991.
278. "commitment to the Amendment." - *Fort Worth Star-Telegram*, June 25, 1992.
278. "fifty-six or fewer seats." - *Grapevine Sun*, Dec. 14, 1997.
279. "override federal law." - *Fort Worth Star Telegram*, Dec. 10, 1997.
279. "to remain competitive." - *Irving News*, Dec. 28, 1997.
279. "some flights to Love Field." - *The Dallas Morning News*, May 8, 1998.
279. "postponed indefinitely." - *Irving News*, Dec. 28, 1997.
279. "by federal law from Love Field." *The Dallas Morning News,* May 8 1998.
279. "so it could begin operations." - Ibid., April 22, 1998.
279. "Mayor Kenneth Barr." - *Fort Worth Star Telegram*, Aug. 31, 1998.
280. "ruling on the matter." - Ibid.
280. "legal questions before the Court." - *The Dallas Morning News*, Sept. 12, 1998.

Index